Facing Up to Modernity

FACING UP TO MODERNITY

Excursions in Society, Politics, and Religion

PETER L. BERGER

Basic Books, Inc., Publishers   New York

Library of Congress Cataloging in Publication Data

Berger, Peter L.
  Facing up to modernity.

  Includes bibliographical references and index.
  1. Sociology—United States—Addresses, essays,
lectures. 2. Political sociology. 3. Religion and
sociology—Addresses, essays, lectures. I. Title.
HM22.U5B39   301   77-74572
ISBN: 0-465-02269-3

10 9 8 7 6 5 4 3 2 1

Contents

III

Transcending Modernity

Preface

Sociology is a systematic attempt to see the social world as clearly as possible, to understand it without being swayed by one's own hopes and fears. This ideal of lucidity (one could even call it selfless lucidity) is intended by what Max Weber called the value-freeness of the social sciences. It is often a difficult and painful business. There are typically two ways of avoiding both the pain and the difficulty. One way is to segregate the process of sociological understanding from all questions of value to the point where the sociologist tries to fashion himself into an utterly detached observer, or, alternatively, adheres to his own values without any reference to his sociological insights. This is either dehumanizing (the individual as such, not just a particular intellectual activity of his, then becomes value-free), or it constitutes a surrender to irrationality (the individual holding on to his values in a realm of the mind that is inaccessible to reasonable argument). The other way, probably the simpler one, is to reject the ideal of value-free understanding, to declare it to be impossible, or undesirable, or both. Such rejection then permits the individual to interpret the social world in accordance with his own value preferences—in effect, to see the world as he would like to see it. It is this latter way of avoiding the tensions of sociological existence that is fashionable today. It transforms the discipline into an instrument of ideological propaganda, a transformation that constitutes the modest contribution of sociologists to the *trahison des clercs* of our time.

I owe to my first teachers in sociology (particularly to Carl Mayer, Albert Salomon, and Alfred Schutz) the strong conviction that both evasions are wrong, intellectually and morally. To be a sociologist need not mean that one become either a heartless observer or a propagandist. Rather it should mean that each act of understanding stands in an existential tension with one's values, even those, indeed especially those, that one holds most passionately. For me, these have mainly been political and religious values. This book, then, represents the particular way in which I have tried to relate sociological understanding to political action and religious commitment. Not for a moment would I claim that I have resolved the tensions inherent in these relationships or put myself forward as an exemplary case. All I can present is one individual's attempt to be a sociologist in the contemporary situation while also seeking to be politically responsible and religiously engaged. This book presumes no more than a certain instructive quality to such a demonstration.

Thus, while the chapters that comprise this book originated at different times, ranging from the early 1960s to the present, the intention is not to present some sort of autobiographical profile. The table of contents reflects this. In one way or another sociology enters into most of the essays. I have placed in section I those in which the main purpose was to understand an existing social situation rather than to draw implications in terms of political or religious commitments. Sections II and III contain essays in which the purpose at hand was to draw such implications (respectively, political and religious ones), even if the underlying argument was sociological. What is at issue here is more than the mechanics of fitting separately produced essays into the contents of a cohesive book. The issue is what it means to be a sociologist, even a value-free one, while also being a concerned citizen of the United States in a very troubled period, as well as being a Christian. Whatever else may or may not be clear in this book, I hope that it is always clear which "hat" I wear at any given moment in these arguments.

The introduction states, as succinctly as I can, my view of the political and moral consequences of sociology as a discipline. It was given as a paper in 1970, on the occasion of my being awarded an honorary degree by Loyola University of Chicago; the juxtaposition of a moment of personal vindication and a period of acute political turbulence seemed conducive to such a statement. The chapters of section I, of course, express not some generalized sociology but my own particular approach to the discipline. This is an approach variously called "humanistic," "phenomenological," or that of the "sociology of knowledge"; all these terms carry a certain freight of ambiguities. In any case, the reader who wants to know more about this approach can satisfy his curiosity relatively painlessly by turning to my book *Invitation to Sociology* (New York: Doubleday-Anchor, 1963); a more systematic initiation can be obtained (with more effort if not necessarily more pain) from *The Social Construction of Reality* (New York: Doubleday, 1966, with Thomas Luckmann).

The theme of modernity is the central one in this book, as it has been central in my thinking over the years: How can one understand that peculiar reality we know as modern society? How can one engage in meaningful political action in modern America? And what does modernity mean for the religious quest? I have explicated my understanding of the impact of modernity on human social existence and consciousness in *The Homeless Mind* (New York: Random House, 1973, with Brigitte Berger and Hansfried Kellner). Finally, the reader who wants to know more about my unapologetically *moraliste* approach to politics may turn to *Pyramids of Sacrifice* (New York: Basic Books, 1974), while *A Rumor of Angels* (New York: Doubleday, 1969) is still the longest statement of how I combine being a sociologist with (I'm afraid) a rather heretical Christianity.

It would be impossible to thank all those whose conversation and criticisms have helped me in developing the particular sensibilities embodied in this book. I do want to acknowledge a special debt to Midge Decter, who helped me see what follows here as a unity rather than a sequence of disparate arguments.

Introduction: Sociology and Freedom

Sociology, greatly to the surprise of most of its older practitioners, has acquired the reputation of a liberating discipline. Sociology courses are crowded with students in search of the intellectual tools to demolish the hypocritical world of their elders and to fashion, for themselves if not for society at large, a new authenticity and a new freedom.

All this is very recent indeed. Only a few years ago most outsiders, if they thought about the matter at all, visualized the sociologist as a dry character, with an insatiable lust for statistics, who at best might dig up some data of use to policy makers, and at worst (in the words of one malevolent commentator) would spend one hundred thousand dollars to discover the local whorehouse. It would have required a wild imagination to conceive of this unexciting type as a potential object of interest either for young seekers after salvation or for the FBI. All the same, it has happened. Especially among the younger members of the profession there are now convincing aspirants to drastically different images of the sociologist. Rampant on the academic scene today is the image of the sociologist as, at any rate, one of several *guru* types, bearing close resemblance to the evangelists of psychedelia, T-group mysticism, and other fashionable gospels from the relatively recent past. There is also the image—perhaps by now it is vestigial—of the sociologist as a carrier of revolutionary doctrine and, at least *in spe,* as a character throwing Molotov cocktails through the windows of the faculty club (in either direction, depending on circumstances). Needless to say, both images have provoked dismay as well as enthusiasm. The former is especially galling for psychologists, who suddenly find themselves challenged in what so recently was a monopoly in the treatment of the metaphysical afflictions of intellectuals. But by far the greatest amount of dismay at all this has been occasioned within the field of sociology itself. Placid purveyors of Parsonian theory or of the higher statistics are suddenly confronted with the demand to become "relevant" to the turbulent and constantly shifting commitments of the young.

Sociology as an instrument for the existential liberation of the individual. Sociology as a weapon in the revolutionary struggle to liberate society. Anyone familiar with the history of the discipline will find these notions startling, if not ironic. At the very origins of sociology, indeed, there was a quasi-religious conception of the new science—that of Auguste Comte and his followers. Even Comte, however, conceived of sociology as an *anti*revolutionary doctrine, as the new church that was to restore order and progress in the wake of the havoc caused by the French Revolution. With few exceptions, the Comtian view of sociology as *Heilswissen* (to use Max Scheler's term) did not survive into the classic age of the discipline, the period (roughly) between 1890 and 1930. None of the classic sociologists would have been able to make much sense of the current notions of sociology as a vehicle of personal liberation. As to the understanding of sociology as a doctrine of revolutionary praxis, it is noteworthy that some of the greatest classic figures (such as Max Weber, Emile Durkheim, and Vilfredo Pareto) invested a good deal of effort in what they considered to be refutations of Marxism. If anything, most of classic sociology in Europe followed a counterrevolutinary and (at least implicitly) conservative doctrine. Early American sociology did indeed have a strong reformist animus, but this was more congenial to YMCA secretaries than to revolutionaries or preachers of spiritual salvation. Even this mild reformism became, at most, a submerged motif as "value-freeness" and technical proficiency became established as binding norms within the profession.

I have no satisfying explanation for the recent dramatic changes in the conception of sociology. One can point, of course, to certain intellectual sources—C. Wright Mills in this country, the so-called "Frankfurt School" in Germany, and in France a number of Marxists-turned-sociologists (such as Henri Lefebvre). This, though, does not explain why these individuals and their ideas have suddenly come to exert such a powerful influence. I strongly suspect that, as often in the history of ideas, there is a strong element of chance in the new affinity between sociology and political radicalism. In any case, I don't intend to devote myself here to speculation about the reasons for this slightly bizarre marriage. Rather than exploring historical causes, I would like to look at the theoretical question at issue. To wit: *In what sense, if at all, can sociology be called a liberating discipline?*

I will approach the question by way of two, seemingly contradictory, propositions: *Sociology is subversive of established patterns of thought. Sociology is conservative in its implications for the institutional order.* I would like to suggest that *both* propositions are correct, and that an understanding of this also entails grasping the relation of sociology and freedom, at least on the level cf politics. (I should add that the *epistemological* problem, of how an empirical science can or cannot deal with man's freedom, is clearly outside the scope of this chapter.)

Sociology is subversive of established patterns of thought: This, of course, is today a favorite notion of those who would marry sociology to radical politics. A few years ago most sociologists would have been either shocked or honestly bewildered by the proposition. Then it was those with a vested interest in established patterns of thought who (if the inelegant simile be forgiven) smelled the rat before those who put it there. I recall a remark made to me in 1956 by a barber in the southern town where I had just started my first teaching job. After I had told him what I was teaching, he paused (more pensively than with hostility) and remarked: "Oh, I know about sociologists. You're the guys who wrote all those footnotes in the Supreme Court decision on getting the colored into the schools." He was right, of course—in an extended sense, if not literally. I wonder how many of the sociologists (some of them southerners living quite comfortably in a segregated society), who busily gathered all those data on the place of the Negro in America, imagined that they were providing the legitimations for one of the great social transformations of our time. Put differently, I would suggest that there is in sociology a subversive impulse that strives for expression regardless of the intentions of individual sociologists.

Every human society rests on assumptions that, most of the time, are not only unchallenged but not even reflected upon. In other words, in every society there are patterns of thought that most people accept without question as being of the very nature of things. Alfred Schutz called the sum of these "the world-taken-for-granted," which provides the parameters and the basic programs for our everyday lives. Robert and Helen Lynd, in their classic studies of *Middletown,* pointed to the same phenomenon with their concept of "of course statements"—statements that people take for granted to such a degree that, if questioned about them, they will preface their answer with "of course." These socially established patterns of thought provide the individual with what, paraphrasing Erving Goffman, we might call his basic reality kit—the cognitive and normative tools for the construction of a coherent universe in which to live. It is difficult to see how social life would be possible without this. But specific institutions and specific vested interests are also legitimated by such taken-for-granted patterns

of thought. Thus a threat to the taken-for-granted quality of the legitimating thought patterns can very quickly become a threat to the institutions being legitimated, and to the individuals who have a stake in
the institutional status quo.

Sociology, by its own intrinsic logic, keeps generating such threats.
Simply by doing its cognitive job, sociology puts the institutional order
and its legitimating thought patterns under critical scrutiny. Sociology
has a built-in debunking effect. It shows up the fallaciousness of socially established interpretations of reality by demonstrating that the facts
do not gibe with the "official" view, or, even more simply, by relativizing the latter (by showing that it is only one of several possible
views of society). *That* is already dangerous enough and would provide
sufficient grounds for sociologists to become what the Prussian authorities used to call *polizeibekannt*—of interest, that is, to the cognitive if
not to the actual police. (Every society has its cognitive policemen who
administer the "official" definitions of reality.) But sociology, at least
in certain situations, is more directly subversive. It unmasks vested interests and makes visible the manner in which the latter are served by
social fictions. At least in certain situations, then, sociology can be political dynamite.

A favorite term of the New Left in Europe and Latin America is derived from the vocabulary of psychoanalysis—*Bewusstmachung* in
German, *concientización* in Spanish—perhaps best translated as
"bringing to consciousness." This is the process of social critique by
which the mystifications of "false consciousness" are demolished and
the way is prepared for the demystified consciousness necessary for revolutionary praxis. I shall return shortly to the question of revolutionary praxis. But as to the first aspect of the term, the subversive effects
of critical social analysis on consciousness, it must be admitted that it
pertains to sociology in a very basic way. Anyone who pursues the sociological perspective to its logical consequences will find himself undergoing a transformation of his consciousness of society. At least potentially, this makes him unsafe from the viewpoint of the guardians of
law and order. It also produces unsafety, sometimes with catastrophic
effects, for his own peace of mind.

"Bringing to consciousness," in this sense, does indeed have a liberating quality. But the freedom to which it leads, apart from its possible
political effects, can be a rather terrible thing. It is the freedom of ecstasy, in the literal sense of *ek-stasis*—stepping or standing outside the
routine ways and assumptions of everyday life—which, let us recall,

also includes routine comforts, routine security. Thus, if there is a relation between "bringing to consciousness" and the ecstasy of liberation,
there is also a relation between that ecstasy and the possibility of desperation. Toward the end of his life Max Weber was asked by a friend
to whom he had been explaining the pessimistic conclusions of his sociological analysis: "But, if you think this way, why do you continue
doing sociology?" Weber's reply is one of the most chilling statements
I know in the history of Western thought: "Because I want to know
how much I can stand." Alfred Seidel, a student of Weber's who was
also greatly influenced by Freud, came to an even more pessimistic
conclusion in his little book appropriately titled *Bewusstsein als Ver-
haengnis—Consciousness as Doom*. Seidel concluded that the combined critical consciousness of sociology and psychoanalysis was not
only politically subversive but inimical to life itself. Whatever other
motives there may have been, Seidel's suicide as a young man in the
1920s was an existential ratification of this view of the "bringing to
consciousness" of sociology.

My purpose is not to suggest that sociologists, if they were only consistent, should all commit suicide. Actually, I have a somewhat more
benign view of the existential possibilities of sociological consciousness.
Rather, I want to point out that the relation between sociology and
freedom is not as simple, or as cheerful, as the radicals in the profession would have us believe. Yes, there is a liberating quality to the discipline of sociology. Yes, there are situations in which sociological understanding can be liberating in a political and (at least in terms of my
own values) morally significant sense—as in the service that sociology
can render to the liberation of American blacks from racial oppression.
But, for the individual, sociology can bring to consciousness aspects of
the world that are profoundly disturbing and a freedom that, in the extreme instance, evokes truly Kierkegaardian terrors.

But let me go on to my second proposition: *Sociology is conservative
in its implications for the institutional order:* Put differently, sociology,
far from leading inevitably to revolutionary praxis, actually inhibits
the latter in most cases. Put differently once more, fomentors of revolution have *as* good reason to be suspicious of sociology as policemen.
This point can be made economically by way of three imperatives
which, in my opinion, sociological understanding can show to be
present in every human community: the imperatives of order, continuity, and triviality. Each one of these imperatives flies in the face of
some of the fondest beliefs of the contemporary left.

After a lecture of mine on sociological theory, a perceptive student remarked to me: "You sure have a hang-up on order, don't you?" I had to concede the description. But I also added that my "hang-up" was not arbitrary or inadvertent. Behind it is the conviction that sociology leads to the understanding that order is *the* primary imperative of social life. There is the additional conviction (which I cannot develop here) that this fact is rooted in the fundamental constitution of man, that is, that not only sociology but philosophical anthropology must lead to a "hang-up on order." Society, in its essence, is the imposition of order upon the flux of human experience. Most people will first think here of what American sociologists call "social control"—the imposition of coercive power upon deviant individuals or groups—and, of course, it is in this sense that radicals will understand, and disagree with, my "hang-up on order." Coercion and external controls, however, are only incidental aspects of society's imposition of order. *Every* social institution, no matter how "non-repressive" or "consensual," is an imposition of order—beginning with language, which is the most basic institution of all. If this is understood, there will then also be the understanding that social life abhors disorder as nature abhors a vacuum. This has the directly political implication that, except for rare and invariably brief periods, the forces of order are always stronger than those of disorder, and, further, that there are fairly narrow limits to the toleration of disorder in any human society. The left, by and large, understands that all social order is precarious. It generally fails to understand that, *just because of this precariousness,* societies will react with almost instinctive violence to any fundamental or long-lasting threat to their order. The idea of "permanent revolution" is an anthropologically absurd fantasy. Indeed, revolutionary movements can be successful only if they succeed fairly rapidly in establishing new structures of order within which people can settle down with some semblance of social *and* psychic safety. Mao Tse Tung's Cultural Revolution can serve as a textbook example of the grotesque failure in store for any revolutionary praxis that fails to grasp this point.

The imperative of continuity is closely related to, but not identical with, the imperative of order. I suppose that, finally, it is rooted in the simple fact that people have children. If one has children, one is required to explain the past to them, and to relate the present to the past. If one loves one's children (and I take it that this is the case with most people who have them), one will want to project into the future whatever good things one has possessed in one's own life—and there are very few people, even among the most oppressed, who have possessed nothing good at all. Conversely, if one loves one's parents (and, the current "generation crisis" notwithstanding, I'm inclined to think that this, too, is something of an anthropological constant), one will not finally want to disparage *everything* that constituted the parents' world—especially if one comes to have children of one's own, who not only ask what will become of them but from what they come. *Children are our hostages to history.* Consequently, to be a parent means (however dimly and on whatever level of intellectual sophistication) to have a stake in the continuity of the social order. As a result, there are limits not only to social disorder but to social discontinuity. The enthusiasts for violent change (most of whom, I have noticed, don't have children) fail to recognize this. Successful revolutionaries find out, usually to their dismay, as they must settle down to govern the society over which they have gained control. The experiences of the Soviet regime with the institutions of the family and of religion are instructive in this regard.

The imperative of triviality is again, I suspect, rooted in some basic facts of the human condition, namely, the facts that man's attention span is limited and that he can only tolerate a limited amount of excitement. Perhaps the physiological foundation of all this is our need to sleep. Social life would be psychologically intolerable if each of its moments required from us full attention, deliberate decision, and high emotional involvement. It is for this reason that I would claim for the following proposition the status of a sociological axiom: *Triviality is one of the fundamental requirements of social life.* It is sociologically, and probably anthropologically, and perhaps even biologically, *necessary* that a goodly portion of social life take place in a state of only dim awareness—if you will, in a state of semisleep. It is precisely to permit this to happen that the institutional order imposes "programs" for the individual's activity.

Society protects our sanity by preempting a large number of choices, not only of action but of thought. If we understand this (the understanding has been worked out systematically in the theory of institutions of the contemporary German sociologist Arnold Gehlen), then we will see that there are limits not only to disorder and discontinuity, but also to the frequency of "significant events." We will then become very careful how we view "meaningless rituals," "empty forms," or "mere routines" in social life—simply because we will recognize that if social life in its entirety were charged with profound meaning, we would all go out of our minds. The "meaninglessness" of so much of social life, which is currently decried as the source of so-called "alienation," is in fact a necessary condition for both individual and collective sanity. The currently fashionable left ideal of "full participation," in the sense that everybody will participate in every decision affecting his life, would, if realized, constitute a nightmare comparable to unending sleeplessness. Fortunately, it is anthropologically unrealizable, though the endless "discussion" that goes on in radical groups gives a certain approximation of the horror that its realization would signify. It is one of the mercies of human nature that, finally, all "participants" and all "discussants" must fall asleep.

I have tried to explicate the conservative bent of sociology by pointing to some basic imperatives of social life that, at the very least, should make the sociologist skeptical of any notions of violent change and thus hesitant to commit himself to revolutionary praxis. I think that similar conclusions can be arrived at by way of empirical analysis, sociological or historical, of the actual processes of revolution. If all this adds up to a conservative propensity, it should be emphasized that the conservatism in question is of a peculiar kind. It is *not* based on the conviction that the institutions of the status quo are sacred, inexorably right, or empirically inevitable. The aforementioned subversive impulse of sociology precludes this type of conservatism. Rather, it is based on skepticism about the status quo in society *as well as* about various programs for new social orders. It is, if you wish, the conservatism in question is of a peculiar kind. It is *not* based on the con-propositions about the subversiveness and the conservatism of sociology thus resolves itself into a paradoxical, but by no means irrational, stance: *the stance of a man who thinks daringly but acts prudently.* This, of course, is exactly the kind of man our young revolutionaries will call a fink. So be it. It is probably one of the unavoidable blindnesses of youth to fail to see that acting prudently in society, while it may be the simple result of wanting to preserve one's little applecarts, may also be motivated quite differently—namely, by carefully thought-through concern to avoid senseless pain and to protect the good things of ordinary life. There is some irony in the fact that a generation which has made a culture hero out of Albert Camus should extol his *Rebel* at the expense of his hymns of praise to the ordinary pleasures of ordinary men on the sun-drenched beaches of a timeless sea.

Sociology, therefore, is a liberating discipline in a very specific way. There can be no doubt about its liberating effects on consciousness. At least potentially, sociology may be a prelude to liberation not only in thought but in action. At the same time, however, sociology points up the social limits of freedom—the very limits that, in turn, provide the social space for any empirically viable expression of freedom. This perspective, alas, is not simple. It requires intellectual effort and is not too easily harnessed to political passions. I would contend that the effort is worth it and that it will serve well precisely those political purposes that come from a concern for living men rather than for abstract doctrines of liberation.

So much for sociology as a discipline. What about the sociologist? A good case can be made that there is a crisis of freedom in the world today. What is to be the place of the sociologist in this crisis?

Questions about the place of sociology and the place of the sociologist are not identical, though they are related. Perhaps the easiest way to show up the difference between the two questions is to answer them in terms of so-called "value-freeness," that Weberian term that has become a sort of middle-echelon devil in the conceptual hell of the sociological left. The *discipline of sociology,* I insist as emphatically as I can, must be value-free, however difficult this might be in some situations. The moment the discipline ceases to be value-free in principle, it ceases to be a science, and becomes nothing but ideology, propaganda, a part of the instrumentarium of political manipulation. On the other hand, the *practitioner of the discipline,* the sociologist who (after all) is also a living human being, must *not* become value-free. The moment he does, he betrays his humanity and (in an operation that can simultaneously be called "false consciousness" and "bad faith") transforms himself into a ghostly embodiment of abstract science. These two statements about value-freeness are made, of course, in discrete frames of reference. The statement about the value-freeness of sociology is methodological; the statement about the value-freeness of the sociologist is ethical. But perhaps it is appropriate to conclude these observations with a little homily.

We may return here to the two images of the sociologist that were conjured up earlier—that of the sociologist as the antiseptically neutral technician and that of the sociologist as the fiercely committed partisan. I think that the sociological left has been largely correct, ethically speaking, in its denunciations of the former type (even if it has been unfair in individual instances). In an age in which not only freedom but the very survival of man is in jeopardy, there is something obscene about the scientist who claims that he is not responsible for the uses to which his science is put. This is not to deny in any way the right of individuals to live the theoretical life or to abstain from political engagement. This right, however, can be exercised more acceptably by Byzantinologists than by most sociologists. Sociology is too much linked to the agonizing dilemmas of our time to permit *most* of its practitioners to pursue their theoretical interests in detachment from the struggles of their fellow men.

I would like to stress that, because of these considerations, I not only believe in the political partisanship of sociologists, but I readily concede that at times this partisanship might be quite fierce. (For example, when it comes to the Pentagon's view of Latin America, my own political reactions tend to be considerably ferocious.) It is equally important to stress, however, that the sociologist has no doctrine of redemption to bring into the political arena. What he has to contribute is precisely the critical intelligence that is, or should be, the foundation of his discipline. This is a political *as well as* a methodological mandate. There are plenty of passions available, and the sociologist may well participate in some of them. His distinctive contribution *to politics* is the consistent, unswerving application of critical intelligence—to the status quo, yes, but also to any challengers of the status quo. Indeed, even in the event that a sociologist may join up with a revolutionary movement (and I have said enough to indicate that I would not normally prescribe this option), his most important political contribution to the movement will be his ongoing critique *of it*. Put differently, my principal objection to most of my radicalized colleagues has not been that they have been engaged in the business of "bringing to consciousness," but that they don't do enough of it.

To whom will such a conception of the sociologist's role have an appeal? Evidently not to those who simply want a career in any kind of establishment, nor to those who see themselves as messianic figures. It is all too clear that both types of ambition are strongly represented in American sociology today. I have found, however, and not least among my own students, that there are others—namely, those still willing to consider a militant commitment to reason. And reason has its own seductiveness.

Facing Up to Modernity

I

UNDERSTANDING

MODERNITY

1

Marriage and the Construction

of Reality

(WITH HANSFRIED KELLNER)

Ever since Durkheim it has been a commonplace of family sociology that marriage serves as a protection against anomie for the individual. Interesting and pragmatically useful though this insight is, it is but the negative side of a phenomenon of much broader significance. If one speaks of *anomic* states, then one ought properly to investigate also the *nomic* processes that, by their absence, lead to the aforementioned states. If, consequently, one finds a negative correlation between marriage and anomie, then one should be led to inquire into the character of marriage as a *nomos*-building instrumentality, that is, of marriage as a social arrangement that creates for the individual the sort of order in which he can experience his life as making sense. It is our intention here to discuss modern marriage in these terms. While this could evidently be done in a macrosociological perspective, dealing with marriage as a major social institution related to other broad structures of society, our focus will be microsociological, dealing primarily with the social processes affecting the individuals in any specific marriage, although, of course, the larger framework of these processes will have to be understood. In what sense this discussion can be described as micro-sociology of knowledge will hopefully become clearer in the course of it.[1]

Marriage is obviously only *one* social relationship in which this process of *nomos*-building takes place. It is, therefore, necessary to look first in more general terms at the character of this process. In doing so

This chapter originally appeared in *Diogenes*, no. 46. Reprinted by permission.

we are influenced by three theoretical perspectives—the Weberian perspective on society as a network of meanings, the Meadian perspective on identity as a social phenomenon, and the phenomenological analysis of the social structuring of reality especially as given in the work of Schutz and Merleau-Ponty.[2] Not being convinced that theoretical lucidity is necessarily enhanced by terminological ponderosity, we shall avoid as much as possible the use of the sort of jargon for which both sociologists and phenomenologists have acquired dubious notoriety.

The process that interests us here is the one that constructs, maintains, and modifies a consistent reality that can be meaningfully experienced by individuals. In its essential forms this process is determined by the society in which it occurs. Every society has its specific way of defining and perceiving reality—its world, its universe, its overarching organization of symbols. This is already given in the language that forms the symbolic base of the society. Erected over this base, and by means of it, is a system of ready-made typifications, through which the innumerable experiences of reality come to be ordered.[3] These typifications and their order are held in common by the members of society, thus acquiring not only the character of objectivity, but being taken for granted as *the* world *tout court,* the only world of which normal men can conceive.[4] The seemingly objective and taken-for-granted character of the social definitions of reality can be seen most clearly in the case of language itself, but it is important to keep in mind that the latter forms the base and instrumentality of a much larger world-erecting process.

The socially constructed world must be continually mediated to and actualized by the individual, so that it can become and remain *his* world as well. The individual is given by his society certain decisive cornerstones for his everyday experience and conduct. Most importantly, the individual is supplied with specific sets of typifications and criteria of relevance, predefined for him by the society and made available to him for the ordering of his everyday life. This ordering or (in line with our opening considerations) nomic apparatus is biographically cumulative. It begins to be formed in the individual from the earliest stages of socialization, then keeps on being enlarged and modified by himself throughout his biography.[5] While there are individual biographical differences making for differences in the constitution of this apparatus in specific individuals, there exists in the society an overall consensus on the range of differences deemed tolerable. Without such consensus, indeed, society would be impossible as a going concern, since it would then lack the ordering principles by which alone experience can be shared and conduct can be mutually intelligible. This order, by which the individual comes to perceive and define his world, is thus not chosen by him, except perhaps for very small modifications. Rather, it is discovered by him as an external datum, a ready-made world that simply is *there* for him to go ahead and live in, though he modifies it continually in the process of living in it. Nevertheless, this world is in need of validation, perhaps precisely because of an ever-present glimmer of suspicion as to its social manufacture and relativity. This validation, while it must be undertaken by the individual himself, requires ongoing interaction with others who coinhabit this same socially constructed world.

In a broad sense, *all* the other coinhabitants of this world serve a validating function. Every morning the newspaper boy validates the widest coordinates of my world and the mailman bears tangible validation of my own location within these coordinates. However, some validations are more significant than others. Every individual requires the ongoing validation of his world, including crucially the validation of his identity and place in this world, by those few who are his truly significant others.[6] Just as the individual's deprivation of relationship with his significant others will plunge him into anomie, so their continued presence will sustain for him that *nomos* by which he can feel at home in the world, at least most of the time. Again in a broad sense, all the actions of the significant others and even their simple presence serve this sustaining function. In everyday life the principal method employed is speech. In this sense, it is proper to view the individual's relationship with his significant others as an ongoing conversation. As the latter occurs, it validates over and over again the fundamental definitions of reality once entered into, not, of course, so much by explicit articulation, but precisely by taking the definitions silently for granted and conversing about all conceivable matters on this taken-for-granted basis. Through the same conversation the individual is also made capable of adjusting to changing and new social contexts in his biography. In a fundamental sense it can be said that one converses one's way through life.

If one concedes these points, one can now state a general sociological proposition: *The plausibility and stability of the world, as socially defined, is dependent upon the strength and continuity of significant relationships in which conversation about this world can be continually carried on.* Or, to put it a little differently: *The reality of the world is sustained through conversation with significant others.* This reality includes not only the imagery by which fellowmen are viewed, but also the way in which one views oneself. The reality-bestowing force of social relationships depends on the degree of their nearness,[7] that is, the degree to which social relationships occur in face-to-face situations and to which they are credited with primary significance by the individual. In any empirical situation there now emerge obvious sociological questions out of these considerations, namely, questions about the patterns of the world-building relationships, the social forms taken by the conversation with significant others. Sociologically, one must ask how these relationships are *objectively* structured and distributed, and one will also want to understand how they are *subjectively* perceived and experienced.

With these preliminary assumptions stated we can now arrive at our main thesis. We would contend that marriage occupies a privileged status among the significant validating relationships for adults in our society. Put slightly differently: *Marriage is a crucial nomic instrumentality in our society.* We would further argue that the essential social functionality of this institution cannot be fully understood if this fact is not perceived.

We can now proceed with an ideal-typical analysis of marriage, that is, seek to abstract the essential features involved. Marriage in our society is a *dramatic* act in which two strangers come together and redefine themselves. The drama of the act is internally anticipated and socially legitimated long before it takes place in the individual's biography, and amplified by means of a pervasive ideology, the dominant themes of which (romantic love, sexual fulfillment, self-discovery, and self-realization through love and sexuality, the nuclear family as the social site for these processes) can be found distributed through all strata of the society. Actualization of these ideologically predefined expectations in the life of the individual occurs to the accompaniment of one of the few traditional rites of passage that are still meaningful to almost all members of the society. It should be added that, in using the term "strangers," we do not mean that the candidates for the marriage come from widely discrepant social backgrounds—indeed, the data indicate that the contrary is the case. The strangeness rather lies in the fact that, unlike marriage candidates in many previous societies, those in ours typically come from different face-to-face contexts—in the terms used above, they come from different areas of conversation. They do not have a shared past, although their pasts have a similar structure. In other words, apart from prevailing patterns of ethnic, religious, and class endogamy, our society is typically exogamous in terms of nomic relationships. Put concretely, in our mobile society the significant conversation of the two partners previous to the marriage took place in social circles that did not overlap. With the dramatic redefinition of the situation brought about by the marriage, all significant conversation for the two new partners is now centered in their relationship with each other—and, in fact, it was precisely with this intention that they entered upon their relationship.

It goes without saying that this character of marriage has its root in much broader structural configurations of our society. The most important of these, for our purposes, is the crystallization of a so-called private sphere of existence, more and more segregated from the immediate controls of the public institutions (especially the economic and political ones), and yet defined and utilized as the main social area for the individual's self-realization.[8] It cannot be our purpose here to inquire into the historical forces that brought forth this phenomenon, beyond the observation that these are closely connected with the industrial revolution and its institutional consequences. Public institutions now confront the individual as an immensely powerful and alien world, incomprehensible in its inner workings, anonymous in its human character. If only through his work in some nook of the economic machinery, the individual must find a way to live in this alien world, come to terms with its power over him, be satisfied with a few conceptual rules of thumb to guide him through a vast reality that otherwise remains opaque to his understanding, and modify its anonymity by whatever "human relations" he can work out in his involvement with it. It ought to be emphasized, against some critics of "mass society," that this does not inevitably leave the individual with a sense of profound unhappiness and lostness. It would rather seem that large numbers of people in our society are quite content with a situation in which their public involvements have little subjective importance, regarding work as a not too bad necessity and politics as at best a spectator sport. It is usually only intellectuals with ethical and political commitments who assume that such people must be terribly desperate.

The point is that the individual in this situation, no matter whether he is happy or not, will turn elsewhere for the experiences of self-realization that do have importance for him. The private sphere, this interstitial area created (we would think) more or less haphazardly as a by-product of the social metamorphosis of industrialism, is mainly where he will turn. It is here that the individual will seek power, intelligibility, and, literally, a name—the apparent power to fashion a world, however lilliputian, that will reflect his own being; a world that, seemingly having been shaped by himself and thus unlike those other worlds that insist on shaping him, is translucently intelligible to him (or so he thinks); a world in which, consequently, he is *somebody*—perhaps even, within its charmed circle, a lord and master. What is more, to a considerable extent these expectations are not unrealistic. The public institutions have no need to control the individual's adventures in the private sphere, as long as they really stay within the latter's circumscribed limits. The private sphere is perceived, not without justification, as an area of individual choice and even autonomy. This fact has important consequences that cannot be pursued here for the shaping of identity in modern society. All that ought to be clear here is the peculiar location of the private sphere within and between the other social structures. In sum, it is above all and, as a rule, *only* in the private sphere that the individual can take a slice of reality and fashion it into his world. If one is aware of the decisive significance of this capacity and even necessity of men to externalize themselves in reality and to produce for themselves a world in which they can feel at home, then one will hardly be surprised at the great importance which the private sphere has come to have in modern society.[9]

The private sphere includes a variety of social relationships. Among these, the relationships of the family occupy a central position and, in fact, serve as a focus for most of the other relationships (such as those with friends, neighbors, and fellow-members of religious and other voluntary associations). Since, as the ethnologists keep reminding us, the family in our society is of the conjugal type, the central relationship in this whole area is the marital one. It is on the basis of marriage that, for most adults in our society, existence in the private sphere is built up. It will be clear that this is not at all a universal or even cross-culturally wide function of marriage. Rather, marriage in our society has taken on a very peculiar character and functionality. It has been pointed out that marriage in contemporary society has lost some of its older functions and taken on new ones instead.[10] This is certainly correct, but we would prefer to state the matter a little differently. Marriage and the family used to be firmly embedded in a matrix of wider community relationships, serving as extensions and particularizations of the latter's social controls. There were few separating barriers between the world of the individual family and the wider community, a fact even to be seen in the physical conditions under which the family lived before the industrial revolution.[11] The same social life pulsated through the house, the street, and the community. In our terms, the family and within it the marital relationship were part and parcel of a considerably larger area of conversation. In our contemporary society, by contrast, each family constitutes its own segregated subworld, with its own controls and its own closed conversation.

This fact requires a much greater effort on the part of the marriage partners. Unlike an earlier situation in which the establishment of the new marriage simply added to the differentiation and complexity of an already existing social world, marriage partners in today's society are embarked on the often difficult task of constructing for themselves the little world in which they will live. To be sure, the larger society provides them with certain standard instructions as to how they should go about this task, but this does not change the fact that considerable effort of their own is required for its realization. The monogamous character of marriage enforces both the dramatic and the precarious nature of this undertaking. Success or failure hinges on the present idiosyncrasies and the fairly unpredictable future development of these idiosyncrasies of only two individuals (who, moreover, do not have a shared past)—as Simmel has shown, the most unstable of all possible social relationships.[12] Not surprisingly, the decision to embark on this undertaking has a critical, even cataclysmic connotation in the popular imagination, which is underlined as well as psychologically assuaged by the ceremonialism that surrounds the event.

Every social relationship requires objectivation, that is, a process by which subjectively experienced meanings become objective to the individual and, in interaction with others, become common property and thereby massively objective.[13] The degree of objectivation will depend on the number and intensity of the social relationships that are its carriers. A relationship that consists of only two individuals called upon to sustain, by their own efforts, an ongoing social world will have to make up in intensity for the numerical poverty of the arrangement. This, in turn, accentuates the drama and the precariousness. The later addition of children will add to the density of objectivation taking place within the nuclear family, thus rendering the latter a good deal less precarious. It remains true that the establishment and maintenance of such a social world make extremely high demands on the principal participants.

The attempt can now be made to outline the ideal-typical process that takes place as marriage functions as an instrumentality for the social construction of reality. The chief protagonists of the drama are two individuals, each with a biographically accumulated and available stock of experience.[14] As members of a highly mobile society, these individuals have already internalized a degree of readiness to redefine themselves and to modify their stock of experience, thus bringing with them considerable psychological capacity for entering new relationships with others.[15] Also, coming from broadly similar sectors of the larger society (in terms of region, class, and ethnic and religious affiliations), the two individuals will have organized their stock of experience in similar fashion. In other words, the two individuals have internalized the same overall world, including the general definitions and expectations of the marriage relationship itself. Their society has provided them with a taken-for-granted image of marriage and has socialized them into an anticipation of stepping into the taken-for-granted roles of marriage. All the same, these relatively empty projections now have to be actualized, lived through, and filled with experiential content by the protagonists. This will require a dramatic change in their definitions of reality and of themselves.

As of the marriage, most of each partner's actions must now be projected in conjunction with those of the other. Each partner's definitions of reality must be continually correlated with the definitions of the other. The other is present in nearly all horizons of everyday conduct. Furthermore, the identity of each now takes on a new character, having to be constantly matched with that of the other, indeed being typically perceived by people at large as being symbiotically conjoined with the identity of the other. In each partner's psychological economy of significant others, the marriage partner becomes the other *par excellence,* the nearest and most decisive coinhabitant of the world. Indeed, all other significant relationships have to be almost automatically reperceived and regrouped in accordance with this drastic shift.

In other words, from the beginning of the marriage each partner has new modes in his meaningful experience of the world in general, of other people, and of himself. By definition, then, marriage constitutes a nomic rupture. In terms of each partner's biography, the event of marriage initiates a new nomic process. The full implications of this fact are rarely apprehended by the protagonists with any degree of clarity. There rather is to be found the notion that one's world, one's other-relationships, and, above all, oneself have remained what they were before—only, of course, that world, others, and self will now be shared with the marriage partner. In should be clear by now that this notion is a grave misapprehension. Just because of this fact, marriage now propels the individual into an unintended and unarticulated development, in the course of which the nomic transformation takes place. What typically *is* apprehended are certain objective and concrete problems arising out of the marriage, such as tensions with in-laws or with former friends, or religious differences between the partners, as well as immediate tensions between them. These are apprehended as external, situational, and practical difficulties. What is *not* apprehended is the subjective side of these difficulties, namely, the transformation of *nomos* and identity that has occurred and that continues to go on, so that all problems and relationships are experienced in a quite new way, within a new and ever-changing reality.

Take a simple and frequent illustration—the male partner's relationships with male friends before and after the marriage. It is a common observation that such relationships, especially if the extramarital partners are single, rarely survive the marriage, or, if they do, are drastically redefined after it. This is typically the result of neither a deliberate decision by the husband nor deliberate sabotage by the wife. What happens, very simply, is a slow process in which the husband's image of his friend is transformed as he keeps talking about this friend with his wife. Even if no actual talking goes on, the mere presence of the wife forces him to see his friend differently. This need not mean that he adopts a negative image held by the wife. Regardless of what image she holds or is believed by him to hold, it will be different from that held by the husband. This difference will enter into the joint image that now must be fabricated in the course of the ongoing conversation between the marriage partners—and, in due course, must act powerfully on the image previously held by the husband. Again, typically, this process is rarely apprehended with any degree of lucidity. The old friend is more likely to fade out of the picture by slow degrees, as new kinds of friends take his place. The process, if commented upon at all within the marital conversation, can always be explained by socially available formulas about "people changing," "friends disappearing," or oneself "having become more mature." This process of conversational liquidation is especially powerful because it is one-sided—the husband typically talks with his wife about his friend, but *not* with his friend about his wife. Thus the friend is deprived of the defense of, as it were, counterdefining the relationship. This dominance of the marital conversation over all others is one of its most important characteristics. It may be mitigated by a certain amount of protective segregation of some nonmarital relationships (say, "Tuesday night out with the boys," or "Saturday lunch with mother"), but even then there are powerful emotional barriers against the sort of conversation (conversation *about* the marital relationship, that is) that would serve as counterdefinition.

Marriage thus posits a new reality. The individual's relationship with this new reality, however, is dialectical—he acts upon it, in collusion with the marriage partner, and it acts back upon both him and the partner, welding together their reality. Since, as we have argued before, the objectivation that constitutes this reality is precarious, the groups with which the couple associates are called upon to assist in codefining the new reality. The couple is pushed toward groups that strengthen their new definition of themselves and the world, and avoids those that weaken this definition. This, in turn, releases the commonly known pressures of group association, again acting upon the marriage partners to change their definitions of the world and of themselves. Thus the new reality is not posited once and for all, but goes on being redefined not only in the marital interaction itself but in the various maritally based group relationships into which the couple enters.

In the individual's biography then, marriage brings about a decisive phase of socialization that can be compared with the phases of childhood and adolescence. This phase has a rather different structure from the earlier ones. There the individual was in the main socialized into already existing patterns. Here he collaborates actively rather than passively accommodating himself. Also, in the previous phases of socialization there was an apprehension of entering into a new world and being changed in the course of this. In marriage there is little apprehension of such a process, but rather the notion that the world has remained the same, with only its emotional and pragmatic connotations having changed. This notion, as we have tried to show, is illusionary.

The reconstruction of the world in marriage occurs principally in the course of conversation, as we have suggested. The implicit problem of this conversation is how to match two individual definitions of reality. By the very logic of the relationship, a common overall definition must be arrived at; otherwise, the conversation will become impossible and, ipso facto, the relationship will be endangered. This conversation may be understood as the working away of an ordering and typifying apparatus—if one prefers, an objectivating apparatus. Each partner ongoingly contributes his conceptions of reality, which are then *"talked through,"* usually not once but many times, and in the process become objectivated by the conversational apparatus. The longer this conversation goes on, the more massively real do the objectivations become to the partners. In the marital conversation a world is not only built, but it is also kept in a state of repair and ongoingly refurnished. The subjective reality of this world for the two partners is sustained by the same conversation. The nomic instrumentality of marriage is concretized over and over again, from bed to breakfast table, as the partners carry on the endless conversation that feeds on nearly all they experience individually or jointly. Indeed, it may happen eventually that no experience is fully real unless and until it has been thus "talked through."

This process has a very important result, namely, a hardening or stabilization of the common objectivated reality. It should be easy to see now how this comes about. The objectivations ongoingly performed and internalized by the marriage partners become ever more massively real, as they are confirmed and reconfirmed in the marital conversation. The world that is made up of these objectivations at the same time gains in stability. For example, the images of other people, which before or in the earlier stages of the marital conversation may have been rather ambiguous and shifting in the minds of the two partners, now become hardened into definite and stable characterizations. A casual acquaintance, say, may sometimes have appeared as lots of fun and sometimes as quite a bore to the wife before her marriage. Under the influence of the marital conversation, in which this other person is frequently "discussed," she will now come down more firmly on one *or* the other of the two characterizations, or on a reasonable compromise between the two. In any of these three options, she will have concocted with her husband a much more stable image of the person in question than she is likely to have had before her marriage, when there may have been no conversational pressure to make a definite choice. The same process of stabilization may be observed with regard to self-definitions as well. The wife in our example will not only be pressured to assign stable characterizations to others but also to herself. Previously uninterested politically, she now identifies herself as a liberal. Previously alternating between dimly articulated religious positions, she now declares herself an agnostic. Previously confused and uncertain about her sexual emotions, she now understands herself as an unabashed hedonist in this area. And so on and so forth, with the same reality- and identity-stabilizing process at work on the husband. Both world and self thus take on a firmer, more reliable character for both partners.

Furthermore, it is not only the ongoing experience of the two partners that is constantly shared and passed through the conversational apparatus. The same sharing extends into the past. The two distinct biographies, as subjectively apprehended by the two individuals who have lived through them, are overruled and reinterpreted in the course of their conversation. Sooner or later they will "tell all"—or, more correctly, they will tell it in such a way that it fits into the self-definitions objectivated in the marital relationship. The couple thus construct not only present reality but reconstruct past reality as well, fabricating a common memory that integrates the recollections of the two individual pasts.[16] The comic fulfillment of this process may be seen in those cases when one partner "remembers" more clearly what happened in the other's past than the other does—and corrects him accordingly. Similarly, there occurs a sharing of future horizons, which leads not only to stabilization but inevitably to a narrowing of the future projections of each partner. Before marriage the individual typically plays with quite discrepant daydreams in which his future self is projected.[17] Having considerably stabilized his self-image, the married individual will have to project the future in accordance with this maritally defined identity. This narrowing of future horizons begins with the obvious external limitations that marriage entails, as, for example, with regard to vocational and career plans. However, it extends also to the more general possibilities of the individual's biography. To return to a previous illustration, the wife, having "found herself" as a liberal, an agnostic, and a "sexually healthy" person, *ipso facto* liquidates the possibilities of becoming an anarchist, a Catholic, or a lesbian. At least until further notice she has decided upon who she is—and, by the same token, on who she will be. The stabilization brought about by marriage thus affects the total reality in which the partners exist. In the most far-reaching sense of the word, the married individual "settles down"—and *must* do so if the marriage is to be viable in accordance with its contemporary institutional definition.

It cannot be sufficiently strongly emphasized that this process is typically unapprehended, almost automatic in character. The protagonists of the marriage drama do *not* set out deliberately to recreate their world. Each continues to live in a world that is taken for granted, and keeps its taken-for-granted character even as it is metamorphosed. The new world that the married partners, Prometheus-like, have called into being is perceived by them as the normal world in which they have lived before. Reconstructed present and reinterpreted past are perceived as a continuum, extending forward into a commonly projected future. The dramatic change that has occurred remains, in bulk, unapprehended and unarticulated. And where it forces itself upon the individual's attention, it is retrojected into the past, explained as having always been there, though perhaps in a hidden way. Typically, the reality that has been "invented" within the marital conversation is subjectively perceived as a "discovery." Thus the partners "discover" themselves and the world, "who they really are," "what they really believe," "how they really feel, and always have felt, about so-and-so." This retrojection of the world being produced all the time by themselves serves to enhance the stability of this world and at the same time to assuage the "existential anxiety" that, probably inevitably, accompanies the perception that nothing but one's own narrow shoulders support the universe in which one has chosen to live. If one may put it like this, it is psychologically more tolerable to be Columbus than to be Prometheus.

Use of the term "stabilization" should not detract from the insight into the difficulty and precariousness of this world-building enterprise. Often enough, the new universe collapses *in statu nascendi*. Many more times it continues over a period, swaying perilously back and forth as the two partners try to hold it up, finally to be abandoned as an impossible undertaking. If one conceives of the marital conversation as the principal drama and the two partners as the principal protagonists of the drama, then one can look upon the other individuals involved as the supporting chorus for the central dramatic action. Children, friends, relatives, and casual acquaintances all have their part in reinforcing the tenuous structure of the new reality. It goes without saying that the children form the most important part of this supporting chorus. Their very existence is predicated on the maritally established world. The marital partners themselves are in charge of their socialization *into* this world, which to the children has a preexistent and self-evident character. They are taught from the beginning to speak precisely those lines that lend themselves to a supporting chorus, from their first invocations of "Daddy" and "Mommy" on to their adoption of the parents' ordering and typifying apparatus that now defines *their* world as well. The marital conversation is now in the process of becoming a family symposium, with the necessary consequence that its objectivations rapidly gain in density, plausibility, and durability.

In sum: The process into which we have been inquiring is, ideal-typically, one in which reality is crystallized, narrowed, and stabilized. Ambivalences are converted into certainties. Typifications of self and of others become settled. Most generally, possibilities become facticities. What is more, this process of transformation remains, most of the time, unapprehended by those who are both its authors and its objects.[18]

We have analyzed in some detail the process that, we contend, entitles us to describe marriage as a nomic instrumentality. It may now be well to turn back once more to the macrosocial context in which this process takes place—a process that, to repeat, is peculiar to our society as far as the institution of marriage is concerned, although it obviously expresses much more general human facts. The narrowing and stabilization of identity is functional in a society that, in its major public institutions, must insist on strong controls over the individual's conduct. At the same time, the narrow enclave of the nuclear family serves as a macrosocially innocuous "play area" in which the individual can safely exercise his world-building proclivities without upsetting any of the important social, economic, and political applecarts. Barred from expanding himself into the area occupied by these major institutions, he is given plenty of leeway to "discover himself" in his marriage and his family, and, in view of the difficulty of this undertaking, is provided with a number of auxiliary agencies that stand ready to assist him (such as counseling, psychotherapeutic, and religious agencies). The marital adventure can be relied upon to absorb a large amount of energy that might otherwise be expended more dangerously. The ideological themes of familism, romantic love, sexual expression, maturity, and social adjustment, with the pervasive psychologistic anthropology that underlies them all, function to legitimate this enterprise. Also, the narrowing and stabilization of the individual's principal area of conversation within the nuclear family is functional in a society that requires high degrees of both geographical and social mobility. The segregated little world of the family can be easily detached from one milieu and transposed into another without appreciably interfering with the central processes going on in it. Needless to say, we are not suggesting that these functions are deliberately planned or even apprehended by some mythical ruling directorate of the society. Like most social phenomena, whether they be macro- or microscopic, these functions are typically unintended and unarticulated. What is more, the functionality would be impaired if it were too widely apprehended.

We believe that the above theoretical considerations serve to give a new perspective on various empirical facts studied by family sociologists. As we have emphasized a number of times, our considerations are ideal-typical in intention. We have been interested in marriage at a normal age in urban, middle-class, Western societies. We cannot discuss here such special problems as marriages or remarriages at a more advanced age, marriage in the remaining rural subcultures, or in ethnic or lower-class minority groups. We feel justified in this limitation of scope, however, by the empirical findings that tend toward the view that a global marriage type is emerging in the central strata of modern industrial societies.[19] This type commonly referred to as the nuclear family, has been analyzed in terms of a shift from the so-called family of orientation to the so-called family of procreation (as the most important reference for the individual).[20] In addition to the well-known socioeconomic reasons for this shift, most of them rooted in the development of industrialism, we would argue that important macrosocial functions pertain to the nomic process within the nuclear family, as we have analyzed it. This functionality of the nuclear family must, furthermore, be seen in conjunction with the familistic ideology that both reflects and reinforces it. A few specific empirical points may suffice to indicate the applicability of our theoretical perspective. To make these we shall use selected American data.

The trend toward marriage at an earlier age has been noted.[21] This has been correctly related to such factors as urban freedom, sexual emancipation, and equalitarian values. We would add the important fact that a child raised in the circumscribed world of the nuclear family is stamped by it in terms of his psychological needs and social expectations. Having to live in the larger society from which the nuclear family is segregated, the adolescent soon feels the need for a "little world" of his own, having been socialized in such a way that only by having such a world to withdraw into can he successfully cope with the anonymous "big world" that confronts him as soon as he steps outside his parental home. In other words, to be "at home" in society entails, *per definitionem*, the construction of a maritally based subworld. The parental home itself facilitates such an early jump into marriage precisely because its controls are very narrow in scope and leave the adolescent to his own nomic devices at an early age. As has been studied in considerable detail, the adolescent peer group functions as a transitional *nomos* between the two family worlds in the individual's biography.[22]

The equalization in the age of the marriage partners has also been noted.[23] This is certainly also to be related to equalitarian values and, concomitantly, to the decline in the "double standard" of sexual morality. In addition, this fact is very conducive to the common reality-constructing enterprise that we have analyzed. One of the features of the latter, as we have pointed out, is the reconstruction of the two biographies in terms of a cohesive and mutually correlated common memory. This task is evidently facilitated if the two partners are of roughly equal age. Another empirical finding to which our considerations are relevant is the choice of marriage partners within similar socioeconomic backgrounds.[24] Apart from the obvious practical pressures toward such limitations of choice, the latter also ensure sufficient similarity in the biographically accumulated stocks of experience to facilitate the described reality-constructing process. This would also offer additional explanation to the observed tendency to narrow the limitations of marital choice even further, for example, in terms of religious background.[25]

There now exists a considerable body of data on the adoption and mutual adjustment of marital roles.[26] Nothing in our considerations detracts from the analyses made of these data by sociologists interested primarily in the processes of group interaction. We would only argue that something more fundamental is involved in this role taking, namely, the individual's relationship to reality as such. Each role in the marital situation carries with it a universe of discourse, broadly given by cultural definition, but continually reactualized in the ongoing conversation between the marriage partners. Put simply: Marriage involves not only stepping into new roles, but, beyond this, stepping into a new world. The *mutuality* of adjustment may again be related to the rise of marital equalitarianism, in which comparable effort is demanded of both partners.

Most directly related to our considerations are data that pertain to the greater stability of married as against unmarried individuals.[27] Though frequently presented in misleading psychological terms (such as "greater emotional stability," "greater maturity," and so on), these data are sufficiently validated to be used not only by marriage counselors but in the risk calculations of insurance companies. We would contend that our theoretical perspective places these data into a much more intelligible sociological frame of reference, which also happens to be free of the particular value bias with which the psychological terms are loaded. It is, of course, quite true that married people are more stable emotionally (*i.e.,* operating within a more controlled scope of emotional expression), more mature in their views (*i.e.,* inhabiting a firmer and narrower world in conformity with the expectations of society), and more sure of themselves (*i.e.,* having objectivated a more stable and fixated self-definition). *Therefore* they are more liable to be psychologically balanced (*i.e.,* having sealed off much of their "anxiety," and reduced ambivalence as well as openness toward new possibilities of self-definition) and socially predictable (*i.e.,* keeping their conduct well within the socially established safety rules). All of these phenomena are concomitants of the overall fact of having "settled down"—cognitively, emotionally, in terms of self-identification. To speak of these phenomena as indicators of "mental health," let alone of "adjustment to reality," overlooks the decisive fact that reality is socially constructed and that psychological conditions of all sorts are grounded in a social matrix.

We would say, very simply, that the married individual comes to live in a more stable world, from which fact certain psychological consequences can be readily deduced. To bestow some sort of higher ontological status upon these psychological consequences is *ipso facto* a symptom of the mis- or nonapprehension of the social process that has produced them. Furthermore, the compulsion to legitimate the stabilized marital world, be it in psychologistic or in traditional religious terms, is another expression of the precariousness of its construction.[28] This is not the place to pursue any further the ideological processes involved in this. Suffice it to say that contemporary psychology functions to sustain this precarious world by assigning to it the status of "normalcy," a legitimating operation that increasingly links up with the older religious assignment of the status of "sacredness." Both legitimating agencies have established their own rites of passage (validating myths and rituals) and individualized repair services for crisis situations. Whether one legitimates one's maritally constructed reality in terms of "mental health" or of the "sacrament of marriage" is today largely left to free consumer preference, but it is indicative of the crystallization of a new overall universe of discourse that it is increasingly possible to do both at the same time.

Finally, we would point here to the empirical data on divorce.[29] The increasing prevalence of divorce might at first appear as a counterargument to our theoretical considerations. We would contend that the very opposite is the case, as the data themselves bear out. Typically, individuals in our society do not divorce because marriage has become unimportant to them, but because it has become so important that they have no tolerance for the less than completely successful marital arrangement they have contracted with the particular individual in question. This is more fully understood when one has grasped the crucial need for the sort of world that only marriage can produce in our society, a world without which the individual is powerfully threatened with anomie in the fullest sense of the word. Also, the frequency of divorce simply reflects the difficulty and demanding character of the whole undertaking. The empirical facts that the great majority of divorced individuals plan to remarry and that a good majority of them actually do, at least in America, fully bear out this contention.[30]

The purpose of this chapter is not polemic, nor do we wish to advocate any particular values concerning marriage. We have sought to debunk the familistic ideology only insofar as it serves to obfuscate a sociological understanding of the phenomenon. Our purpose has been twofold. First, we wanted to show that it is possible to develop a sociological theory of marriage that is based on clearly sociological presuppositions, without psychological or psychiatric categories that have dubious value within a sociological frame of reference. We believe that such a sociological theory of marriage is generally useful for a fully conscious awareness of existence in contemporary society, and not only for the sociologist. Second, we have used the case of marriage for an exercise in the sociology of knowledge, a discipline that we regard as most promising. Hitherto this discipline has been almost exclusively concerned with macrosociological questions, such as those dealing with the relationship of intellectual history to social processes. We believe that the microsociological focus is equally important for this discipline. The sociology of knowledge must not only be concerned with the great universes of meaning that history offers up for our inspection, but with the many little workshops in which living individuals keep hammering away at the construction and maintenance of these universes. In this way, the sociologist can make an important contribution to the illumination of that everyday world in which we all live and which we help fashion in the course of our biography.

2

Toward a Sociological
Understanding of Psychoanalysis

Psychoanalysis has become a part of the American scene. It is taken for granted in a way probably unparalleled anywhere else in the world. This can be asserted without hesitation even if one means psychoanalysis in its narrower, proper sense, that is, as a form of psychotherapy practiced both within and beyond the medical establishment. But psychoanalysis in this narrower sense constitutes only the institutional core of a much broader phenomenon. Within this core we find the highly organized structures of psychoanalytically oriented psychiatry, with its networks of hospitals, research agencies, and training centers, the various psychoanalytic associations (both those which deny and those which admit nonmedical practice), and wide sectors of clinical psychology. The prestige and privilege of this institutional complex in America are already a remarkable matter, not least for the sociologist. Yet, if we take psychoanalysis in a more general sense, that is, as an assortment of ideas and activities derived in one way or another from the Freudian revolution in psychology, then we find ourselves confronted in this country with a social phenomenon of truly astounding scope.[1]

Surrounding the institutional core of psychoanalysis there is a ring of satellite organizations and activities that may be called, loosely, the counseling and testing complex. Here we find entire professions, young in age and peculiar to this country, the most important among them being social casework, which only in America has taken on the character of a psychotherapeutic activity.[2] The counseling and testing complex, increasingly professionalized in its staff, extends into large areas

This chapter originally appeared in *Social Research*, vol. 32, no. 1 (Spring, 1965): 26-41. Reprinted by permission of The Graduate Faculty, New School for Social Research, New York.

of the total institutional structure of the society, its heaviest sedimentation being in the areas of welfare organization (both public and private), education, and personnel administration.[3] Yet even this much more extended perspective by no means exhausts our phenomenon. For we are not dealing only, or even primarily, with institutions and organizations. More importantly, psychoanalysis has become a cultural phenomenon, a way of understanding the nature of man and an ordering of human experience on the basis of this understanding. Psychoanalysis has given birth to a psychological model that has influenced society far beyond its own institutional core and surrounding fringe. American law, especially in such new branches as juvenile and domestic relations courts, but by no means only there, is increasingly permeated with psychoanalytically derived conceptions.[4] American religion, both in its thought and in its institutional activities, has been deeply influenced by the same psychological model.[5] American literature, both "high" and "low," would be unthinkable today without it. The media of mass communication are filled with materials derived from the same source.

Most importantly, everyday life, as expressed in the common speech, has been invaded by the terminology and interpretative schemes of psychoanalysis. Terms such as "repression," "frustration," "needs," and "rationalization," not to mention the key concept of "unconscious," have become matter-of-course expressions in broad strata of the population. While we cannot be sure to what extent this linguistic usage is merely rhetorical and to what extent it has actually influenced the conduct it purports to describe, we are probably on safe ground if we assume that at least three areas of everyday life have been significantly affected by psychoanalytically derived ideas—sexuality, marriage, and child rearing. Both the so-called sexual revolution and the so-called family renascence in America have been accompanied by a flood of psychoanalytically inspired interpretations, which, by the nature of such processes, have increasingly become self-interpretations of those engaged in these activities. If we accept Robert Musil's observation that 90 percent of human sex life consists of talk, then we may add that in America this talk has become more and more Freudian. And if we may believe John Rechy's novel, *City of Night,* even the young male prostitutes on Times Square worry about their narcissism.

A phenomenon of such magnitude becomes part of what Alfred Schutz has called the world-taken-for-granted, that is, it belongs to those assertions about the nature of reality that every sane person in a society believes as a matter of course. Only a madman would have denied the existence in medieval Europe of demoniacal possession; demoniacal possession was a self-evident fact of everyday life. Today, only a madman would assert this once self-evident fact as against, say, the germ theory of disease. Sane people in our society take the germ theory of disease for granted and act accordingly, although, naturally, most of them have to defer to experts for proof of this theory. It would seem that a number of root assertions of psychoanalysis have come to be taken for granted in a similar way. Thus, the questioning of the existence of the unconscious in a gathering of college-educated Americans is likely to be as much a self-certification of derangement as would be the questioning of the germ theory of disease. Insofar as college-educated Americans interpret themselves, they know themselves to be equipped with an unconscious as a sure fact of experience; what is more, they also have specific notions as to how this appendage is furnished. For example, they are predisposed to admit the existence of unconscious guilt and to anticipate its eventual eruption. Only in America could James Baldwin have converted this predisposition into a political strategy.

Sociology, like psychoanalysis, occupies a unique position in the American cultural situation. There is probably a common reason behind the cultural prominence of these two disciplines of collective introspection. It would be surprising if they had not influenced each other, and, as we know, the mutual influence has been massive.[6] There has been a strong sociological undercurrent in the development of psychoanalytic theory in this country, especially in the neo-Freudian schools, which have transformed the gloomy vision of the great Viennese pessimist into a bright, uplifting, and social-engineering-oriented program of secularized Methodism. The influence in the other direction has been no less remarkable, although American sociology is still probably less influenced by psychoanalytic theory than is its sister discipline, cultural anthropology. What is interesting is the range of this theoretical acculturation within the field of sociology. Although individual sociologists differ in their views concerning the feasibility of integrating psychoanalytic ideas with sociological theory, those who have a strongly positive opinion pretty much cover the spectrum of contemporary positions in the field. Thus Talcott Parsons, who has gone very far in incorporating psychoanalytic conceptions within his sociological system, shares this predilection with some of his sharpest critics.[7] Whatever else may be in dispute between the struc-

tural-functional school and its antagonists, the propriety of the sociological employment of psychoanalysis is not. Those sociologists who
have kept aloof from psychoanalysis, for instance, those who prefer to
draw upon George Herbert Mead rather than Freud for the psychological underpinnings of their sociological work, have generally done
so without directly questioning the validity of the interdisciplinary in-
termarriage.

If one is married, one may describe precisely this or that facet of the
marriage partner's conduct, but apprehension of the latter's total *ges-
talt* becomes ever more difficult. A similar difficulty of perception has
been the result of the American liaison between psychoanalysis and sociology. Thus we have excellent analyses by sociologists of specific,
partial aspects of the psychoanalytic phenomenon. There is a whole
literature which concerns itself with various social dimensions of the
psychotherapeutic enterprise. There are studies of the social distribution of various psychiatrically relevant conditions, intensive analyses of
the social structure of the mental hospital (these investigations now
adding up to a sort of subdiscipline within the subdiscipline of medical
sociology), studies of attitudes toward various psychotherapeutic procedures in different social strata, and studies of the social processes going on in the course of psychotherapy.[8] In recent years much of this
work has been generously subsidized by the National Institute of Mental Health, as well as by private foundations. We would not disparage
these studies, which have greatly enriched our knowledge of many facets of the phenomenon and in some cases have yielded insights of much
wider theoretical import (as, for example, the work of August Hollingshead and Erving Goffman).[9] All the same, there remains an enormous gap when it comes to the sociological analysis of the phenomenon as a whole. Three attempts at such analysis which have achieved
a measure of comprehensiveness are Richard LaPiere's *The Freudian
Ethic,* Eric Larrabee's *The Self-Conscious Society,* and Philip Rieff's
Freud—The Mind of the Moralist.[10] LaPiere's work is burdened with
a heavy political bias (because the author looks upon Freudianism as
some sort of socialistic subversion of American free enterprise—hardly
a helpful suggestion), Larrabee's does not go much beyond description,
and Rieff's is in the main an exegetical enterprise, with some general
observations on what its author calls "the emergence of psychological
man" in the concluding chapter.

Obviously, the present chapter cannot even begin to fill this gap.
What it does attempt is to outline some of the presuppositions for the

needed task of sociological analysis and to venture some tentative hypotheses on the possible results of such an analysis. The first presuppositions are negative. It goes without saying that a sociological analysis will have to bracket, or avoid passing scientific judgment on, the practical utility of the various psychotherapeutic activities. The sociologist qua sociologist can be of no assistance to distressed individuals hesitating before the multiplicity of healing cults available on the market today, just as he can be of no assistance in the choice of the many religious or quasi-religious *Weltanschauungen* which are engaged in pluralistic competition in our society. In addition, a sociological analysis of our phenomenon will have to bracket the question of the scientific validity of the psychological model under scrutiny. This might be a task for sociological theory or social psychology, but it is an unnecessary burden for the study of the empirical phenomenon itself. The sociologist qua sociologist need not serve as arbiter among competing psychologies, just as, to return to the previous analogy, the sociologist of religion does not have to concern himself with the question of whether God exists. It should be strongly emphasized that this bracketing can occur even if the sociologist believes, as most American sociologists evidently do, that the psychoanalytic understanding of man is somehow true. Ideas do not succeed in history by virtue of their truth but of their relationship to specific social processes. This, as it were, root platitude of the sociology of knowledge makes it imperative that a phenomenon such as ours be investigated in an attitude of rigid abstinence from epistemological judgments about it.

The most important positive presupposition for such a sociological analysis is that it proceed within a frame of reference that is itself sociological. This means that sociological modes of analysis must be pushed to their own intrinsic limits and not be blocked by limits stipulated by another discipline. This procedure excludes the common practice of American sociologists of conceding to the psychologists extraterritorial preserves within the sociological universe of discourse (a courtesy, by the way, rarely reciprocated by the psychologists). Whatever may be the methodological merits of other disciplines, the sociologist cannot allow the scope of his work to be dictated by the latter. Thus, in different areas of investigation, the sociologist cannot allow the jurist or the theologian to put up "no trespassing" signs on territory that, by the rules of his own game, is legitimate sociological hunting ground. In terms of the phenomenon that interests us here, the sociologist cannot concede to the psychologist exclusive rights to that vast area we commonly call "psychological." It was precisely the great achievement of George Herbert Mead to show how the sociologist may enter this area without abandoning the presuppositions of his own discipline.

This is hardly the place to argue in what sense a sociological psychology may be constructed on the basis of Mead's work. Two crucial propositions of a sociological approach to psychological phenomena must, however, be explicated (in this context, of necessity, in an abbreviated and axiomatic fashion). The first proposition asserts that there is a dialectical relationship between social structure and psychological reality, the second that there is, similarly, a dialectical relationship between psychological reality and any prevailing psychological model. It must be emphasized that, in either proposition, psychological reality does not mean some givenness that may be uncovered or verified by scientific procedures. Psychological reality means the way in which human beings in a specific situation subjectively experience themselves. The dialectical relationship between psychological reality, in this sense, and social structure is already implied in the fundamental Meadian theory of the social genesis of the self. A particular social structure generates certain socialization processes that, in their turn, serve to shape certain socially recognized identities, with whatever psychological configuration (cognitive and emotive) appertains to each of these identities. In other words, society not only defines but shapes psychological reality. Just as a given psychological reality originates in specific social processes of identity production, so the continued existence and subjective plausibility of such a psychological reality depend upon specific social processes of identity confirmation. Self and society, as Mead understood, are inextricably interwoven entities. The relationship between the two, however, is dialectical rather than mechanistic, because the self, once formed, is ready in its turn to react upon the society that shaped it. This understanding, which we would regard as fundamental to a sociological psychology, provides the sociologist with his logical starting point in the investigation of any psychological phenomenon—to wit, the analysis of the social structures of the situation in question.

The second proposition concerns the relationship of this psychological reality with whatever theories have been concocted to explain it. Since human beings are apparently destined not only to experience but also to explain themselves, we may assume that every society provides a psychological model (in some cases possibly more than one) precisely for this purpose of self-explanation. Such a psychological model may take any number of forms, from highly differentiated intellectual constructions to primitive myths. And once more we have here a dialectical relationship. The psychological reality produces the psychological model, insofar as the latter is an empirical description of the former. But the psychological reality is in turn produced by the psychological model, because the latter not only describes but defines the former, in that creative sense of definition intended in W. I. Thomas' famous statement that a situation defined as real in a society will be real in its consequences, that is, will become reality as subjectively experienced by the members of that society. Although we have jumped many steps of argumentation here, it may be clear that our second proposition follows of necessity from our first; both propositions spring from the same underlying understanding of the structuring of consciousness as a social process. As far as the second proposition, an important one for our phenomenon, is concerned, it may be paraphrased at least partially by saying that psychological models operate in society as self-fulfilling prophecies.

The phenomenon that interests us here is a particular psychological model, acculturated and institutionalized in American society in particular ways. The sociological analysis must then revolve around the question of to what social structures, with their appropriate psychological realities, this particular psychological model corresponds (or, if one wishes to use a Weberian term, with what social structures this model may have an elective affinity). Before we turn to some hypothetical reflections on this question, it will be advisable to clarify the character of the psychological model a little further. It must be emphasized strongly that in the characterization to follow it is not our intention to reduce the various psychoanalytic theories to some sort of common denominator. Indeed, at this point we are not primarily interested in theories at all, but in the much broader sociocultural configuration outlined in our opening remarks, a configuration that has its historical origin and its theoretical as well as institutional core in the psychoanalytical movement, but which is no longer coextensive with this movement. The following, then, is an attempt to isolate some key propositions of a psychological model operative in the taken-for-granted world of everyday life in our society, a phenomenon that (perhaps *faute de mieux*) we would designate as "psychologism."[11]

Only a relatively small segment of the total self is present to consciousness. The unconscious is the matrix of decisive mental processes. The conscious self is moved out of these unknown depths into actions the true meaning of which it does not understand. Men are typically ignorant of their own motives and incapable of interpreting their own symbolizations. Specific and scientifically verifiable hermeneutic procedures have to be applied for such interpretation. Sexuality is a key area of human conduct. Childhood is the key phase of human biography. The ongoing activity of the self may be understood in terms of the operation of scientifically ascertainable mechanisms, of which the two most important are repression and projection. Culture may be understood as the scene of interaction between unconscious motor forces and consciously established norms.

What structural developments have a bearing on the success of this psychological model in our society? In the argument to follow we are strongly indebted to Arnold Gehlen's and Thomas Luckmann's contributions to a social psychology of industrial society.[12]

The fundamental structurizing force in modern society is industrialization. In rationalizing and fragmenting the processes of production industrialization has autonomized the economic area of the institutional fabric. This autonomous economic area has then become progressively segregated from the political institutions on the one hand and from the family on the other. The former segregation does not concern us here. The segregation between the economic complex and the family, however, is relevant for our considerations, for it is closely connected with the emergence of a novel social phenomenon—the sphere of the private. A modern industrial society permits the differentiation between public and private institutional spheres. What is essential for the psychological reality of such a society is that its members experience this dichotomization as a fundamental ordering principle of their everyday life. Identity itself then tends to be dichotomized, at the very least, in terms of a public and a private self. Identity, in this situation, is typically uncertain and unstable. In other words, the psychological concomitant of the structural patterns of industrial society is the widely recognized phenomenon of identity crisis. In even simpler words, individuals in this sort of society do not know for certain who they are or, more accurately, do not know to which of a number of selves which they experience they should assign priority status. Some individuals solve the problem by identifying themselves primarily in terms of their public selves. This solution, however, can be attractive only to those whose roles in the public sphere (usually this means occupational roles) allow such identification in the first place. Thus one might perhaps decide that one's real self is identical with one's role as a top business executive or as some kind of professional. This option is not very seductive for the great masses of people in the middle and lower echelons of the occupational system. The typical option for them has been to assign priority to their private selves, that is, to locate the "real me" in the private sphere of life. Thus an individual may say, "Don't judge me by what I do here—on Madison Avenue I only play a role—but come home with me to Darien and I'll show you who I *really* am."

This privatization of identity has its ideological dimension and its psychological difficulties. If the "real me" is to be located in the private sphere, then the activities of this sphere must be legitimated as decisive occasions for self-discovery. This legitimation is provided by interpreting sexuality and its solemnization in the family as precisely the crucial tests for the discovery (we would say, the definition) of identity. Expressions of this are the ideologies of sexualism and familism in our society, ideologies that are sometimes in competition (say, *Playboy* magazine against the *Ladies' Home Journal*) and sometimes merge into synthesis (the sensible-sex-for-young-couples constellation). The psychological difficulties stem from the innate paucity of firm social controls in the private sphere. The individual seeking to discover his supposedly real self in the private sphere must do so with only tenuous and (in terms of his total life) limited identity-confirming processes to assist him. There appears then the need for identity-maintenance agencies in the private sphere. The family is, of course, the principal agency for the definition and maintenance of private identity. However, for many reasons that cannot be developed here, the family alone is insufficient. Other social formations must fill this gap. These are the agencies designed to meet the psychological needs of the identity market. Variously organized, some of these agencies are old institutions transformed to fulfill new functions, such as the churches, while others are institutional novelties, such as the psychotherapeutic organizations that interest us here. All reflect the overall character of the private identity market, that of a social sphere poor in control mechanisms (at least as compared with the sphere of public institutions) and permissive of a considerable measure of individual liberty. The various identity-marketing agencies thus tend to be voluntary, competitive, and consumer oriented, at least insofar as their activity is restricted to the private sphere.

If we now turn briefly to the public sphere, with its central economic and political institutions, we are confronted with yet another structural consequence of industrialization—the prevalence of bureaucratic forms of administration. As Max Weber showed long ago, bureaucracy is one of the main results of the profound rationalizations of society necessitated by modern industrial capitalism. Bureaucracy, however, is much more than a form of social organization. Bureaucracy also entails specific modes of human interaction. Broadly speaking, one may say that bureaucracy tends to control by manipulative skill rather than by outright coercion. The bureaucrat is thus not only a sociological but also a psychological type. The psychological reality brought about by bureaucratically administered institutions has been studied by a good number of recent sociologists, the concepts of some of them having actually gained broad popular familiarity; we need only mention David Riesman's "other-directed character" and William Whyte's "organization man" by way of illustration.

With this excursus of sociologizing behind us it is not difficult to return to the phenomenon that concerns us here. In view of the structural configuration and its psychological concomitants just outlined one would like to say, "If Freud had not existed, he would have had to be invented." Institutionalized psychologism, as derived directly or indirectly from the psychoanalytic movement, constitutes an admirably designed response to the needs of this particular sociohistorical situation. Unlike some other social entities involved in the modern identity crisis (such as the churches on one side and political fanaticisms on the other), institutionalized psychologism straddles the dividing line between the public and private spheres, thus occupying an unusually strategic position in our society. In the private sphere it appears as one of the agencies supplying a population of anxious consumers with a variety of services for the construction, maintenance, and repair of identities. In the public sphere it lends itself with equal success to the different economic and political bureaucracies in need of nonviolent techniques of social control. The same psychological practitioner (psychiatrist, clinical psychologist, psychiatric social worker) can in one role assist the privatized suburbanite in the interior decorating of his sophisticated psyche, and in another role assist him (let us assume that he is an industrial relations director) in dealing more effectively with actual or potential troublemakers in the organization. If one may put it this way, institutionalized psychologism is in a probably unique position to commute along with its clientele. It is capable of doing just what institutionalized religion would like to do and is increasingly unable to do—accompany the individual in both sectors of his dichotomized life. Thus the symbols of psychologism become overarching collective representations in a truly Durkheimian sense—and in a cultural context singularly impoverished when it comes to such integrating symbols.

Sociological analysis, however, can penetrate even further into the phenomenon, to wit, it can clarify the social roots of the psychological model itself. Thus we can now go back to our characterization of this model and ask how its central themes relate to the social situation in which the model has been so eminently successful. We would suggest, first, that a psychological model that has as its crucial concept a notion of the unconscious may be related to a social situation in which there is such complexity in the fabric of roles and institutions that the individual is no longer capable of perceiving his society in its totality. In other words, we would argue that the opaqueness of the psychological model reflects the opaqueness of the social structure as a whole. The individual in modern society is typically acting and being acted upon in situations the motor forces of which are incomprehensible to him. The lack of intelligibility of the decisive economic processes is paradigmatic in this connection. Society confronts the individual as mysterious power, or, in other words, the individual is unconscious of the fundamental forces that shape his life. One's own and the others' motives, meanings, and identities, insofar as they are comprehensible, appear as a narrow foreground of translucency, the background of which is provided by the massive structures of a social world that is opaque, immensely powerful, and potentially sinister. The interpretation of one's own being in terms of the largely submerged Freudian iceberg is thus subjectively verified by one's ongoing experience of a society with these characteristics.

As the crucial psychologistic concept of the unconscious fits the social situation, so do the other themes used in our previous characterization of the model. The theme of sexuality fits the requirements of the social situation in which the essential self is located in the private sphere. In consequence, the identity-defining functions of contemporary sexual myths are legitimated by psychologism on various levels of intellectual sophistication. Again, the theme of childhood serves to establish the primacy of the private sphere in the hierarchy of self-definitions. This theme has been particularly significant in the psychologistic legitimation of contemporary familism, an ideology that interprets the family as the most "healthy" locale of identity affirmation. The understanding of the self as an assemblage of psychological mechanisms allows the individual to deal with himself with the same technical, calculating, and "objective" attitude that is the attitude *par excellence* of industrial production. Indeed, the term "productivity" has easily found its way from the language of the engineer to that of the psychologist. In consequence, psychologism furnishes the *(nota bene)* "scientific" legitimation of both inter- and intrapersonal manipulation. Furthermore, the interpretation of culture as a drama between individual "needs" and social realities is a fairly accurate reflection of the ongoing balancing act between "fulfillment" and "frustration" in the everyday life of individuals in a high-level consumers' society. In consequence, psychologism again provides a "scientific" legitimation to the adjustment technology without which such a society could hardly get along.

Finally, psychologism provides a peculiar combination of soberness and fantasy that would seem to correspond to profound aspirations of people living in a highly rationalized society. Psychologism presents itself as a science and as a technique of rational control. Conversely, psychologism makes possible once more the ancient fascination with mystery and magic. Indeed, one is tempted to speak here of a form of neo-mysticism. Once more the true self is to be discovered through a descent into the presumed depths of one's own being, and, even if the ultimate discovery is not that of the divine (at least not anywhere this side of Jungianism), it still has the old flavor of the *numinous*. Psychologism thus brings about a strange reversal of the disenchantment and demythologization of modern consciousness. The other world, which religion located in a transcendental reality, is now introjected within human consciousness itself. It becomes that other self (the more real, or the healthier, or the more mature self, or however it may be called by the different schools) which is the goal of the psychologistic quest.

Our considerations here have had to be distressingly abbreviated. And, we would emphasize once more, our argument has been tentative and hypothetical in its intention. However, it is our hope that we have been able to indicate the scope of the analytic task to be undertaken. Thomas Szasz has spoken of the emergence of the "therapeutic state." It may well be that the latter is but one aspect of the emergence of a "psychological society." It is all the more important that the full weight of sociological understanding be brought to bear on this monumental phenomenon.

3

The Blueing of America

(WITH BRIGITTE BERGER)

A sizable segment of the American intelligentsia has been on a kick of revolution talk for the last few years. Only very recently this talk was carried on in a predominantly left mood, generating fantasies of political revolution colored red or black. The mood appears to have shifted somewhat. Now the talk has shifted to cultural revolution. Gentle grass is pushing up through the cement. It is "the kids," hair and all, who will be our salvation. But what the two types of revolution talk have in common is a sovereign disregard for the realities of technological society in general, and for the realities of class and power in America.

Only the most religious readers of leftist publications could ever believe that a political revolution from the left had the slightest prospects in America. The so-called black revolution is at a dividing fork, of which we shall speak in a moment. But as to the putatively green revolution, we think that the following will be its most probable result: It will accelerate social mobility in America, giving new opportunities for upward movement of lower-middle-class and working-class people, and in the process will change the ethnic and religious composition of the higher classes. Put differently: Far from "greening" America, the alleged cultural revolution will serve to strengthen the vitality of the technological society against which it is directed, and will further the interests of precisely those social strata that are least touched by its currently celebrated transformations of consciousness.

The cultural revolution is not taking place in a social vacuum, but has a specific location in a society that is organized in terms of classes. The cadres of the revolution, not exclusively but predominantly, are the college-educated children of the upper middle class. Ethnically, they tend to be WASPs and Jews. Religiously, the former tend to belong to the main-line Protestant denominations, rather than to the more fundamentalist or sectarian groups. The natural focus of the revolution is the campus (more precisely, the type of campus attended by this population), and such satellite communities as have been springing up on its fringes. In other words, the revolution is taking place, or minimally has its center, in a subculture of upper-middle-class youth.

The revolution has not created this subculture. Youth, as we know it today, is a product of technological and economic forces intimately tied to the dynamics of modern industrialism, as is the educational system within which the bulk of contemporary youth is concentrated for ever-longer periods of life. What is true in the current interpretations is that some dramatic transformations of consciousness have been taking place in this sociocultural ambience. These changes are too recent, and too much affected by distortive mass-media coverage, to allow for definitive description. It is difficult to say which manifestations are only transitory and which are intrinsic features likely to persist over time. Drugs are a case in point. So is the remarkable upsurge of interest in religion and the occult. However, one statement can be made with fair assurance: The cultural revolution has defined itself in diametric opposition to some of the basic values of bourgeois society, those values that since Max Weber have commonly been referred to as the "Protestant ethic"—discipline, achievement, and faith in the onward-and-upward thrust of technological society. These same values are now perceived as "repression" and "hypocrisy," and the very promises of technological society are rejected as illusionary or downright immoral. A hedonistic ethic is proclaimed in opposition to the "Protestant" one, designed to "liberate" the individual from the bourgeois inhibitions in all areas of life, from sexuality through aesthetic experience to the manner in which careers are planned. Achievement is perceived as futility and "alienation," its ethos as "uptight" and, in the final analysis, inimical to life. Implied in all this is a radical aversion to capitalism and the class society that it has engendered, thus rendering the subculture open to leftist ideology of one kind or another.

Its radicalism, though, is much more far-reaching than that of ordinary, politically defined leftism. It is not simply in opposition to the particular form of technological society embodied in bourgeois capitalism but to the very idea of technological society. The rhetoric is Rousseauean rather than Jacobin, the imagery of salvation is intensely bucolic, the troops of the revolution are not the toiling masses of the Marxist prophecy but naked children of nature dancing to the tune of primitive drums.

When people produce a utopia of childhood it is a good idea to ask what their own childhood has been like. In this instance the answer is not difficult. As Philippe Ariès has brilliantly shown, one of the major cultural accomplishments of the bourgeoisie has been the dramatic transformation of the structure of childhood, in theory as well as in practice. Coupled with the steep decline in child mortality and morbidity that has been brought about by modern medicine and nutrition, this transformation is one of the fundamental facts of modern society. A new childhood has come into being, probably happier than any previous one in human society. Its impact, however, must be seen in conjunction with another fundamental fact of modern society—namely, the increasing bureaucratization of all areas of social life. We would see the turmoil of youth today as being rooted in the clash between these two facts—paraphrasing Max Weber, in the clash between the new "spirit of childhood" and the "spirit of bureaucracy." However one may wish to judge the merits of either fact, both are probably here to stay. Logically, the clash almost invariably erupts when the graduates of the new childhood first encounter bureaucracy in their own life—to wit, in the educational system.

We cannot develop this explanation any further here, though we would like to point out that it is almost exactly the opposite of the Freudian interpretations of the same clash provided, for example, by Lewis Feuer or Bruno Bettelheim: Rebellious youth is not fighting against any fathers; on the contrary, it is outraged by the *absence* of parental figures and familial warmth in the bureaucratic institutions that envelop it. The point to stress, though, is that the transformation of childhood, born of the bourgeoisie, today affects nearly all classes in American society—*but it does not affect them equally*. As, for example, the work of John Seeley and Herbert Gans has demonstrated, there exist far-reaching differences between the child-rearing practices of different classes. The transformation, and with it the new "spirit of childhood," developed most fully and most dramatically in the upper middle class—that is, in the same social context that is presently evincing the manifestations of "greening."

To say this is in no way to engage in value judgments. If value judgments are called for, we would suggest calibrated ones. Very few human cultures (or subcultures) are either wholly admirable or wholly execrable, and the intellectuals who extoll this particular one are as much *terribles simplificateurs* as the politicians who anathematize it. In any case, our present purpose is to inquire into the probable consequences of the cultural changes in question.

The matrix of the green revolution has been a class-specific youth culture. By definition, this constitutes a biographical way station. Long-haired or not, *everyone*, alas, gets older. This indubitable biological fact has been used by exasperated over-thirty observers to support their hope that the new youth culture may be but a noisier version of the old American pattern of sowing wild oats. This is probably true for many young rebels, especially those who indulge in the external paraphernalia and gestures of the youth culture without fully entering into its new consciousness. But there is evidence that for an as yet unknown number, the way station is becoming a place of permanent settlement. For an apparently growing number there is a movement *from youth culture to counterculture*. These are the ones who drop out permanently. For yet others, passage through the youth culture leaves certain permanent effects, not only in their private lives but in their occupational careers. As with the Puritanism that gave birth to the bourgeois culture of America, this movement has its fully accredited saints and those who only venture upon a *halfway covenant*. The former, in grim righteousness, become sandal makers in Isla Vista. The latter at least repudiate the more obviously devilish careers within "the system," namely, those in scientific technology, business, and government that lead to positions of status and privilege in the society. They do not drop out, but at least they shift their majors—in the main, to the humanities and the social sciences, as we have recently seen in academic statistics.

The overall effects of all this will, obviously, depend on the magnitude of these changes. To gauge the effects, one will have to relate them to the class and occupational structures of the society. For those who become permanent residents of the counterculture, and most probably for their children, the effect is one of downward social mobility. This need not be the case for the halfway greeners (at least as long as the society is ready to subsidize, in one way or another, poets, T-group leaders, and humanistic sociologists). But they, too, will have been deflected from those occupational careers (in business, government, technology, and science) that continue to lead to the higher positions in a modern society.

What we must keep in mind is that whatever cultural changes may be going on in this or that group, the personnel requirements of a technological society not only continue but actually expand. The notion that as a result of automation fewer and fewer people will be required to keep the technological society going, thus allowing the others to do their own thing and nevertheless enjoy the blessings of electricity, is in contradiction to all the known facts. Automation has resulted in changes in the occupational structure, displacing various categories of lower-skilled labor, but it has in no way reduced the number of people required to keep the society going. On the contrary, it has increased the requirements for scientific, technological, and (last but not least) bureaucratic personnel. The positions disdained by the aforementioned upper-middle-class individuals will therefore have to be filled by someone else. The upshot is simple: *There will be new "room at the top."*

Who is most likely to benefit from this sociological windfall? It will be the newly college-educated children of the lower-middle and working classes. To say this, we need not assume that they remain untouched by their contact with the youth culture during their school years. Their sexual mores, their aesthetic tastes, even their political opinions might become permanently altered as compared with those of their parents. We do assume, though, that they will, now as before, reject the antiachievement ethos of the cultural revolution. They may take positions in intercourse that are frowned upon by Thomas Aquinas, they may continue to listen to hard rock on their hi-fi's, and they may have fewer racial prejudices. But all these cultural acquisitions are, as it were, functionally irrelevant to making it in the technocracy. Very few of them will become sandal makers or farmers on communes in Vermont. We suspect that not too many more will become humanistic sociologists.

Precisely those classes that remain most untouched by what is considered to be the revolutionary tide in contemporary America face *new prospects of upward social mobility*. Thus, the "revolution" (hardly the word) is not at all where it seems to be, which should not surprise anyone. The very word *"avant-garde"* suggests that one ought to look behind it for what is to follow—and there is no point asking the *avant-gardistes*, whose eyes are steadfastly looking forward. Not even the Jacobins paid attention to the grubby tradesmen waiting to climb up over their shoulders. A technological society, given a climate of reasonable tolerance (mainly a function of affluence), can afford a sizable number of sandal makers. Its "knowledge industry" (to use Fritz Machlup's term) has a large "software" division which can employ considerable quantities of English majors. And, of course, the educational system provides a major source of employment for non-technocratic personnel. To this may be added the expanding fields of entertainment and therapy, in all their forms. All the same, quite different people are needed to occupy the society's command posts and to keep its engines running. These people will have to retain the essentials of the old "Protestant ethic"—discipline, achievement orientation, and also a measure of freedom from gnawing self-doubt. If such people are no longer available in one population reservoir, another reservoir will have to be tapped.

There is no reason to think that "the system" will be unable to make the necessary accommodations. If Yale should become hopelessly greened, Wall Street will get used to recruits from Fordham or Wichita State. Italians will have no trouble running the Rand Corporation, Baptists the space program. Political personnel will change in the wake of social mobility. It is possible that the White House may soon have its first Polish occupant (or, for that matter, its first Greek). Far from weakening the class system, these changes will greatly strengthen it, moving new talent upward and preventing rigidity at the top (though probably having little effect at the *very* top). Nor will either the mechanics or the rewards of social mobility change in any significant degree. A name on the door will still rate a Bigelow on the floor, only there will be fewer WASP and fewer Jewish names. Whatever other troubles "the system" may face, from pollution to Russian ICBMs, it will not have to worry about its being brought to a standstill by the cultural revolution.

It is, of course, possible to conceive of such economic or political shocks to "the system" that technological society, as we have known it in America, might collapse, or at least seriously deteriorate. Ecological catastrophe on a broad scale, massive malfunction of the capitalist economy, or an escalation of terrorism and counterterror would be cases in point. Despite the currently fashionable prophecies of doom for American society, we regard these eventualities as very unlikely. If any of them should take place after all, it goes without saying that the class system would stop operating in its present form. But whatever else would then be happening in America, it would *not* be the green revolution. In the even remoter eventuality of a socialist society in this country, we would know where to look for our greeners—in "re-habilitation camps," along the lines of Castro's Isle of Pines.

We have been assuming that the children of the lower-middle and working classes remain relatively unbitten by the "greening" bug—at least sufficiently unbitten so as not to interfere with their aspirations of mobility. If they, too, should drop out, there would be literally no one left to mind the technological store. But it is not very easy to envisage this. America falling back to the status of an underdeveloped society? Grass growing over the computers? A totalitarian society, in which the few remaining "uptight" people run the technocracy, while the rest just groove? Or could it be Mongolian ponies grazing on the White House lawn? Even if the great bulk of Americans were to become "beautiful people," however, the rest of the world is most unlikely to follow suit. So far in history, the uglies have regularly won out over the "beautiful people." They probably would again this time.

The evidence does not point in this direction. The data we have on the dynamics of class in a number of European countries would suggest that the American case may not be unique. Both England and western Germany have been undergoing changes in their class structures very similar to those projected by us, with new reservoirs of lower-middle-class and working-class populations supplying the personnel require-ments of a technological society no longer served adequately by the old elites.

What we have described as a plausible scenario is not terribly dra-matic, at least compared with the revolutionary visions on which intel-lectuals so often thrive. Nor are we dealing with a process unique in history. Vilfredo Pareto called this type of process the "circulation of elites." Pareto emphasized (rightly, we think) that such circulation is essential if a society is going to survive. In a Paretian perspective, much of the green revolution would have to be seen in terms of deca-dence (which, let us remark in passing, is not necessarily a value judg-ment—some impressive flowerings of human creativity have been de-cadent in the same sociological sense).

But even Marx may, in a paradoxical manner, be proven right in the end. It may be the blue-collar masses that are, at last, coming into their own. "Power to the people!"—nothing less than that. The "class struggle" may be approaching a new phase, with the children of the working class victorious. These days we can see their banner all over the place. It is the American flag. In that perspective, the peace em-blem is the old bourgeoisie, declining in the face of a more robust adversary. Robustness here refers, above all, to consciousness—not only to a continuing achievement ethos, but to a self-confidence not unduly worried by unending self-examination and by a basically intact faith in the possibilities of engineering reality. Again, it would not be the first time in history that a declining class leaned toward pacifism, as to the "beautiful things" of aesthetic experience. Seen by that class, of course, the blue-collar masses moving in suffer from considerable aesthetic deficiencies.

"Revolutionary" America? Perhaps, in a way. We may be on the eve of its blueing.

4

The Assault on Class

(WITH BRIGITTE BERGER)

Of all evils in American society, racial oppression is the most intolerable. Of all priorities for American society, the attainment of racial justice is the most urgent. The issue of race touches on the very heart of the moral values by which the society lives. Martin Luther King understood this, and the same understanding illuminates his ideal of an integrated American society. The ideal is not only the integration of black Americans in terms of all the rights and privileges promised by the society's political creed—and it is not at all integration in the sense of depriving blacks of their cultural identity, as King's detractors (including the posthumous ones) have falsely claimed. Very importantly, the ideal also refers to the integration of all Americans in a moral community, and thus to the integration of American society with its historic moral purposes. Nothing in the turbulence of the last few years has invalidated this ideal. It is the only one, today as much as in 1962, which makes sense in terms of the self-interest of blacks, the self-interest of society, and not least, the imperatives of decency.

This is why the present (1972) situation is so serious, not only for blacks but for the entire society. For the first time in almost twenty years there is the widespread impression that the national government is turning away from the cause of racial justice. Rightly or wrongly, many people feel that the inability or unwillingness of the Nixon administration to provide moral leadership in this area brought on a new era of Reconstruction. Rightly or wrongly, there is the widespread notion that the goal of integration is being abandoned in an unholy and ironic collusion between white backlash and black separatism. All this, however, is happening while at the same time the courts and at least

This chapter originally appeared in *Worldview* (July, 1972). Copyright ⁶ 1972 by The Council on Religion and International Affairs. Reprinted by permission.

elements of the national government are continuing to push radical measures inspired by the integrationist ideal. Thus, for example, former president Nixon issued a statement against busing while a certain Mr. J. Stanley Pottinger, an official of the same administration, bombarded private universities with peremptory demands to prove innocence of racial bias in employment. Is it just that the right hand does not know what the left hand is doing? Could there be some deeper confusions at work here? Or is everything to be explained by way of *realpolitik*?

We do not claim to know the political strategies of the Nixon administration. We do claim some expertise on the sociological misconceptions of liberal intellectuals. We would contend that these misconceptions are, at the very least, one important factor in the present situation. More specifically, we would argue that there has been widespread confusion of the issues of race and class. The assault on racial injustice has, without this being really noticed, turned into an assault on some of the basic presuppositions of the class system. We think that this has been a mistake. Since the class system in America is a vigorous social reality, we expect that the mistake will be costly and that programs based on it will fail. The sooner this is recognized, the sooner will it be possible to return to the agenda of racial integration set in motion by the Supreme Court decision of 1954. We would make it very clear that, in what follows, we are not seeking to eulogize the existing class system. Rather, we intend to clarify certain social realities by cutting through confusing rhetoric.

The three issues currently in the forefront of public attention that are most relevant to our theme are those of busing school children for purposes of racial integration, introducing lower-class housing into middle-class residential areas as a matter of public policy, and establishing group quotas in certain sectors of employment through government pressure. Each of these issues is today primarily understood in terms of race. The opposition to such programs is widely labeled as "racism." There can be no doubt that the motive to remedy long-lasting injustices to nonwhites has been crucial in the inauguration of these programs, nor can there be any doubt that racial prejudice is a factor to be taken seriously in the resistance to them. Nevertheless, to view these issues exclusively in terms of race is to misunderstand what is going on in such a fundamental way as to merit the appellation "false consciousness." Perhaps what has been going on in the public mind on these issues is a domestic equivalent to the preoccupation with

Vietnam in the field of foreign affairs. Certainly race is as much a crucial problem in the domestic affairs of the United States as is the Indo-Chinese debacle in the country's foreign policy. It is impossible to understand either except in a perspective that transcends each.

The busing of schoolchildren to achieve a more balanced representation of racial groups was conceived as part of a general plan to improve the situation of racial minorities, particularly blacks, in American society. The institution of public education was to be employed as an important instrument of social change. It may be asked (as, indeed, it has been) whether this was not based on an overestimation of this particular institution in terms of its power to effect societal change. Be this as it may, the policy has now made public education a primary focus of assault on the class system.

This point becomes clearer if one looks for the class premise touched upon in the issue. The premise is simply that parents are entitled to hand on to their children the benefits of their class position (a position which in the case of many is the result of social mobility achieved within their own lifetimes). It hardly needs emphasis that this premise constitutes an important motive for people to exert themselves for the achievement or maintenance of a privileged position within the class system. As far as schools are concerned, the benefits in question are far more complex than those relating to the physical paraphernalia and educational quality (whatever that may mean these days) of the particular school. The benefits that parents have in mind clearly include the association of their children with children of comparable class position. Putting the same thing negatively, it means that parents want to shield their children from the social and cultural realities of lower-class life—realities that the parents themselves have often escaped as a result of long-lasting and hard effort. Nor is there any great mystery as to what are those lower-class realities that are foremost in parents' minds. They are above all physical violence, high incidence of crime and hard drugs, and the prevalence of cultural attitudes that are uncongenial to a middle-class way of life. It is undoubtedly true that, particularly in many urban areas of the country, the lower-class associations from which parents shrink as a result of these implications have racial connotations, that is, in many cases the lower-class milieu which parents want to keep away from their children is *also* a nonwhite milieu. It may also be assumed beyond much doubt that racial fears and antagonism aggravate the class antagonism that would be there in any case. To argue, however, that all opposition to the breakdown of class differentiation between schools is therefore "racism" is to obfuscate the issue. There are large numbers of white middle-class parents with impeccable liberal credentials and no empirically observable racial prejudice who wish to preserve their children from situations in which they might risk physical harm or in which they might acquire attitudes or habits that are contrary to the families' life style.

Contrary to what is still the liberal rhetoric on this issue, we would maintain that the major opposition to enforced busing is not due to the fact that America is a "racist" society, but rather that it is a class society. What is more, the widespread failure of these particular efforts to achieve racial integration is due to the fact that the class system, while under assault, continues to be a fundamental social fact. As a result of these considerations, it is possible to consider two scenarios in this area. If we assume that the American class system will continue, then the aforementioned policies will continue to be frustrated. Whatever their professed ideology may be, very few middle-class parents will be willing to abandon the premise that their children are entitled to whatever benefits their class position can obtain. There will then continue to be efforts to defeat busing by political and legal means. If these efforts fail, those middle-class parents who can afford it financially will continue to do in greater numbers what they are already doing now—either move to areas beyond the offending bus routes or take their children out of the public schools. Those unable to afford these maneuvers will produce growing tensions in a situation in which they feel trapped. It is hard to see how either eventuality will further racial integration; the former has so far tended to produce more rather than less segregation in the schools.

The alternative to this scenario is one of increasing political compulsion. The end point of such compulsion (hardly a plausible one under present circumstances) would be that people would be prevented by the government from choosing their place of residence or that private schools would be abolished unless they conform to the racial balances prescribed for public education. For the former eventuality one might imagine a new federal offense, "flight to avoid racial integration," somewhat comparable to the offense of *Republikflucht* in the German Democratic Republic. This is not a likely development in the United States. Should one really be sorry that this is so?

The motive of redressing injustice to racial minorities has also been foremost in the policies now underway to scatter low-income housing across middle-class residential areas and to challenge zoning codes that tend to foster class homogeneity in housing. Yet the assault on the class system in this area is similar to what has occurred in education, and the particular class premise under attack is almost identical with the aforementioned one. The physical and social quality of one's place of residence has been one of the most tangible benefits of class position and one of the foremost rewards of class mobility. The choice of one's neighbors in terms of class compatibility has been an integral part of these benefits. Once more the category of "racism" serves to mystify the basic motives involved in this issue. Almost certainly these motives are rooted in the underlying reality of social differentiation, no matter how the latter is defined. We may assume that comparable motives would reassert themselves even if the class system were destroyed and some other system of differentiation put in its place. There is, of course, the ancient and powerful dream of an undifferentiated and un-stratified society, a dream that has taken various ideological forms in the course of history. Fortunately or unfortunately, this dream has little bearing on either the present reality or any likely future of Ameri-can society.

The plausible scenarios for future developments in this area are also quite similar to those mentioned in the case of education. If one as-sumes that the class system will continue, then almost inevitably ways will be found to frustrate or avoid those policies which are conducive to eroding the system at its roots. The alternative to this scenario is once more the massive application of political compulsion to change the rules of the class game.

The assault on class in the area of employment derives directly from Title VII of the Civil Rights Act of 1964. This law, as is well known, prohibited employment discrimination not only in tax-supported em-ployment but by any employers working under contract for the govern-ment. As a result of various policy initiatives of the federal govern-ment, this original proscriptive barrier against discrimination gave birth to demands for "affirmative action." In the recent past this trend has achieved a certain climax in the moves by the Department of Health, Education, and Welfare to combat "racism" and "sexism" in private universities that receive federal funds under any programs. Whatever the liberal rhetoric under which these government moves continue to be legitimated, the almost inevitable effect of these policies would be the establishment of systems of group quotas in wide sectors of the labor market and their enforcement by government bureau-cracies. To the extent that social mobility is primarily linked to an individual's relationship to the occupational system and its opportunities, this third area of assault on the class system is probably the most serious of the three discussed here. If it were pushed to its final logical consequence, it would destroy the class system and replace it with a new pattern that at this point is hard to foresee in detail. The class premise at issue here is the fundamental one of individual competition and individual achievement. This premise has provided a basic motivating force for the individual seeking to improve or maintain his position in society. The new pattern in its final consequence would substitute for this premise a new principle by which both status and the opportunities for status change would be politically allocated and bureaucratically administered by government agencies (which, presumably, would themselves by organized by quota principles).

This third avenue of assault on class is so recent and novel that it is difficult to envisage to what scenario it may lead. Compared to the first two discussed here, this particular assault could be harder to resist because fewer escapes are possible from its impact. A middle-class individual (white *or* nonwhite) can take a number of actions to avoid lower-class incursions in the education of his children and in his choice of residential neighborhood. Similar moves would become very difficult if his entire profession were subject to a federally imposed quota system. The most likely scenario here is mounting political resistance, similar to the resistance to busing and residential scattering. Labor unions are likely to be in the forefront of this resistance (the progress of unions in organizing college faculties is an important fact in this connection). Another scenario would be an intensification of conflict between different groups (as well as *within* groups) over the allocation of quotas and indeed over the criteria by which individuals are to be assigned to this or that group. Such conflict would be ferocious in occupations that find themselves in a tight spot on the labor market. The institutionalization that might emerge from the conflict would be hair-raising in its political and legal complexities. At a recent party at which some academics were discussing the HEW questionnaires sent to universities, one of those present said that his sister could not get into the astrology major at her college because the Polish quota was filled; he added that she was now trying to get into home economics as a lesbian. The laughter was uneasy, and the joke wasn't really very good. But Mr. Pottinger's project to replicate the Hindu caste system in American academia isn't all that funny either. Nor is it very likely to succeed. Again, should one be sorry about this prospect?

So much for these three issues. Underlying them and their attendant rhetorical turbulence, however, is a peculiar twist in the recent course of liberal egalitarianism. Since this twist is closely connected with the overall assault on class, its general implications are worth scrutinizing.

It is significant, we think, that in each of these three issues one may observe a progression from *pro*scriptive to *pre*scriptive political and legal positions. It was one thing for the Supreme Court to say in 1954 that to bar a child from a particular school solely because of his race was a violation of the child's rights; it is quite another thing for the federal courts and for agencies of the federal government to impose specific patterns of racial "balance" on school systems. It was one thing when both federal and state fair housing laws prohibited discrimination against individuals on the basis of race in the renting or selling of housing; it is quite another thing if political and legal power should now be used to design a demographic composition of a community or an entire region. Similarly, it was one thing for the Civil Rights Act of 1964 to prohibit racial discrimination in employment; the establishment of a system of racial and other group quotas by government fiat bears little resemblance to that original intention. One further commonality should be noted in each of these three cases. The original proscriptive actions were designed to protect the rights of individuals; the prescriptive policies now coming to the fore no longer focus on individuals but on collectivities. Indeed, it is becoming popular to cite the social desirability of furthering the collectivities in question (be they racial, ethnic, or other groups) in cases where the rights of an individual seem to be infringed upon. In other words, injury to the individual, regrettable though it may be, is legitimated in terms of this or that collective destiny. This constitutes not only a fundamental change in policies but an ideological reversal. Concern for the rights and the welfare of the individual, regardless of his or her group membership, has been one of the great moral themes of modern liberalism. It is deeply ironic that a moral impetus rooted in this same liberalism should now be in the process of giving birth to an ethic of collectivities that is profoundly illiberal in its implications.

We have already indicated that we do not believe that the current assault on class will be successful. It is a useful exercise, though, to stop for a moment and envisage such success. In that event, what would American society look like?

The most immediate implication would be a *quality* jump in the scope of political controls. To the extent that these and similar policies

continue and are accompanied by a serious governmental effort at enforcement, they would not only create vast new bureaucratic agencies
of government; but they would also entail an extension of governmental power into previously nonpoliticized sectors of social life to
such a degree that the quantitative accretion would result in a quali-
tative change. The consistent movement from proscriptive legislation
in the area of social justice is a good portent of what could lie in store
here. There are, of course, ample precedents for this tendency in
American history. Since at least the 1930s there has been a strong tendency of liberally inspired legislation to produce gigantic new bureaucracies and thus increase the scope of governmental power. This obvious fact has repeatedly been characterized by liberal intellectuals as
right-wing fantasy and hysteria, but these ideological incantations do
not change the historical record. Almost certainly there are even deeper roots to all this in the history of this country. The demon of "racism" has quite logically replaced the old demon of rum, and the new
Prohibition requires an extension of police powers at least equal to
those that were made necessary by the old. The liberal penchant to
prescribe morality regardless of cost may be seen as a late if somewhat
bizarre flowering of a hoary Puritan ambition. Nor would it be the
first time in American history (or for that matter in general history)
that actions inspired by a passionate morality would have led to thoroughly unforeseen consequences, some of them diametrically opposed
to the original moral intentions.

The implications of those policies are considerably broader than a
simple extension of the powers of government. One of the most important structural characteristics of modern society, especially since the industrial revolution, has been the dichotomization of social life into a
public and private sphere. Although the relationship between these
two spheres has been far from stable, there has been a general tendency
to recognize a bifurcation of values dominating those two spheres.
What is more, liberal ideology has generally legitimated this bifurcation. The public sphere, with its central political and economic institutions, has been dominated by the abstract relations of what (since
Ferdinand Toennies) sociologists have called *Gesellschaft*. It was further assumed that these abstract relations were related to formal rights
and obligations of the individual *abstracted from* any particular collective identities. This state of affairs was codified in a legal tradition of
civil liberties and legitimated by the liberal ideology of the rights of the
individual. The private sphere, on the other hand, while embedded

within the social and legal structures of the public world, continued to be a sector of life dominated by the particularistic values of *Gemeinschaft*. In the family, in the private relations of friendship and neighborhood, in voluntary religious associations, and through a variety of other collective affiliations, the individual was very largely left free to fashion for himself experiences of community that were not formally recognized within the public order (the legal status of the family, with its profound roots in the most ancient traditions of our civilization, is the major exception to this trend). The classical formula for the public morality brought about by this dichotomization of social life is the liberal article of faith that the public rights of the individual exist "irrespective of race, color, or creed."

The trends under discussion here indicate a reversal in this area. Communal identities previously defined as belonging to the private sphere (such as the individual's racial, ethnic, religious, or sexual identity) are now to be embodied in specific allocations of public status. Conversely, the intrusion of public power into areas of the individual's life previously considered to be none of the former's business (such as the individual's decisions where to educate his children or where to live) are legitimated by the new priority of the rights of collectivities over the rights of the individual. Behind all this lies another ancient dream—that of the all-embracing society. It is the dream of a world in which the individual will feel equally "at home" in all areas of his social involvement. Whatever may have been the conditions for the realization of this dream in other periods of history, it is fairly clear that under modern conditions it is only the state that has appeared as a plausible candidate for this role of redemptive agent. Thus this dream of a new *Gemeinschaft* spanning both the public and private spheres has invariably been the prelude to totalitarian developments in the modern world, regardless of whether the dreamers range themselves on the right or left of the political spectrum.

Modern society in general, and its class system in particular, has been accurately described by sociologists as being based on a principle of achieved rather than ascribed status. Needless to say, this principle has often been violated, and contemporary American society can certainly not be sociologically understood as a realization of it. Many critics have pointed this out. Nevertheless, the principle of achieved status has not simply operated as a free-floating idea devoid of empirical social reality. Rather it has served as a motivating force, both in the biography of individuals and in political efforts to change the social order.

In labor practices, in access to educational opportunity, in the civil service, and in the treatment of defendants and litigants in court, a vast variety of actions were taken to insure that individuals be treated equally, on the basis of abstract and formal rights pertaining to them as *individuals* and not by virtue of their ascriptive membership in this or that collectivity. Indeed, where such ascription took place it was widely understood as an injustice to the individual and a corruption of the institutions in question. The dynamics of the class system were likewise understood in terms of this principle of achieved status. Injustices of the class system were understood precisely in terms of violation of this principle, as in cases where an individual, because of his ascribed background (that is, because of the "accident of birth"), was denied some right or opportunity pertaining to him as an individual. Consequently, liberal efforts to combat social injustices were generally conceived as a further opening up of the class system, and it was widely assumed that this would actually make the system work better.

By contrast, what happens now is not an improvement of the class system but an incipient assault upon its fundamental logic. Part and parcel of this is a shift from the principles of achievement and merit to a principle of ascription in the allocation of social privilege. The notion that the individual should achieve a position in society as far as possible by his own individual effort is increasingly questioned on moral grounds. Instead, the individual's social destiny is morally tied to the destiny of whatever collectivity to which he is defined as primarily belonging. It follows that status, instead of being achieved, comes to be ascribed. Put simply, it will matter less what individuals *do* than what they *are*, or, more precisely, than what they are deemed to be. If status is to be ascribed, the logical question to ask is: *Who will do the ascribing?* There can be little doubt as to the answer: It will be the government. The foregoing trends therefore point toward a totalitarian future which is the diametrical opposite of the liberal vision. It is a future in which not only are the resources and benefits of society allocated politically, but in which the very identity of the individual is politically assigned.

It is important to underline that the illiberal implications of the current assault on class cannot be compared with earlier attempts to remedy the injustices of the class system. The liberal reforms of the New Deal period, whatever other defects they may have had, were certainly not designed to put the principles underlying the class system in question. The class premise of individual competition for the benefits of

achieved status remained unchallenged even within the ranks of organized labor. Rather, the welfare measures instituted by the New Deal
could be described as the establishment of a "floor" at the lower reach-
es of the class system. No one should be permitted to fall beneath that
"floor." While the benefits of society should continue to be the objects
of competitive striving, it was deemed morally intolerable that anyone
in the society should live in outright misery. Similarly, the movement
for racial justice embodied in the civil rights movement of the early
1960s did not constitute an attack on the class system as such. On the
contrary, it was designed to open up the class system to those who had
previously been excluded from its competitive game, and it could actually be maintained with some plausibility that such opening up would
benefit the very dynamics of class. Discrimination against individuals
on the basis of race could be designated quite correctly as an irrational
inconsistency injected into the dynamics of class. Thus the great liberal
reform impulses since the 1930s were designed to make the same system more inclusive.

To sum up the argument of the preceding paragraphs: If the implicit thrust of the current attacks on class were crowned with success,
both the vision and the (admittedly imperfect) empirical reality of an
"open society" would be laid to rest. We think that this would be a
most undesirable state of affairs. We should add that our reason for
thinking this is *not* a belief that there is something intrinsically wonderful about the class system, *nor* are we committed to the egalitarian
doctrine of liberal ideology. Rather, we are convinced that the only
likely alternative to the liberal design in our present situation is some
variety of totalitarianism. We are quite capable of imagining forms of
Gemeinschaft that we would find more appealing than the American
class system. Unfortunately, these are not realistic options. The realistic alternative is between the class system and the all-encompassing
modern state—or, more precisely, the realistic question is the extent to
which the totalitarian tendencies of the latter may still be curbed. It is
for these reasons (admittedly pessimistic) that we would opt for modifications of the class system rather than for its dismemberment.

At the same time, we are convinced that no political conception is
morally acceptable if it posits the price of continuing racial injustice for
the maintenance of the class system, or, for that matter, any other aspect of the society. Fortunately, we do *not* think that in this we confront an alternative. On the contrary, we are persuaded that the problems of racial injustice can be solved within the structures of the class

system and, indeed, that such solution will finally turn out to be in the interest of those who are present victims of racial injustice. We believe that the goals of justice and freedom are not incompatible, and that *both* can be attained by the individual "irrespective of race, color, or creed." We reject a design in which the state will allocate to each race its slice of the collective servitude.

If one takes this position, the strategic goal will be quite clear, even though there may be uncertainty on tactics. The strategic goal will continue to be that of the early civil rights movement—an integrated and open class society. This goal certainly does not preclude energetic government action. We incline to the view that the major crisis facing the class system, and indeed American society as a whole, in the coming years will stem from very different sources, namely, from the difficulties of absorbing the available labor supply (especially the supply of highly educated labor—all those college graduates with exorbitant expectations for their personal futures) in an economy of limited growth. If government is to move constructively in this situation, it will not be by meddling in the private sphere but by opening up new economic opportunities. Contrary to the currently fashionable fantasies of "no growth," every hope for greater justice (for blacks, for women, or for anyone else in the society) will be shattered unless continuing economic growth permits the *reality* of social mobility. Manipulation of the symbols of mobility and encroachment upon the private life of individuals by government actions simply detract from those things that have to be done. Indeed, quota systems as now being fashioned, and the general assault on class and its presuppositions of merit, are conducive to the undermining of the motives for economic effort. Ultimately, these are policies conducive to both social and economic stagnation. But this would be the topic for another discussion.

If one wants to modify the class system by ensuring wider and more equitable participation in it, rather than to destroy the system, it would seem to follow that one's tactical focus will be economic. The basic "engine" of class mobility is the individual's relation to the economy. The basic mechanism of racial oppression has been economic, too, namely, the exclusion of racial minorities from access to the economic benefits of the society. This fact, we think, has become much more obvious as a result of the rapid collapse of legally instituted racial segregation. We doubt, therefore, that blacks will benefit in the long run (perhaps not even in the short run) by political allocations of status that are unrelated to the achievement ethic of the class system. If this is so, then the focus of policy should be on employment and income. There must be a continuation of measures that forcefully proscribe racial discrimination in every category of employment. There must be income policies that greatly elevate the "floor" below which no one in the society may be permitted to sink. Nor would we do away with the concept of "affirmative action," even such as may be termed "race conscious" in that it makes special provision for previously excluded groups, as long as this action does not contravene the intrinsic logic of the class system. There should be special training programs in the areas of employment, special programs for better housing, special educational efforts on behalf of racial minorities—all forms of "affirmative action" beyond the proscriptive measures barring discrimination or segregation. But if such programs keep their attention on the economic "engine," they will avoid confusing symbolic and real gains. They will also cost a lot of money. Symbolism is attractive to politicians because it is (or seems to be) inexpensive. This is why the major political problem in this area is the marshaling of the resources needed for the real tasks before us.

5

The Socialist Myth

It is widely believed that the radicalism of the late 1960s is over. Those who identified with it regret its passing (not least, one supposes, because with it seems to have passed so much of their youth); others are consoled and reassured. But both are mistaken. The more tumultuous manifestations of that period have indeed become rarer—but primarily because so many of the radical impulses of ten years ago have now become firmly institutionalized. To be sure, the rhetorical goals of the "revolution" have not been achieved; the goals of revolutionary rhetoric are never achieved. Yet the "revolution" has succeeded beyond its wildest expectations in the social milieu that, from the beginning, provided both its place of origin and its principal audience—the milieu of the intellectuals, of the cultural elite.

This success has been spectacular in Western Europe, where various forms of *gauchisme* are culturally dominant—in some countries to the point of a near monopoly. This dominance is not just a matter of intellectual climate or mood; it is exercised through job networks and career channels, through the control of institutions in education, publishing, the media, and the general "culture business." The aftereffects of the late 1960s are somewhat less dramatic in the United States. Yet here, on the cultural scene, there has also been a massive shift to the left which has found a variety of institutional expressions, many of them of great political relevance. Domestic politics continues to be dominated by egalitarian, redistributionist, and liberationist ideas and programs conceived in the late 1960s. Foreign policy is undergoing a convulsive and possibly permanent change as a result of one of the major radical formulations of the late 1960s—the proposition that American world power is immoral and ought therefore to be curtailed, if not dismantled. Most important, within the intellectual milieu there has been a far-reaching delegitimation of some of the key institutions and

This chapter originally appeared in *The Public Interest*, no. 44 (Summer 1976).

values of American society: There is probably growing consensus to the effect that the market economy is intrinsically evil, that the culture of the mass of the American people ("Middle America") is inferior and pathological, and, most ominously of all, that the political system of liberal democracy is a corrupt sham.

This body of political and cultural attitudes is not new. It represents merely the latest eruption of a powerful, deeply running current within Western civilization that goes back at least to the early nineteenth century. This particular eruption, however, comes at a critical moment in world affairs and may have decisive consequences for a very long time to come. For this reason, an understanding of the peculiar affinity of intellectuals for such beliefs is very far from merely an abstract academic concern. It is timely, politically significant, even urgent.

Intellectuals and the Left

Le coeur est à la gauche. As a tendency, at the very least, this has been true of intellectuals for a long time. To understand why it helps to ask two questions: What does the "left" mean in this context? And who are the "intellectuals"? Both terms, needless to say, have been the subject of endless definitions and redefinitions. Yet, when all is said and done, the terms refer to empirical phenomena that are readily available and, much of the time, fairly clear. If the left is often fractioned and shifting along its own boundaries, it is always definable in terms of what it opposes: the socioeconomic system of capitalism and its historical correlate, the culture of the bourgeoisie. Whatever else it may mean, to be "on the left" is to be antagonistic to capitalism and to bourgeois culture. Put positively, to be "on the left" is to participate, in whatever manner and to whatever degree, in one of the great myths of modern history—the myth of socialism. As for the "intellectuals," it will suffice to describe them as that social stratum whose principal activity is the production and distribution of ideas. One of the important processes of the twentieth century has been the vast increase in the population of this stratum, a development resulting from the growth of what Fritz Machlup has called the "knowledge industry." Daniel Bell has persuasively argued that this development is one of the constitutive features of contemporary Western society.

There have been intellectuals with no tendency toward socialism, as there have been nonintellectual socialists. The affinity between intellectuals and the socialist myth is nevertheless one of long standing, and the recent population explosion of the intellectual stratum has intensified that relationship—an interesting phenomenon in itself, which also suggests that the reasons for the attraction are unlikely to be superficial. The simplest explanation for the affinity (and the one most congenial to those who are "on the left" themselves) would be that socialism just happens to be the only rational conclusion for an informed understanding of the modern world. Thus the increased attraction of socialism could be directly attributed to the spread of the relevant information and insight in an increasingly literate and educated population.

But this explanation will not do. Even if it were true that socialism is the only rational conclusion, this would not explain its dissemination among specific social groups. Modern science, for example, may also be described as the only rational conclusion for certain questions about nature—and yet it took millennia before it came to be established in specific groups in a specific corner of the world. Ideas neither triumph nor fail in history because of their intrinsic truth or falsity. Furthermore, the affinity between intellectuals and socialism is clearly more than a matter of rational arguments. It is suffused with values, with moral passion, in many cases with profoundly religious hope—in sum, with precisely those characteristics which permit speaking of a socialist *myth* (in a descriptive, nonpejorative sense).

The affinity between intellectuals and the left has been noted many times, and there have been various attempts to explain it. Most of the explanations have been in terms of the vested group interests and/or psychological propensities of intellectuals. Vilfredo Pareto viewed socialism as but another rationalization of what he termed "spoliation"—the process by which one group seeks to plunder another; in this view, the intellectuals identifying with socialist movements are simply trying to join what they (rightly or wrongly) believe to be the future elite, and their ideology is nothing but a smokescreen for their ambition. Joseph Schumpeter sought the clue to the affinity in the material interest of intellectuals as a group in the expansion of the modern "tax state"; put simply, intellectuals prefer socialism, and all steps in the direction of socialism, because they expect a socialist system to provide them with a more satisfactory subsidization than a market economy (the likelihood that they are mistaken in this assessment does not invalidate the argument). F. A. Hayek, on the other hand, offered an

explanation in terms of the intellectuals' propensity for abstract speculation; socialism seduces less by the riches it promises than by the neat-
ness of its theoretical constructions, its apparent rationality. Bertrand
de Jouvenel approached the question along similar lines, and the same
interpretation underlies David Caute's treatment of the long flirtation
of Western intellectuals with the Soviet Union, which he calls a "post-
script to the Enlightenment."

There have been comparable analyses of the leftward shift on the intellectual scene since the late 1960s. Irving Kristol has argued persuasively that there is a kind of class struggle in America today between the intellectuals (now a bloated group numbering in the millions) and the business elite; as always, this class struggle is over privilege and power. Raymond Aron and Helmut Schelsky have interpreted
the leftward tendency of Western European intellectuals in essentially
similar ways. Daniel Bell, in his most recent work, has ingeniously
combined an analysis of class interests with Lionel Trilling's conception of the "adversary culture": Capitalism suffers from a profound
contradiction between the rationale of its technoeconomic structure
and the cultural ethos of liberationism brought about by the very success of that structure.

The Costs of Modernization

Clearly, intellectuals have vested interests like any other social
group (leaving aside the question as to whether intellectuals can actually be called a "class"), and it is inconceivable that such interests
should not enter into their ideological preferences. It is also plausible
that the psychological traits associated with their role as society's full-
time theorizers should influence their perceptions of the world. What
must be added to the foregoing, however, is a closer look at the mythic
qualities of socialism. Put differently, specific characteristics of the socialist myth have a bearing on the specific affinity between it and Western intellectuals.

Much has been written, at least from Georges Sorel on, about the
mythic quality of socialism. One important element should be added to
this line of interpretation: *The socialist myth derives much of its power
from its unique capacity to synthesize modernizing and countermodernizing themes.* Modernization—its ideas, values, as-

pirations—continues to be the dominant theme of our time, and it is fully integrated into all the various versions of socialism. The socialist program is based on all the standard cognitive assumptions of modernity—history as progress (an idea which must be understood as a secularization of biblical eschatology), the perfectibility of man, scientific reason as the great liberator from illusion, and man's ability to overcome all or nearly all of his afflictions by taking rational control of his destiny. In these assumptions, socialism, like liberalism, is the child of the Enlightenment. Unlike liberalism, however, socialism has also successfully incorporated the themes that have arisen in protest of the discontents of modernity, notably the theme of renewed community. Both liberalism and socialism have upheld the threefold promise of the French Revolution—of liberty, equality, and fraternity (although they have very different definitions for these terms). But liberalism has rarely had much to say about fraternity; socialism, by contrast, has made this one of its most inspiring ambitions.

Modernity is brought about only at great costs, costs exacted at the time of its inception in Europe and continuing to be exacted today. The forces of modernization bring on massive material sacrifices and dislocations, from the destruction of English village life in the past to remarkably similar cataclysms in the Third World today. There are large numbers of people who suddenly lose their traditional livelihood and are plunged into acute misery, large migrations of people under conditions of great deprivation, and even mass hunger and virulent new epidemics. But what is more, economic and social dislocations of such magnitude frequently necessitate a quantum jump in the repressive measures of the political order. This aspect of modernization is apparent from the notorious "black codes" of eighteenth-century England (which, among other innovations, increased enormously the number of offenses, compared to medieval common law, that were punishable under the death penalty) to the luxuriant growth of repressive regimes in the contemporary Third World. But there are also subtler, though by no means less important, costs of modernization. Most of these relate directly or indirectly to the loss of community.

Through most of human history, most human beings have lived in small social settings marked by a plenitude of ongoing face-to-face contacts and by intense solidarity and moral consensus. It would be false to idealize this condition. It was by no means characterized at all times by general happiness; it included every variety of suffering and oppression. But one kind of suffering that it almost never included was what moderns have come to know as alienation, or *anomie*. Community was real and all-embracing, for better or for worse. The individual was thus rarely, if ever, thrown back upon himself. There were few, if any, uncertainties about the basic cognitive and moral framework of life, hardly any crises of meaning, practically no crises of identity. Individuals knew their world, and they knew who they were. Institutional order, collective meanings, and individual identity were firmly and reliably integrated in the sacred order provided by religious tradition. Human beings were at home in reality—even if, perhaps especially if, this home was often a less than satisfactory place.

Modernity, by contrast, is marked by homelessness. The forces of modernization have descended like a gigantic steel hammer upon all the old communal institutions—clan, village, tribe, region—distorting or greatly weakening them, if not destroying them altogether. The capitalist market economy, the centralized bureaucratic state, the new technology let loose by industrialism, the consequent rapid population growth and urbanization, and finally the mass media of communication—these modernizing forces have caused havoc to all the social and cultural formations in which human beings used to be at home, creating a radically new context for human life. It is hardly surprising that this transformation caused severe discontents, giving birth to countermodernizing impulses that consistently expressed themselves in movements that invoked the old solidarities, from the Fronde in the seventeenth century to the latest "nativisms" of the contemporary Third World. Even where there were no organized movements, there was a sense of longing for the restoration of community, for redemption from the alienating power of modernity.

In its political manifestations, countermodernization is usually perceived as backward looking, as "reactionary." This perception is often adequate, but it is important to see that it can also be forward looking, "progressive"—whenever the longed-for community is located in the future rather than the past. There are religious prototypes (Jewish as well as Christian) for either type of antimodern sentiment. Socialism is the secular prototype *par excellence* of projecting the redemptive community into the future. The genius of socialism, though, is that its secularized eschatology incorporates in addition the central aspirations of modernity—a new rational order, abolition of material want and social inequality, and complete liberation of the individual. Socialism, in other words, promises all the blessings of modernity and the liquidation of its costs, including, most importantly, the cost of alienation. To grasp this essentially simple fact about the socialist myth and to recall at the same time that modern secularism has greatly weakened the plausibility of competing religious eschatologies is to remove the mystery of the magnetic appeal of socialism. Indeed, if any mystery remains, it is that socialism has not yet triumphed completely.

"Scientific" Socialism

Marxism has been the most comprehensive intellectual formulation (or, if one prefers, legitimation) of the socialist myth. The decisive clue to its tenacious hold on the imagination of large numbers of people is precisely its claim, from the beginning, to be *scientific socialism*. The act of mythological synthesis, so to speak, was accomplished at the very moment when Marx turned the fire of his messianic hope on the dry bones of Manchester economics. To be able to retain all the redemptive expectations of socialism, and to do so on the basis of a "scientific" theory (the more difficult, the better!)—*that* is the central clue to the seductiveness of the Marxist message. Marxism, of course, has separated into different sects (in that, too, it stands in apostolic succession to Judaeo-Christian messianism), and the synthesis has taken correspondingly different forms. A history of Marxism in terms of the permutations of the two components of the socialist myth—the modernizing and the countermodernizing impulses—remains to be written. Some branches of Marxism have submerged the messianic component in a pedantic "scientism," others have gone the opposite route. It is safe to say, though, that wherever Marxism has maintained a wide appeal, it has sought to keep the two themes in some sort of balance. Put differently, in the face of the dislocations and discontents of modernity, Marxism has always held out the promise that people may eat their cake and have it, too.

Thus the view of Marxism as an offspring of the Enlightenment is as one-sided as the contrary view of it as nothing but a quasireligion. It is *both*, and in this duality lies its enduring appeal. The socialist myth promises the fulfillment of *both* the rational dreams of the Enlightenment *and* the manifold aspirations of those to whom the Enlightenment has been an alienating experience. Such a promise inevitably grates against its imperfect realization in empirical reality, frustrating and often enraging its believers. This is nothing new in the long history

of eschatologies, which is inevitably a history of the psychology of disappointment. It is all the more important to understand that, given the
inherent plausibility of the mythic vision, no amount of empirical disappointments can conclusively invalidate it. Myths are falsification-
proof. After all, the disciples of Jesus of Nazareth expected his return
in glory within their own lifetimes; Christians are still waiting, despite
what Protestant theologians have so nicely called the *Parousiever-
zoegerung* (freely translated, the slight delay in the Second Coming).
The socialist *parousia,* too, has been delayed; claimants to that status
have so far been a big disappointment. Socialists are still waiting, even
if they feel compelled by the empirical evidence to shift the direction of
their eschatological anticipation from time to time.

The Soviet Union has been a major disappointment to many, and
the psychological drama of the resulting ambivalences, denials of reality, and ideological reconstructions has been fully documented. All the
same, keeping in mind the peculiar synthesis of modernizing and
countermodernizing impulses in the socialist myth, the Soviet Union
has realized its promise in instructive, if somewhat surprising, ways. It
was Lenin who, in 1920, characterized Communism as "Soviet power
plus electrification"; over fifty years later, Russian reality could be described as "Middle Ages plus intercontinental missiles" (and it is not
irrelevant that the countermodern imagination has repeatedly invoked
medieval imagery—as indeed did Marx, in his few lyrical descriptions
of life after the socialist revolution). A very short list of these medieval-
isms will have to suffice here: the restoration of the essentially feudalis-
tic merger of political and economic institutions (the disjunction of
these two by nascent capitalism marked the beginning of the modern
era); the abolition, at least in theory, of the postmedieval split between
public and private life; the governing of society by the party aristocracy
(in this respect, one might say that contemporary Russia is actually
one up on the Middle Ages—there is now only one aristocracy, uniting
within itself the elite functions of both clergy and nobility); and last,
but not least, the creation of a new serfdom, which ties the peasant to
the land (it was only recently that residents of collective farms, who
make up close to half the Soviet population, received the right to the internal passports necessary for travel). In other words, the dominant
trait of Soviet life that Zbigniew Brzezinski has so aptly called the
"bureaucratization of boredom" is not all that far removed from
Marx's "idiocy of village life," the sophistication of Soviet technology
notwithstanding.

This is obviously not exactly what the original promise was all about. Believers have consequently looked elsewhere for the realization of the socialist myth—of late, mainly to various Third World countries, with China currently heading the list. This is not the place to discuss the bizarre reiteration concerning China of all the old stratagems of wishful thinking that had previously been directed toward the Soviet Union. The main point is that many, if not all, of these socialist regimes can also be described quite well as "neomedieval" (Shmuel Eisenstadt has suggested "neo-patrimonial," Pierre Bourdieu "socialo-feudal"). The basic formula for coping with the various disappointments is always the same (after, that is, the customary prior denial that there is anything to be disappointed about): The disappointing country does not embody "true socialism"; therefore, it does not falsify the socialist vision; "true socialism" is either still in the future, or must be looked for elsewhere—if not in Russia then in China, if not in China then in Vietnam, and so on *ad infinitum*. An excellent illustration of this procedure is the designation of the Soviet system as "state capitalism," thus setting it off against the allegedly different system of the Chinese.

Modernity and its Discontents

If these are some of the key features of the socialist myth, the question remains why intellectuals should have a particular affinity to it. As already suggested, the material interests of intellectuals as a "class" may well predispose them toward socialism. But an understanding of the mythic dimension of socialism suggests an additional explanation: *Intellectuals constitute a group particularly vulnerable to the discontents of modernity.*

To some extent this vulnerability is shared by the upper middle class as a whole, the wider stratum within which intellectuals are found as a result either of birth or of social mobility. It is the upper middle class that has evolved out of the old bourgeoisie, which had been the historical "carrier" of industrial capitalism and thus had been closer than any other group to the primary processes of modernization. There were others, to be sure, who suffered materially from the birth pangs of modern society while the bourgeoisie reaped the material benefits—the impoverished and displaced rural populations, the new urban working class, the marginal groups generally subsumed under the category of *lumpenproletariat,* and even the sectors of the aristocracy for whom modernization meant a decline in power and privilege. But the more subtle costs of modernization, involving meanings and norms, were exacted of the class closest to the inner turbulence of the process. It was the bourgeoisie who initially and most directly experienced the impact of rapid mobility, urbanization, pluralism, and affluence. Historians are not in agreement concerning the social, psychological, and ideological consequences of these experiences. It seems plausible, however, that the earlier version of the bourgeoisie succeeded in "containing" the disruptive effects of modernization mainly with the help of two crucial institutions—the family and the church. These two were the pillars of the world of bourgeois respectability, offering shelter to the individual from the alienating forces of modernization. It is precisely these two institutions that have been the major targets of the "adversary culture" of the intellectuals.

The bourgeoisie transformed the larger society in a cataclysmic manner, while at the same time it created a new form of the family, which functioned for its members as an island of tranquillity at the very heart of the cataclysm. The "invention of childhood" (as recorded, for instance, by Philippe Ariès) was probably the most important institutional innovation in this respect, with far-reaching consequences for socialization and character formation. At the same time, especially in Protestant countries, the bourgeoisie was infused with a religious ethic that gave coherence and significance to the struggles in the economic, social, and political arenas. It is also probable that the bourgeois family and bourgeois religion were important factors in the very rise of the bourgeoisie to power. Significantly, bourgeois intellectuality turned against these institutions only after the historic victory of the bourgeoisie. In other words, the "adversary culture" arose within the bosom of a world that was already bourgeois in its dominant features.

The Adversary Intellectuals

At this point, the differentiation between two segments within the bourgeoisie becomes important—the much larger group of those continuing to live within the respectabilities of bourgeois culture, and the initially small minority of intellectual adversaries. A question which cannot be answered here is the extent to which this distinction resulted from the respective relations of these two groups to the "mode of production"—the production of "things" by the former, as against the manipulation of symbols by the latter. In any event, this distinction still exists today in the upper middle classes of contemporary Western societies—but with the exceedingly important difference that the numerical proportion of the two segments has changed drastically. (For the American situation, one may again turn to Kristol and Bell for the most persuasive interpretations of this change.)

Thus there still exists today an upper-middle-class stratum, broadly identified with business and with scientific/technological activities, which continues to "contain" the discontents of modernity within the old bourgeois structures of respectability. This stratum is still animated by the norms of the "Protestant ethic," is antiliberationist in its family and personal values, and is still strongly attached to religion (not only ideologically, but through institutional participation). By contrast, there is a burgeoning "new class" of intellectuals deeply antagonistic to virtually all the old norms of respectability. It is consumption-oriented rather than production-oriented. Its values for private life are ever more radically liberationist. It is pervasively secularized, often evincing a violent antipathy to all the traditional forms of Christian and Jewish religiosity. And, as a result, this stratum has come to be progressively deprived of the earlier protections against the discontents of modernity. Put simply, the old upper middle class still manages to be "at home" in the modern world, but the intellectuals suffer increasingly from a profound sense of homelessness—and the socialist myth meets their needs directly.

This is not to argue that there is something inevitable to this particular affinity. Other myths could, and indeed did, meet the same needs. Both conservative and nationalistic ideologies have had an appeal to intellectuals, as in Europe before World War II. It is very instructive that these were similar to socialist ideologies in that they were also "adversary" to the old bourgeois world—they were anticapitalist, opposed to liberal democracy, and contemptuous of the respectabilities of bourgeois culture. Yet none of them was able to accomplish the peculiar synthesis of modernity and countermodernity characteristic of the socialist myth. It is certainly possible that new myths will arise on the right, with a new charisma and a strong appeal to intellectuals; the Third World is a likely locale for this. In the West, at this time, there is no sign of a new myth. The socialist myth is virtually without effective competition.

The Power of Myths

If the foregoing analysis is correct, there is no reason to expect the dominance of the left on the Western intellectual scene to be reversed. The intrinsic power of the socialist vision appears as strong as ever. The new position of the "knowledge industry" has given intellectuals more influence than ever before and has thus given the socialist myth an unprecedented institutional base. Indeed, the myth has achieved a sort of cultural establishment. To be sure, there are great variations within the ecclesiastical community gathered around the myth, and there will continue to be variations. The myth may or may not be couched in terms of Marxist theory; it may be pro-Soviet or anti-Soviet, pro-Maoist or anti-Maoist; it may enter into shifting alliances with other ideologies (such as the counterculture, or politically active Christian groups); it may have different postures toward the norms and institutions of liberal democracy. Yet, in all these transmutations, the myth retains—must retain—its essential antagonism to the world of capitalism and bourgeois culture. Thus to the extent that Western societies continue to be organized by the institutions of that world, those who adhere to the socialist vision will also retain their anti-Western animus.

Myths are not easily generated or manipulated. They have their own dynamics, their own "truth." What can be termed the mythic deprivation of Western societies in the face of the socialist vision thus cannot be remedied by an effort of the will. It is one thing for the historian or social scientist to diagnose the condition, quite another to devise plausible remedies. With socialism as the only good myth going, the political and economic elites of Western societies have become remarkably demoralized. The old rhetoric in defense of free enterprise, of the American way of life, and even of the institutions of liberal democracy, has come to sound hollow—it increasingly lacks the capacity to convince and inspire. Calls for a revival of liberalism or of the American creed, however well reasoned, will be ineffective unless they can be "fueled" by the power of mythic plausibility. It seems unlikely that, on its own, liberalism—least of all in its social-democratic versions—is capable of regaining such power (in Western Europe the mythic edge is unmistakably held by the *left* wings of the social-democratic parties, that is, by those elements least connected with the liberal tradition). It remains possible that there will come a new upsurge of mythical nationalism in the West—even new forms of fascism—but even then it is likely that the essential elements of the socialist vision will be retained. In all likelihood, such an upsurge would take the form of *national socialism* (the terminological likeness to what emerged under this same label in the 1920s and 1930s in Europe is not at all accidental).

There is, however, one fairly effective remedy against the power of the socialist myth—the experience of living in a society where that myth has been politically elevated to the status of official doctrine. One of the savage ironies of the times is that, ideologically, Marxism is on the ascendancy everywhere—*except* in the countries that call themselves Marxist. One cannot lure a cat from behind the chimney with Marxist rhetoric in the Soviet Union or in Eastern Europe. There Marxism is ceremony, the myth has become a petrified ornament. On the basis of that empirical evidence, one prediction is fairly certain: Western intellectuals will cease to be fascinated by the socialist myth soon after Western societies are taken over by socialist regimes. It must be added, however, that in the not improbable case that these regimes will resemble Soviet totalitarianism, this belated conversion will have little, if any, political significance. For totalitarian regimes, it appears, can survive for a long time without plausible myths and in a cultural climate of pervasive cynicism.

There is one more possibility: a reversal of the long-standing trend of secularization in the Western world generally, and particularly in its cultural elite. Throughout most of human history the myths that guided life, including political life, sprang from the soil of religious faith. The possibility of such a revival is nowhere more relevant than in America, where religion has had a unique relationship to the social realities of pluralism and political freedom. Religious faith, it need hardly be added, cannot be decided upon or engineered merely through rational insight into its importance. The spirit blows where it wills. However, those who have a stake in the future of liberal democracy, and who are troubled by the delegitimations it has recently undergone, would do well to ponder its relationship to the vital forces of religion still existing in American society.

None of this has an immediate bearing on the *gauchiste* extravaganza now sweeping the intellectual scene in Western countries. The reasonable expectation is that it will continue, though its ideological details may change from time to time. Those who have come under the sway of the socialist myth are not likely to be dissuaded by arguments, for they have a seemingly unending capacity to reinterpret evidence. They will not be appeased by reforms within Western societies or by protestations of humane concern by those who do not share their ultimate vision. Nor is any of this surprising, once it is understood that they are under the sway of a myth. Myths derive their power from those realms of the mind in which the gods used to dwell, and the gods have always been relentless.

6

Toward a Critique of Modernity

As so often, the problem begins with language. In this instance the very term "modernity" has been given a significance both normative and distortive by the myth of progress which has crucially shaped Western thought since the Enlightenment. It is a normative significance because modernity is understood as intrinsically superior to whatever preceded it—the opposite of being modern is being backward, and it is difficult to entertain the notion that backwardness may have something to say for itself. And, ipso facto, it is a distortive significance because such a perspective makes it very hard to see modernity for what it is—_a historical phenomenon_, in principle like any other, with an empirically discernible beginning and set of causes, and therefore with a predictable end. Minimally, a critique of modernity must begin with a bracketing of the normative assumptions about it.

Marion Levy has defined modernization as "the ratio of inanimate to animate sources of power." This is not an altogether satisfactory definition, but it is useful in pointing to the core of the phenomenon, namely, the transformation of the world brought about by the technological innovations of the last few centuries, first in Europe and then with increasing rapidity all over the world. This transformation has had economic, social, and political dimensions, all immense in scope. It has also brought on a revolution on the level of human consciousness, fundamentally uprooting beliefs, values, and even the emotional texture of life. A transformation of such vastness could not have taken place without profound anguish, first of all material (due to the exploitation and oppression that have accompanied modernization virtually everywhere), but also cultural and psychological. It should not be surprising, therefore, that from the beginning modernization has been in a seesaw dynamic with forces opposing it.

In the contemporary world this dynamic of modernization/countermodernization is readily visible. There continue to be aggressive ideologies of modernity, confidently asserting that the transformations of our age are the birth pangs of a better life for humanity. These modernizing ideologies span the great political divide; there are capitalist as well as socialist versions. There also exist a variety of countermodern ideologies, both in the so-called advanced industrial societies (as in the counterculture and in segments of the ecology movement—I need only refer here to the debate over the limits of growth) and in the countries where modernization is a more recent event (as in miscellaneous blends of neotraditionalism, nationalism, and indigenous modifications of the socialist vision). A critique of modernity requires further an act of deliberate detachment from these polemical positions, at least on an ad hoc basis. A critique is not an attack, but rather an effort to perceive clearly and to weigh the human costs. It should be stressed that such a critical attitude *in no way* precludes the existential possibility of other attitudes as well, including the attitudes of moral judgment and political engagement.

Only the barest outline of such a critique can be offered here. The focus will be on five dilemmas that modernity has imposed on human life. Each of these dilemmas can be studied (and, I believe, to a degree explained) by historical and social-scientific methods. Each of them touches on profound philosophical questions as well as on very practical questions.

The first dilemma is brought on by the *abstraction* that is one of the basic characteristics of modernity. It is also, perhaps, the most intensely studied aspect of the phenomenon, especially by sociologists. Georg Simmel put it at the center of his analysis of modern society, an emphasis that has recently been reiterated by Anton Zijderveld. But, in the guise of different terminologies, most of the classical theorists in the sociological tradition have attempted to grasp this aspect of the phenomenon—Karl Marx (capitalism as the source of "alienation" and "reification"), Emile Durkheim (the relation between "organic solidarity" and *anomie*), Max Weber (the discontents of "rationalization"), and others.

The abstraction of modernity is rooted in the underlying institutional processes on which modernity rests—the capitalist market, the bureaucratized state (as well as the numerous nonstate bureaucracies of more recent origin), the technologized economy (as well as the domination by technology of noneconomic sectors of society), the large city with its heterogenous agglomeration of people, and the media of mass communication. On the level of social life, this abstraction has entailed the progressive weakening, if not destruction, of the concrete and relatively cohesive communities in which human beings have found solidarity and meaning throughout most of history. On the level of consciousness, the same abstraction has established forms of thought and patterns of emotionality that are profoundly inimical (if you will, "repressive") with regard to broad sectors of human experience. Specifically, a quantifying and atomizing cognitive style, originally at home in the calculations of entrepreneurs and engineers, has invaded other areas (from the theory of political ethics to the praxis of the bedroom) in which that style has produced severe discontents. In the highly modernized Western countries the process of abstraction has gone so far that a great effort is required to wrench free of it, even in a simple act of perception (let alone in actual living). In the countries of the Third World the collision between modernizing abstraction and older, more concrete forms of human thought and experience can be observed every day, often in dramatic situations.

It is certainly too much to say that all the facets of this process of abstraction are fully understood, although all are "empirically available" and especially accessible to the methods of the social sciences. In any case, the process is sufficiently understood, I think, to permit a passage from description to critique. Philosophically, the critique will have to face a deceptively simple question: To what extent is the cognitive style of abstraction adequate for an understanding of the world and of human experience? This question has repeatedly been asked in various ways from within Western philosophy; it seems to me that today it may be asked in a much richer way as a result of the encounter with non-Western traditions of thought. Practically and politically, the question is once more deceptively simple: Given the fact that modern man must live in a number of inevitably abstract structures (notably those given with technology and bureaucracy), how can there also be room in society for the rich concreteness of human life? Once more, the scope of this question ranges from the constructions of political order to the way in which men and women go to bed together. And let me make just one slightly polemical observation here: Contrary to current intellectual fashion, the question cannot be resolved by a critique of capitalism alone. To date, in any event, socialist societies have exchanged the "alienations" of the market for the "alienations" of bureaucracy (leaving aside whatever else may be the gains or costs of socialism). In this matter, it is still timely to recall what H. L. Mencken said some fifty years ago: "To believe that Russia has got rid of the evils of capitalism takes a special kind of mind. It is the same kind that believes that a Holy Roller has got rid of sin."

The second dilemma is that of *futurity*—a profound change in the temporal structure of human experience, in which the future becomes a primary orientation for both imagination and activity. Of all the simplifications one may commit in describing the process of modernization, perhaps the least misleading is to say that modernization is a transformation in the experience of time. John Mbiti asserts that he knows of not a single African myth that deals with the future. I cannot evaluate this assertion, but it is clear that modernization everywhere (not just in Africa) means a powerful shift in attention from past and present to the future. What is more, the temporality within which this future is conceived is of a very peculiar kind—it is precise, measurable, and, at least in principle, subject to human control. In short, it is time to be mastered. This temporal transformation takes place on three levels. On the level of everyday life, clocks and watches become dominant (it is no accident that the wristwatch is a prime symbol of being modern in many Third World countries, and what a potent symbol it is—a machine strapped onto the naked skin, machine time superimposed upon the organic rhythms of the body). On the level of biography, the individual's life is perceived and actively planned as a "career" (say, in terms of a sequence of steps in a biographical project of upward social mobility). On the level of an entire society, national governments or other large-scale institutions map out projects in terms of a "plan" (say, a five-year plan, a seven-year plan, or even more long-range scenarios such as "stages of economic growth" or the "transition to communism"). On all three levels, this new temporality is in sharp conflict with the way in which human beings have experienced time before the advent of modernity.

In premodern China the clock was a harmless toy; in Europe it became what Baudelaire called *"un Dieu sinistre, effrayant, impossible."* The same institutional forces that produced Western abstraction gave birth to this sinister divinity in the West. The clock as well as the calendar come to dominate human life as the latter is technologized and bureaucratized. Within the spheres of technology and bureaucracy there is little chance of escaping this domination. But this peculiar temporality has gone far beyond these limited spheres. To a remarkable degree we have become engineers and functionaries even in the most intimate aspects of our lives. There is a powerful nexus between "time engineering" in industry and in the nursery, as there is among the "planning" of military strategists, guidance counselors, and sex therapists.

The philosophical questions that must be addressed to modern futurity are, I think, fairly obvious (though I'm not at all sure that they are easily answered). The practical and political questions are no less important. There is no reason to doubt what battalions of psychologists have been telling us for decades, namely, that the pace of modern living is detrimental to mental well-being and may also be harmful to physical health. Futurity means endless striving, restlessness, and a mounting incapacity for repose. It is precisely this aspect of modernization that is perceived as dehumanizing in many non-Western cultures. There have also been strong rebellions against it within Western societies—a good deal of both youth culture and counterculture can, I think, be understood as insurrections against the tyranny of modern futurity, not to mention the current vogue of "transcendental-meditation" and similar mystical aspirations toward a liberating, timeless "now." I would contend that these movements are to be taken very seriously. To be sure, there is no alternative to the dominance of futurity in certain areas of social life. To bring this point home, one has only to imagine public utilities operated by hippies and government agencies by contemplative monks. (Sometimes it seems that such takeovers have in fact taken place. But that's another story.) A romantic rejection of futurity may be aesthetically attractive, but it has little practical value. The critical task is rather a painstaking analysis of the possible *limits* of this particular temporal mode. Put simply, the question is how and in what areas of social life it may be possible to do without clocks and calendars.

The political component of such a critique must, above all, deal with the human costs of every long-range project or plan that bases itself on an allegedly certain future. The world is full of people (most of them intellectuals, bureaucrats, and politicians) who claim to know the future by this or that allegedly scientific method—and who impose enormous sacrifices on the putative beneficiaries of their wonderful programs. These people (latter-day secularized proponents of Biblical eschatology) range from left to right on the political spectrum. Their claims regarding the future must be subjected to ruthless scrutiny. It seems to me that sociology, with its habits of irreverence and debunking, is particularly suited for this critical task.

The dilemma is that posed by the modern process of *individuation*. Modernization has entailed a progressive separation of the individual from collective entities, and as a result has brought about a historically unprecedented counterposition of individual and society. This individuation is, as it were, the other side of the coin of the aforementioned abstraction, and it relates to the latter in a paradoxical way. The external, social-structural causes are the same—to wit, the weakening of the all-embracing, all-containing communities that used to sustain the individual in premodern societies. The paradox is that, at the same time as these concrete communities have been replaced by the abstract megastructures of modern society, the individual self has come to be experienced as both distinct and greatly complicated—and, by that very fact, in greater need of the personal belonging which is difficult in abstract institutions. It is likely that this paradox has taken a particularly virulent form in Western societies because of some factors that are not intrinsic to the modernizing processes as such—for example, the factor of the Christian tradition in the West, which made possible the development of a highly sophisticated conception of individual rights, and the factor of what (following Philippe Ariès) one may call the "invention of childhood" by the rising bourgeoisie of Europe, which resulted in peculiarly individuating patterns of socialization. If that is so, one may conceive of modernization *without* Western-type individuation in societies lacking these factors in their history (Japan is an instructive case in point; China may turn out to be another). Even in such societies, however, there is the problem of mediating between the new megastructure and the communities which order individual life. Thus it is relatively easy to teach people with (let us say) a medieval self-image to fly jet planes; it is more difficult to build medieval notions of personal loyalty and obligations into bureaucratic institutions (both the Japanese and the Chinese have had interesting problems of this kind).

Be this as it may, modernity, by simultaneously making institutions more abstract and the people in them more individuated, has enormously aggravated the threat of what sociologists call *anomie*. Once again this dilemma has both philosophical and practical-political dimensions. The current debate over the meaning of equality at least has the merit of having made more people aware of the philosophical dimension. It may also serve to uncover an underlying ambiguity of people wanting *both* individual autonomy (often pushed to an extreme libertarian pole) *and* communal solidarity. Only by understanding this dilemma of individuation can one understand the recurring propensity of Western intellectuals (who, for reasons that cannot be elaborated here, experience the anomic threat more sharply than other people) to be fiercely committed to individual rights and at the same time to be uncritically admiring of totalitarian societies that deprive the individual of all rights in the name of the collectivity. There are vital questions here of philosophical anthropology and of political ethics: Is the modern conception of the individual a great step forward in the story of human self-realization (as liberal thought since the Enlightenment has maintained), or is it, on the contrary, a dehumanizing aberration (as it would appear to be in the perspective of most non-Western traditional cultures)? These questions, as should be clear, also have a practical side in public policy and in the way people manage their personal lives.

Those who view modern individuation as an aberration have no real problem. They just have to decide which system of collectivism appeals to them most. Those who value the rights and liberties of the individual, despite the high price in *anomie* and occasional anarchy, face practical and political problems of staggering scope. The overriding problem is the search for social arrangements that will at least partially satisfy the yearning for community without dismantling the achievements of individuation. Such a search will take different forms in different countries, and it is by no means limited to the West or necessarily dependent on a Western-type political order (as ethnocentric Western social scientists continue to maintain). Thus this search is at the heart of what has been called "socialism with a human face" in Eastern Europe. In parts of the Third World there is the problem of the still powerful presence of those who want to opt out of much or most of modernization, including modern individuation. In all of this there is ample room for that combination of theoretical questioning and practicality which has always been the hallmark of the "sociological imagination" at its best.

The fourth dilemma is that of *liberation*. An essential element of modernization is that large areas of human life, previously considered to be dominated by fate, now come to be perceived as occasions for choice—by the individual, or by collectivities, or by both. This is the, if you will, Promethean element in modernity, which has always been seen by the adherents of traditional religious world views as a fundamental rebellion against the divinely instituted human condition. Modernization entails a multiplication of options. One of the most seductive maxims of modernity is that *things could be other than what they have been.* This is the turbulent dynamism of modernity, its deeply rooted thirst for innovation and revolution. Tradition is no longer binding; the status quo can be changed; the future is an open horizon. This dynamism can be traced back to early developments in Western history, but there are more proximate institutional causes. Today it is not so much that individuals become convinced of their capacity and right to choose new ways of life, but rather that tradition is weakened to the point where they *must* choose between alternatives whether they wish it or not. The existentialist dictum of freedom as a condemnation is peculiarly and revealingly modern. The sociological theories of Arnold Gehlen have gone furthest, in my opinion, in shedding light on this transition from fate to choice. Gehlen also makes understandable why this change produces tensions and discontents of great severity. He has shown persuasively that one of the most archaic functions of society is to take away from individuals the burden of choice. With modernization, this "unburdening" function becomes progressively weakened—fate is challenged, the social order ceases to be taken for granted, and both individual and collective life come to be more and more uncertain. To be sure, there is an exhilarating quality to this liberation. There is also the terror of chaos.

The philosophical question, of course, concerns the limits, if any, of human liberation. It is once more the classical question of discerning between what may and what may not be changed in the human condition—but it is a question that looks very different today than it did in the time of the Stoics, because today we have a vastly different view both of the relativity and the manipulability of the human world. The practical question is how to sustain (or, for that matter, to construct *de novo*) social arrangements that provide at least a modicum of stability in an age of dynamic uncertainties. This is a problem for the revolutionary no less than for the conservative; indeed, it could be argued that the problem is even graver for the revolutionary, because the social arrangements that he constructs do not have even the remnants of traditional taken-for-grantedness still available to the conservative, and are therefore all the more precarious in a world in which fate has been abolished.

The liberation from all bonds that limit choice (be it individual or collective) continues to be one of the most powerful inspirations of modernity. Its price is precisely that "anguish of choice" which existentialists have described so well. The latter phenomenon has brought about that peculiarly modern paradox that Erich Fromm has called the "escape from freedom"—an escape which actually views *itself* as a liberation. This may not be very logical, but it makes much sense psychologically. Thus there are two quite contradictory notions of liberation in the world today (not only in the West): liberation of the individual from fate of any kind (social, political, even biological), and liberation of the individual from the *anomie* of a condition without fate. Put simply, there is the ideal of liberation *as* choice and the ideal of liberation *from* choice. The two ideals crisscross contemporary values and ideologies, and it is of great importance that their social and psychological presuppositions be clearly understood; otherwise, all becomes confusion.

Finally, there is the dilemma of *secularization*. Modernization has brought with it a massive threat to the plausibility of religious belief and experience. Put differently, modernity, at least thus far, has been antagonistic to the dimension of transcendence in the human condition. Again one may ask whether the distinctive cultural conditions of the Western culture that served as the matrix of modernity have led to this result; conversely, one may ask whether modernization *without* secularization is possible in different cultural contexts. But even in Third World countries, where traditional religion has shown great resilience and even the capacity for strong resurgences (for instance, in the Islamic world), the secularizing effects of modernization have been felt. The reasons for this are not at all mysterious. The common explanation of secularization in terms of the impact of modern science and technology undoubtedly has much merit; I think that equally important are the consequences of the pluralizing and ipso facto relativizing forces of modernization. Secularization, of course, has not meant that religious belief and practice have disappeared, and not even the most thorough proponents of so-called secularization theory regard such disappearance as a likely outcome in the foreseeable future (the reappearance of strong religious impulses in the Soviet Union, after half a century of intense antireligious propaganda backed up by repressive actions of all kinds, is very suggestive on this point). But secularization *has* meant a weakening of the plausibility of religious perceptions of reality among large numbers of people, especially as the world view of secularity has come to be "established" by the intellectual elites and in the educational institutions of modern societies.

Obviously, religious and nonreligious observers will differ in the assessment of this phenomenon. For those who see transcendence as a necessary (because true) constituent of the human condition, secularization is an aberration, distortive of reality and dehumanizing. For them, the critique of modernity will have a crucially important theological dimension; indeed, their critique will probably both begin and end with theological propositions. But those who do not have such religious commitments (say, agnostic sociologists, or even atheistic ones) can also see the dilemma posed by secularization. The dilemma comes from the fact (an empirically "available" fact, *not* a theological proposition) that secularization frustrates deeply grounded human aspirations—most important among these, the aspiration to exist in a meaningful and ultimately hopeful cosmos. This dilemma is closely related to what Max Weber called the need for "theodicies," that is, for satisfactory ways of explaining and coping with the experiences of suffering and evil in human life. There are, of course, secular "theodicies," and they clearly work for some people. It appears, however, that they are much weaker than the religious "theodicies" in offering both meaning and consolation to individuals in pain, sorrow, or doubt.

This last dilemma, more than the preceding four, raises more philosophical than practical problems, although it, too, has its practical side. The question here is, quite simply, that of the rights of religion in a modern society. I think it is no accident that countermodernizing trends and movements have frequently been characterized by powerful reaffirmations of transcendence. The experiential realities of mystery, awe, and transcendent hope are hard to eradicate from human consciousness. Yet, even in Western countries with strong legal safeguards for religious liberty, there is an Enlightenment tradition of "delegitimating" these experiences; the tradition, of course, is strongest in the cultural and educational elites. For very sociological (that is, *non*theological, *non*philosophical) reasons, I doubt that this is a viable state of affairs. It goes without saying that there are issues of public policy involved in this (in the United States, most of these relate to the question of how the constitutional separation of church and state is to be interpreted).

I believe that the critique of modernity will be one of the great intellectual tasks of the future, be it as a comprehensive exercise or in separate parts. The scope is broadly cross-cultural. It will be a task that, by its very nature, will have to be interdisciplinary; I'm enough of a parochialist to believe that sociology has a uniquely useful contribution to make. It will also be a task linking theory and praxis, touching, as it does, certain fundamental philosophical as well as highly concrete practical-political questions. The task is also of human and moral urgency. For what it is finally all about is the question of how we, and our children, can live in a humanly tolerable way in the world created by modernization.

II

ACTING IN
MODERN AMERICA

7

Languages of Murder

In early 1971 national attention was focused on two trials, the court-martial of Lieutenant William Calley for the Mylai massacre, and the trial of Charles Manson and associates for the grisly two-day mass-murder spree known as the Tate/LaBianca murders. Two books were published in close succession about these two trials—Richard Hammer's *The Court-Martial of Lt. Calley*[1] and George Bishop's *Witness to Evil*.[2] The two books are unequal in merit. Hammer's account is well written, tautly organized, and gives the reader an at times unbearable sense of participation in the courtroom drama at Fort Benning. Bishop's book is very poorly written and organized, and it succeeds (no mean achievement in view of its subject matter) in both boring and confusing the reader for long stretches. Fortunately, both books contain long excerpts of courtroom testimony, allowing the protagonists to take the stage away from the two reporters. In any case, the purpose of the following comments is *not* to review the aforementioned books. Rather, it is to take them as an occasion for reflecting about the significance of the two trials.

Both trials were widely perceived as paradigmatic, though different people had different paradigms in mind. In the paradigm of the left, it was American society as such that was on trial in Fort Benning. In the paradigm of the right, the Manson trial signified the trial of the counterculture. For those convinced of the imminent demise of American society, both trials together were paradigmatic of America's descent into a jungle of murderous irrationality; this last paradigm was especially prominent in foreign commentary, as, for example, in that of the German news magazine *Der Spiegel*. The characters, and even the physical appearance, of the two major defendants facilitated these symbolic perceptions. It was not difficult to perceive Calley as the pro-

This chapter originally appeared in *Worldview* (January, 1972). Copyright 1972 by The Council on Religion and International Affairs. Reprinted by permission.

totype of murderous *Amerika*—the ineffective martinet, blandly un-repentant, an almost too obvious incarnation of the "banality of evil." And there was Manson, hairy apparition from unspeakable depths of countercultural dementia, in each detail the figure of terror evoked in the rhetoric of law-and-order politicians and haunting the nightmares of Middle America. Both figures were so true to type, so bereft of indi-vidual reality, that one could not help wondering whether, perhaps, the one had been specially constructed by the *New York Review of Books* and the other by Spiro Agnew's ghostwriters. It should hardly come as a surprise, then, that Nixon, as always finely attuned to popu-lar paradigms, intervened in both cases. It was probably a simple gaffe when Nixon spoke of Manson as a guilty man while the trial was still in process, but it left little doubt as to the enemies stalking through Nixon's nightmares. It was anything but a gaffe when Nixon inter-vened *after* Calley's conviction in order to assuage the emotional tur-moil in that Middle America with which Nixon's imagination shares both enemies and heroes. Finally, the macabre occurrence of Christ-ological symbolism underlined the paradigmatic character of these clashing perceptions. To his "family," Manson was a Christ-figure. It was left to Calley's biographer John Sack to exclaim, after the con-viction, "I see Rusty as Christ on the cross being crucified" (Hammer, p. 374). There is hardly a better metaphor of our present political situ-ation than this polarization in the imagery of redemptive suffering.

To anyone capable of a measure of detachment from the polarized passions of the day, these paradigms are hardly convincing as referring to presently existing sociocultural contexts. Middle America is not in-habited by Calleys, nor the counterculture by Mansons. Neither figure is objectively representative of his respective social milieu—*at the present time*. If one reflects about the latter phrase, however, the sub-jective perception of the two figures as such representatives becomes ominously significant. The significance deepens as one recalls that Cal-ley and Manson were not only perceived as demonological counter-images; there was also positive identification with what they were per-ceived to represent. Such identification was all too apparent in the pop-ular outcry following Calley's conviction, making Aubrey Daniel, Cal-ley's prosecutor, question rather optimistically whether these people were aware of the evidence presented at the trial. There was, to be sure, no comparable popular identification with Manson in the counterculture. But some identification with Manson as a sort of revo-lutionary hero is part and parcel of a widespread legitimation of violence and crime by radical spokesmen. It is in this sense that Calley and Manson are, indeed, both paradigmatic and representative: *They represent possibilities of the American spirit today.* The degree of identification with these representations by polarized segments of the American people will decide whether they will turn from paradigms of possibility to paradigms of objective social reality.

Precisely because of the polarization of imagery it is important to ask, with as much detachment as one can muster, what the two crimes have in common and where they differ. Both Calley and Manson were convicted of massacres of helpless people, without provocation and without mercy. The Mylai massacre far exceeded the Tate/LaBianca murders in the number of victims. The former called up older visions of monumental horror—Lidice, Katyn, Oradour; the latter, however horrible, remained within the parameters of what one might call non-apocalyptic criminology. Moreover, the larger settings differed greatly. The Mylai murders took place in a setting of actual war, the Tate/LaBianca murders in a war of Manson's fantasy. Thus Mylai was an event within a much larger setting of systematic brutality—of free-fire zones, of body counts, of the "mere gook rule." The Tate/LaBianca murders took place in a setting of peace, or "normal life"—it was Manson and his associates who "brought the war home." It is not too obvious which of the two settings brings with it the greater gravamen of guilt. Calley's crime must be seen in the setting of a much wider inhumanity, and might thus be taken as both more serious in its implications and (as the defense argued) less culpable by the same token. The American military had in actual fact been waging a war of systematic inhumanity in Vietnam (regardless of the question of the typicality or uniqueness of the particular horror of this massacre), and to the extent that American society is responsible for its military it must share in that responsibility, too. While the zones that the counterculture has "liberated" from the larger society can hardly be held up as exemplars of humane living (one may simply refer here to the Haight-Ashbury and the East Village as they now appear after several years of "liberation"), no comparable charge of inhumanity can be made against the counterculture. Thus Manson's crime took place in a setting of (at the very least) relative civilization, and might thus be viewed as both less serious in its implications and (as the prosecution argued) more heinous.

It would be thus as simplistic to equate the two crimes morally as it is to see them as objective representations of their respective sociocultural worlds. Nevertheless, it is instructive to look at the continuities that exist between the two crimes both in spirit and in the shape of action. As these continuities are perceived, the import of both crimes for the future of America may be seen in a profoundly disturbing conjunction.

The essential continuity is that both crimes consisted of *impersonal killings*. It is worth quoting in full a particular exchange between Daniel and Calley to make this point. Daniel was questioning Calley about his men firing as they moved into Mylai:

DANIEL: What were they firing at?
CALLEY: At the enemy, sir.
DANIEL: At people?
CALLEY: At the enemy, sir.
DANIEL: They weren't human beings?
CALLEY: Yes, sir.
DANIEL: They were human beings?
CALLEY: Yes, sir.
DANIEL: Were they men?
CALLEY: I don't know, sir. I would imagine they were, sir.
DANIEL: Didn't you see?
CALLEY: Pardon, sir?
DANIEL: Did you see them?
CALLEY: I wasn't discriminating.
DANIEL: Did you see women?
CALLEY: I don't know, sir.
DANIEL: What do you mean you weren't discriminating?
CALLEY: I didn't discriminate between individuals in the village, sir. They were all the enemy, they were all to be destroyed, sir. (Hammer, p. 263)

And in case anyone suspects that this formulation was only elicited from Calley by the hostile questioning of the prosecution, here is what Calley said earlier under examination by the defense and what he said in his final plea to the court:

I was ordered to go in there and destroy the enemy. That was my job on that day. That was the mission I was given. I did not sit down and think in terms of men, women and children. They were all classified the same, and that was the classification that we dealt with, just as enemy soldiers. (Hammer, p. 257)

Nobody in the military system ever described them as anything other than communism. They didn't give it a race, they didn't give it a sex, they didn't give it an age. . . . That was my enemy out there. (Hammer, p. 367)

A similar procedure of "no discrimination" characterizes the "mission" of Manson's little platoon. Indeed, the following summary of testimony of the manner in which its victims were selected may well be described as an operation in Manson's own free-fire zone:

> The witness then described what was, in many ways, the most chilling aspect of the whole affair. With Manson driving, Linda, Tex, Clem Tufts, Patricia Krenwinkel and Leslie Van Houten wandered at random around the city seeking, in military kill terms, targets of opportunity. They could have stopped at anyone's house to carry out their mission. At one point Manson spotted a man driving a white Volvo sport car. He told Linda, who was now driving, to pull up beside the car at the next light and he, Manson, would kill him. She did and Manson was out of the car, apparently ready to commit murder, when the light changed and the man drove off. The objective was quickly forgotten and Charlie next told her to stop at a church they happened to be passing. They parked in the parking area, Manson got out and tried the doors but they were locked. He got back in and they drove away. (Bishop, p. 163)

In other words, neither Calley nor Manson were killing individual human beings. Calley was killing "the enemy," or even "communism." Manson, on the other hand, was killing "pigs." This is how one witness reported Manson's definition of this term: "Asked what he meant by pigs, Manson had said that, 'Pigs were anyone that gave consent to support the system'." It follows logically that the killers feel innocent of any crime. Calley repeatedly, and dramatically in his final plea, asserted his innocence. In answer to questioning by Daniel, he even achieved the memorable sentence, "There wasn't any big deal, no sir" (Hammer, p. 276). Manson, a commander sensitive to the morale of his troops, asked each participant in the murders whether they felt remorse; each answered "No" (Bishop, p. 162).

The killers feel innocent because their victims have, by "classification," been deprived of humanity. They are also absolved of guilt because they acted under orders. As Calley put it:

> I felt then and I still do that I acted as I was directed, and I carried out the orders that I was given, and I do not feel wrong in doing so, sir. (Hammer, p. 257)

This is how, on the other hand, Linda Kasabian described the command structure of the "family":

q: Did you disagree with his philosophy in some respects?
a: Yes, I did.
q: And you told him that you disagreed with it when he told you?
a: No. Because I was always told, "Never ask why."
q: Were you also told that you couldn't disagree?

A: The girls used to always tell me that. "We never question Charlie. We know that what he is doing is right." (Bishop, p. 209)

Faced with acts such as those committed in these two crimes, a commonsense reaction is to assume that the perpetrators must somehow be "crazy," or at least were so at the time. In both trials psychiatrists entered the scene—to the considerable annoyance of the defendants, who insisted on their sanity. Calley completely lost his temper when he was referred to a sanity board:

> Outside the courtroom in the corridors, Calley was enraged. He chain-smoked cigarettes, paced up and down, and railed. "I think it's unwarranted and unnecessary. I don't think we're trying to say I was insane. So I don't like it." (Hammer, p. 221)

Manson thus described himself ("with quiet dignity," one is tempted to say) in one of his statements to Judge Older: "I am a reasonable human being, a reasonable person" (Bishop, p. 275). In both trials there was psychiatric evidence to suggest that there were conditions tending to reduce the moral capacity of anyone subjected to them. In the Calley trial these were the overall circumstances of the Vietnam war; in the Manson trial the demoralization was linked to drugs. In both trials the image of the "robot" was invoked in this connection. Albert LaVerne, a psychiatrist called by Calley's defense (Calley himself pithily remarked of LaVerne, "He's nuts" [Hammer, p. 217]), thus characterized Calley's state of mind at the time when, according to the defense, he was under an order to destroy Mylai:

> He could not disobey that order. He was like an automaton, a robot. When the order came to stop shooting, the party's over, he stopped. (Hammer, p. 219)

A. R. Tweed was a psychiatrist called in by defense lawyers to cast doubt on the testimony of Linda Kasabian, the prosecution's star witness in the Manson trial. His comments on the moral effects of drug use were immediately relevant to this issue, but since drugs had been an important ingredient in the overall life style of the "family," the comments have a broader relevance:

> The habitual long-term use of LSD for pleasure or escape produces the possibility for the impairment of good sense and maturation. . . . Individuals so affected may become confused and disorganized and are usually markedly suggestible. (Bishop, p. 120)

One of the defense lawyers summarized the psychiatric evidence by saying that LSD use "led to the disturbance of the so-called super-ego functions, which is the conscience or moral functioning area of the brain" (Bishop, p. 121). Later on the prosecution, in something of a lapse of logic (as the defense pointed out), described the Manson "family" as "a closely knit band of vagabond, mindless robots" (Bishop, p. 399). Whatever the moral implications of psychiatric diagnosis, legal insanity was not invoked as a defense in either trial. And, common sense notwithstanding, Calley and Manson were tried as they wanted to be regarded—as "reasonable persons." In doing so, the courts were affirming once again a fundamental principle of Western law, simply stated by Aubrey Daniel in his final charge to the jury:

> When the accused put on the uniform of an American officer. . .he was not relieved of his conscience, he was not relieved of his responsibility to make appropriate moral judgments. (Hammer, p. 347f)

It is not irrelevant to point out in this connection that, through much of the trial, the members of Manson's "family" appeared in a "uniform" of their own. (Bishop, p. 194)

Killing impersonally, "without discrimination," does not come easily to Americans. Despite the currently fashionable descriptions of American culture as peculiarly prone to violence, there are powerful inhibitions against indiscriminate violence in the culture. This was poignantly revealed during the Korean war, when the military turned to the psychiatrists in desperation about the incredibly high proportion of soldiers who, even in combat, were simply unable to press the trigger on their weapons. Americans mostly murder their relatives, close friends, and neighbors, as the crime statistics show; they have difficulties when it comes to killing "the enemy." An intensive "basic training" is required to overcome these difficulties. The fundamental psychological principles of this training correspond closely to the previously mentioned legitimations of innocence: *The victims must be dehumanized and the killers deprived of individuality.*

The military does its best to accomplish the latter in its training procedures; the stress of combat conditions, especially in a war such as the one in Vietnam, goes far to achieve the former. The Manson "family" had its own "basic training" for deindividuation. The most important training devices here were drugs and orgiastic sex. One of the essential features of the drug experience (as indeed of other forms of ecstasy) is that the borderlines between self and others, and between self and world, become blurred. All merge into oneness, and in that oneness there can be no evil—and, therefore, no evildoing. This is not an argument from morality against the drug experience as such; it may well have emotional and even cognitive values. The moral argument only turns against the drug experience becoming a dominant theme and organizing principle of life as a whole. At that point, the deindividuation induced by the experience threatens to obliterate all moral distinctions (which, *mutatis mutandis*, is one of the reasons why the Judaeo-Christian tradition, with its intense moral concern, has always been wary of ecstatic mysticisms). Similarly, an essential element of orgiastic sex is the elimination of individual distinctions. Again, to say this is not in itself a moral argument against the orgy as an occasional release from the inhibitions of "normal" life (as, say, in the Bacchanalia of classical antiquity); the moral question arises when the orgy becomes a primary and continuous mode of sexual conduct in a group. At that point, the orgiastic experience, like the drug experience, serves as a training device for deindividuation. It is in this sense that the following testimony about the patterns of "making love" in the Manson commune is relevant:

> We all shed our clothes, and we were laying on the floor, and it was just like—it didn't matter who was beside you, if it was a man or a woman, you just touched each other and made love with each other, and the whole room was like this. It was sort of just like one. (Bishop, p. 140)

In other words, Manson's troops "made love" in a manner instructively similar to the one in which they, as well as Calley's troops, "made war"—*without discrimination*. It is of considerable moral importance that this particular continuity be understood. It then becomes clear that "making love" need not necessarily be as far removed from "making war" as the self-congratulatory propaganda of the counterculture suggests. One may further recall that, in the very midst of the Mylai massacre, one of Calley's soldiers forced a Vietnamese woman to perform what one of the witnesses in the Manson trial disarmingly called "that oral whatchamacallit."

Beyond the justifications of murder provided by the dehumanization of the victims and the deindividuation of the killer there are what we may call the political legitimations. In Calley's case these are simple. They are the ancient legitimations of patriotism, which Calley's defense paraded with high emotionality in its final plea:

> Good men, these boys. You find they were boys trained to kill, sent overseas to kill. . . .Are they to be labeled murderers at My Lai or are they entitled to consideration from the fact that they were doing their job as they saw it? Perhaps they acted too aggressively, perhaps they were trying too hard,

perhaps they were not using good judgment. But do the facts warrant hang-
ing a young American lieutenant by the neck until dead because he was trying to do his job? (Hammer, p. 338)

The jury, to its historic credit, was not swayed by this plea. An
alarmingly large segment of the American public was. And indeed, in a
political world view in which America is identical with the forces of
light struggling, in untarnished purity, with the forces of darkness, the
massacre of unarmed and unresisting civilians is an uncomplicated
part of "doing the job."

The political legitimations available in Manson's bizarre universe
are not terribly different. The "family" represents a holy remnant in a
world of evil. It can do no wrong, because its ultimate cause is universal love. Linda Kasabian tells us all about it:

> There's different degrees of love. There is an earthly love between people, a
> physical love. There is also an important love where, you know, you feel
> love towards all living things, which is more of a universal love. (Bishop, p.
> 279)

And again later:

Q: When did Mr. Manson turn into a devil-like man?
A: Well, he was a devil-like man the whole time, but I saw him differently.
Q: You loved him then?
A: Yes.
Q: Do you love him now?
A: Yes.
Q: Do you love the girls now?
A: Sure, I love everybody. (Bishop, p. 283f)

It is important to stress that this language of universal love was not invented by Linda Kasabian on the witness stand. All along, *this was the
language of the murderers.* Put differently: The same people who proclaimed an ideology of universal love could, without remorse, "waste"
those they regarded as "the enemy" (to mix their syntax with Calley's
for a moment):

> "Charlie said pigs were police," DeCarlo said. "They were white collar
> workers, ones that work from eight to five."
> And what should be done with pigs?
> "They otta have their throats cut and be hung up by their feet." (Bishop,
> p. 328)

In this universe of political legitimations, it is always *the others* who
are the murderers. It is perhaps the final touch in the profound conjunction of the two crimes that, in each trial, the *other* crime was referred to as an argument of defense. George Latimer, one of Calley's

defense attorneys, directly referred to the other trial in his plea to the jury:

> He talked about the trial of Charles Manson for the murder of Sharon Tate in California, which was then also coming to its end, and he talked about "draft evaders and that part of the citizenry that try to destroy our courts and turn our courtrooms into barrooms. They can always find someone to represent them all the way to the Supreme Court of the United States. Why deride someone who helps a man who tried to defend his country?" (Hammer, p. 336)

Mylai was not referred to directly in the Manson trial. But this is Manson's reported comment on the speech in which Nixon mentioned him: "Here is a man. . .who is accused of hundreds of thousands of murders, accusing me." (Bishop, p. 230)

If the killers are innocent, who then is to blame? Wilbur Hamman, one of the psychiatrists testifying in the Calley trial, suggested God, surely the most time-honored legitimator of the world's evils:

> I do not believe that we should hold any one person responsible for My Lai. . . .I do not believe that we should hold any one person or the nation responsible. If you want to hold someone responsible, I think the only one you could point to would be God. (Hammer, p. 238)

One may recall here the inscription on the executioner's sword in Freiburg, cited by Albert Camus in his denunciation of capital punishment: "Thou, Lord Jesus, art the judge!" This particular piece of blasphemy has often enough been a favorite excuse of conservative souls. The final excuse in the Manson defense is more modern. Manson himself stated it, in a perfect parody of the liberal theory that finally it is "society" that must be blamed for everything:

> I am not allowed to be a man in your society. I am considered inadequate and incompetant [sic] to speak or defend myself in your court. You have created the monster. . . .You have never given me the constitution you speak of. . . .I do not accept what you call justice. (Bishop, p. 103)

And here is Manson later on, in what sounds like a mad paraphrase of some recent pronouncements of Tom Wicker's:

> "These children that come at you with knives," he said, "they are your children. You taught them. I didn't teach them. These children, everything they have done, they have done for love of their brother." (Bishop, p. 386)

Like a distortion mirror, Manson's world view reflects not only bits and pieces of liberal ideology; even more interestingly, it accommodates elements of the radical picture of American society. In Manson's own mind, his crimes were the first act in a political scenario he called

"Helter Skelter." Here is how the chief prosecutor summarized this scenario:

> The evidence will show that one of Manson's principal motives for the Tate/LaBianca murders was to ignite Helter Skelter, in other words, start the black-white revolution by making it look like the black people had murdered the five Tate victims and Mr. and Mrs. LaBianca, thereby causing the white community to turn against the black man and ultimately lead to a civil war between blacks and whites, a war Manson foresaw the black man winning. (Bishop, p. 98)

"Crazy"? Perhaps so. But thus far the scenario has an uncanny similarity to what passes for "revolutionary strategy" among many radical intellectuals today. Unfortunately, Manson had an ulterior motive in all of this:

> Manson envisioned that black people, once they destroyed the white race and assumed the reins of power, would be unable to handle the reins because of inexperience and would have to turn over the reins to those white people who had escaped from Helter Skelter, that is, turn over the reins to Manson and his followers. (Bishop, p. 98)

Here, alas, Manson turns out to be too "crazy" for the radical imagination. Or could it be that he is not quite "crazy" enough? But when it comes to Manson's image of blacks, he is safely back in the universe of discourse of liberal wisdom. Here is Linda Kasabian's description of Manson's racial views—once more, it is hard to avoid the impression that one is listening to deliberate parody:

> He used to say that blackie was much more aware than whitey and super together, and whitey was just totally untogether, just would not get together; they were off on these side trips, and blackie was really together. (Bishop, p. 142)

It is all there, jumbled together, the bits of liberal masochism and of radical mayhem. There can be no doubt that everything is distorted, mixed up, coming out in demented gibberish. Yet there is one moral implication that is lucid and unambiguous: *Crime is legitimated as a necessary step in the strategy of revolution.* In this "revolutionary morality," the details apart, Manson is in fairly large company.

On the face of it, both culture and counterculture have an easy way out of the confrontation with these two figures. Each can plausibly dismiss its "assigned" figure as an aberration. In that case, though, the argument cuts both ways: If denizens of Middle America can dismiss "their" Calley as a morally irrelevant exception, they must concede the same right to the counterculture with "its" Manson—and vice versa. This evasion is the less ominous option. Far more terrible is that other option, in which there is positive identification with these figures of murderous violence, be it in the name of a beleaguered patriotism or of the necessities of revolution. One may open the newspaper almost any morning and discover that this second option is uncomfortably close.

The time for self-righteousness is long past for *any* sector of the political spectrum. Conservatives, liberals, and radicals alike have shown an unlimited capacity for humanitarian rhetorics—and each rhetoric has revealed its potential for the legitimation of inhumanity. If "they" have their murderers, so have "we." If there is any future short of totalitarian nightmare for either "them" or "us," it will be by way of a return to moral sanity. The underlying option for America is between the sacredness of human life to which Aubrey Daniel appealed in his summation to the jury and the various ideologies of death, no matter under what cultural or political guise they may present themselves.

8

The Greening of American Foreign Policy

Nearly everyone agrees that Vietnam represents a watershed in American foreign policy. Then the interpretations diverge. Some would see these events as a great victory for the forces of morality in American public life; for people holding this view, the main problem in the future is to make sure that the "lesson of Vietnam" is not forgotten and that American actions in the world do not slide back into their allegedly habitual immorality. Others would see Vietnam as a decisive defeat of American power and self-interest; in this view the victory domestically was one of isolationism, and the problem is how to reverse or at least mitigate the debacle of American foreign policy. It is worth noting that these two interpretations are not necessarily contradictory: Morality is not a recipe for political success, and it would not be the first time in history that a nation developed its finest moral sensibilities just before its destruction (indeed, there are theories of history that see a causal connection between the moral refinement and the destruction). My purpose here, however, is not to adjudicate between these two views, but rather to integrate them (*aufheben*, if you will, since the intellectual scene is crawling with crypto-Hegelians) in a more comprehensive frame of reference.

It has been observed by quite a few commentators on the American situation (most lucidly by Irving Kristol) that the Vietnam events mark the advent of a new elite. This elite has been given different names, none satisfactory. Perhaps the easiest course is to follow diplomatic usage and employ the name by which this group likes to call itself, and that is "intellectuals." It is a large group, variegated within itself, by no means fixed either sociologically or ideologically. Yet its basic char-

This chapter originally appeared in *Commentary* (March, 1976).

acteristics are readily stated: These are people who, largely as a result of having successfully passed through the higher levels of the educational system, make their living in what Fritz Machlup has aptly designated the "knowledge industry"—the educational system proper, the communications media in their full variety (from Hollywood, via Madison Avenue, to the smoke-filled rooms in which New York publishers hold their sales conferences), the world of think tanks and research institutions (though probably one would have to exclude those that are concerned only with technology and the natural sciences), and various layers of bureaucracy (both inside and outside government) where it is expected that people have "ideas." In terms of conventional stratification categories, the group is clearly upper middle class, but it is so distinctive in comparison with other groups on this class level (notably those in the business world) that other categories seem more useful. To call the group an elite sidesteps the question of whether it is or is not a new class and points directly to the most important fact, namely, that there is here a new constellation of political power.

The new elite exercises a good deal of political power at this point. That much is clear. It is also clear, though, that there are competing elites. Most important among those is the economic elite—the world of Wall Street, of the big corporations (national and multinational), and their allies in the political system. Kristol has argued persuasively that there is a kind of "class struggle" going on between these two elites. I have no quarrel with this interpretation (though, perhaps, I would put greater stress on the fact that this political struggle is accompanied by a *Kulturkampf*—"by their reading you shall know them"). My thesis, however, is this: *The antagonism between the two elites is over domestic issues. On international issues there is a convergence of perceptions and interests. As this convergence becomes established, a new fact will increasingly become evident—to wit, the influence of a new intellectual-industrial complex on American foreign policy.*[1] Furthermore, the international agenda proceeding from this somewhat bizarre convergence may be stated quite simply: *The agenda is to substitute moral rhetoric and commercial activity for military and political power.* Or, in other words: *The agenda is the dismantling of the American empire.*

To avoid misunderstanding, let me hasten to say that this thesis in no way implies a conspiracy. It is not at all dependent on the assumption (though it may be a correct one, for all I know) that top executives of multinational corporations are engaging in earnest dialogue with editorial writers of the *New York Times*. Current fashion to the contrary, history rarely moves through conspiracies. Nor is it my assumption that the convergence is based on some sort of theoretical agreement. Rather, perceptions and interests converge in an unintended way, possibly even in a way that contradicts the theories held by the two parties. Max Weber used the term "elective affinity" to describe such a process: Specific ideas and specific interests come together at certain moments of history, they "fit" with each other, and it is this "fit" which becomes a real factor in the course of events.

The United States came out of World War II as an imperial power. For a quarter of a century this power, maintained through a network of military and political commitments, has been a key element in what international order there has been. The American empire has derived its legitimacy from the idea that it served to defend freedom (in this respect the analogy is with the Athenian rather than the Roman empire). It hardly needs emphasis at this late date that the concept of freedom in this legitimation has had a good deal of elasticity: The so-called free world contains, or contained (it is indicative of our situation that one is uncertain as to what tense to use), a good many dictatorships as well as genuine democracies. All the same, it *was* a free world in two senses: Contained within it were *all* the democracies, and, while it contained dictatorships, it did *not* contain any totalitarian society (is it necessary to explain that crucial distinction, so ably made by Hannah Arendt?). Until the late 1960s, the great majority of American intellectuals accepted the essential legitimacy of the American empire, even if they had objections to certain manifestations of it. Equally important, the economic elite operated on the notion that the maintenance of American imperial power was in their interest (in *that* respect, at any rate, being in full accord with the Marxists). Vietnam has changed all this. Most American intellectuals have come to believe that the American empire is immoral. This change of mind is now highly visible. But Vietnam has also changed the mind of what may well be the majority of the economic elite—Vietnam has given rise to the idea that the American empire is *unprofitable*. The two shifts in perception are very different in quality. One, grounded in ethical considerations, has an ideological, sometimes almost religious fervor. The other, based on empirical considerations, is (or at least considers itself to be) hardnosedly realistic. Nevertheless, the two converge in the reassessment of America's place in the world—and, I submit, this convergence is now beginning to have real political consequences.

What are the interests at work? At first glance, the interests of the intellectual elite appear to be primarily ideological. One does not have to be a Marxist to suspect that this is not the whole story. Broadly speaking, the major alternatives for the direction of modern societies are between a system favoring market mechanisms in the distribution of whatever good things are available and a system favoring mechanisms of political allocation. These alternatives are inadequately described by the terms "capitalism" and "socialism," since neither system exists in its ideal-typical form, and existing societies are best seen by being located on a continuum between the two ideal-typical poles. On the American political spectrum, the right favors market mechanisms, the left mechanisms of political allocation (*mutatis mutandis,* the same division holds for other countries, especially for Western Europe). A good case can be made for the proposition that intellectuals tend to be on the left because they expect to profit in material terms from a system in which mechanisms of political allocation are favored over market mechanisms. Once again, this case has been made by Kristol; more recently, it has been made eloquently by the German sociologist Helmut Schelsky. It is probable that intellectuals are mistaken in this expectation, at least in the long run, but this is irrelevant at present. It is certainly correct that, in this country, intellectuals have felt that their interests were better served by liberal than by conservative political forces. The "knowledge industry," like any other, gravitates politically toward its most reliable sources of subsidization.

It would be excessively cynical and ipso facto distortive, however, to understand ideological trends in the intellectual elite as being *nothing but* a reflection (to use Lenin's term) of its material interests. Not only are there sincerely held beliefs (almost all ideologies are believed in sincerely, no matter how convenient they may be to the material interests of the believers), but there are also elements of faith, of myth, that transcend concrete interests. "Socialism" is the only good myth going in the world today, and intellectuals are its most important protagonists. To be on the left politically is to participate in this myth, and the satisfactions derived from this participation cannot be explained in terms of interest alone. Different groups in different countries vary, of course, in their understanding of the left vision. Everywhere it is a vision of a society in which the alienations of modernity are overcome, in which there is not only a high degree of equality but also a new ethic of human community. It is this common mythical vision that allows individuals with divergent positions on concrete political issues to perceive each other as belonging together; in *that* sense, if in no other, the adage *pas d'ennemis à la gauche* expresses a profoundly correct insight.

This left ideological tendency (which, *au fond*, is the participation in whatever manner in the myth of "socialism") is an international phenomenon. It is now dominant in most of Western Europe and in most of the Third World as far as the intellectual elites are concerned, even in countries where governments are animated by other ideas and where the influence of intellectuals over "the masses" is slight. The American situation is different in a number of respects: The left tendency is more recent, therefore more precarious. There continue to be countervailing tendencies, even among intellectuals. Also, aside from a still small minority of explicit Marxists, the American left is comparatively open, less doctrinaire, "softer" than its counterparts in Europe and the Third World. More pacifist than militant, it recoils from the uglier realities of "revolutionary necessity," and in the classical trade-off between equality and liberty it continues to hold on tenaciously to *both* ideals.

The intellectual elite dominated by this ideological tendency, despite all sorts of factions within it, has in common the outline of both a domestic and a foreign program. Domestically, the program has probably been caught most accurately in the title of a recent book by Herbert Gans: *More Equality*. The phrase covers not only the egalitarian thrust in economic and social policies, but also expresses a cultural orientation of "liberationism." Conversely, the program is antagonistic to market forces and their alleged inequities—broadly speaking, it is anti-"capitalist." It is also anti-"repression" (in the area of penology as well as with regard to various deviances in personal life style), secularist (sometimes downright antireligious), and imbued with a classically Enlightenment faith in the powers of reason. Perhaps its most attractive feature is a strong capacity to respond compassionately to situations of human misery. The sometimes complicated details and dilemmas of this domestic program need not concern us here. But there is also the outline of a foreign program. This also has its contradictions and ambiguities, but its fundamental thrust could also be captured in a pithy phrase: *Less power!* Or, at least: Less *American* power!

The view of the international scene held within this group is curiously ethnocentric. International developments are perceived as if they were taking place in an American context, and a basically domestic political posture is extended into foreign policy. The results are also curious, which should not be surprising. There is a strong belief in the potency of public opinion—heedless of the fact that, strictly speaking, there *is* no public opinion in much of the world outside the West, since all communications are tightly controlled by government. Concomitantly, there is a belief in the efficacy of moral example and suasion—a belief that assumes a commonality of moral values between American intellectuals and the rest of mankind. International disputes are viewed as if they were conflicts between interest groups within the borders of the United States. Thus the international order toward which American policy should be geared is to be based on trust. It follows that there is a strong antagonism toward the deployment of military force in any way. Most in this group are not recommending abolition of the American military establishment; rather, it is to be cut down as much as possible, and, very importantly, not to be relied upon as a means of influence and persuasion. Needless to say, there is even stronger antagonism to covert operations of any kind. In all of this, there is hardly any sympathy for the major foreign adversary of the United States; the group under discussion here is certainly *not* pro-Soviet. There is, however, a pronounced tendency to underestimate Soviet power and to overestimate the reasonable character of Soviet intentions. When it comes to admiring foreign regimes, the propensity is to choose regimes that call themselves "socialist" and that are (or are thought to be) different from the Soviet type of "socialism"—China, North Vietnam, and Cuba have been the major beneficiaries of this quest for new friends.

Very important in this connection are two cognitive quirks in this view of the world. One is a pronounced reluctance to perceive the world in terms of the distribution of free institutions. These American intellectuals do, of course, believe in such classical democratic values as freedom of speech, freedom of worship, individual protection against arbitrary arrest, and due process. But there is an unwillingness to classify countries in these terms, probably because such a classification would be reminiscent of the "cold war mentality," which has been "discredited," and, more significantly, because it would make painfully clear that virtually everywhere such free institutions as remain in the world do so behind a shield of American power. The other peculiarity of perception is an inability to grasp the difference between dictatorship and totalitarianism (which is probably why the lesson taught by Hannah Arendt has to be repeated periodically)—the difference, say, between North Korea and South Korea, between (before the fall of Saigon) North Vietnam and South Vietnam, between Castro's Cuba and Batista's, between Spain and Czechoslovakia. In editorial after editorial, commentary after commentary, these completely discrepant realities are subsumed jointly under the category of "nondemocratic," and, more often than not, the totalitarian regime comes off better because, supposedly, it does more to alleviate misery or is more egalitarian. Closely linked to this incapacity to perceive the reality of totalitarianism is the failure to understand the quality of information emanating from totalitarian societies. How, for example, is one to know that there is less misery than there used to be in a country where all communications are government controlled and all visitors are restricted to government-controlled tours? The surrealistic absurdity of statements made in this group in recent years about China may serve as the principal illustration.

Until very recently the intellectuals' view of the world was in sharp opposition to that prevailing among the economic elite in this country. If the latter was seen by the former as caught in a "cold war mentality" or an ideology of "imperialism," the reverse perception was one of "utopianism," "idealism," and "softness on communism." Put simply: Intellectuals were losing faith in the American empire while businessmen were still holding on to it. I believe that this balance has been changing since the debacle of the American imperial adventure in Indochina. It is *not*, let me hasten to stress, that businessmen have become latter-day converts to McGovernism. But, at any rate in the area of foreign policy, the perceived self-interest of the economic elite is leading it to a posture that, while not identical, is highly congruent with the posture of the intellectuals. Again, this is not to suggest that businessmen are exclusively motivated by material interests. Like everyone else, businessmen have beliefs, values, moral and cognitive prejudices, and these have an influence on their actions. When businessmen are compared with intellectuals, it is hard to say who has the edge in the matter of ideology. However, I think that the following distinction can be made: The economic elite operates in a context where the penalties for false perceptions are quicker and more easily seen than in the context of the intellectual elite. This means that ideological tendencies are more rigorously controlled by a "reality principle"—to wit, the principle of perceived economic interest.

The shift in perception that is now taking place within this group can be described rather simply: The American empire, previously perceived as an economic asset, is now coming to be perceived as an economic liability in many parts of the world. It is inflationary (Vietnam was *not* "good for Wall Street"). It is an insufficient guarantee for the safety of foreign investments. It unnecessarily antagonizes an important sector of foreign trade partners. This shift may not pertain to all parts of the world equally; an exception may be some areas of Latin America. But it pertains, I think, to most of the rest of the Third World. Most importantly, it has affected the perception of American economic interests vis-à-vis the communist countries. And I shall argue that it may have a decisive effect on the perception of American economic interests in Europe.

From the standpoint of *any* economic elite, political stability is a prime desideratum. It must be, since only in a politically stable situation can long-range economic strategies pay off. The modern corporation is compelled, most of the time, to think in long-range terms; that is, only rarely can it afford quick in-and-out economic adventures. This concern with political stability has led repeatedly to a readiness to do business with all sorts of morally distasteful regimes, as long as those regimes had a control over their respective countries that seemed reasonably long range. Indeed, as intellectual critics of American business abroad have pointed out, there has been the propensity to prefer stable dictatorships to unstable democracies. There is no need to repeat here the uninspiring record of American corporations meddling in the internal affairs of foreign countries to insure a profitably stable political environment. The one big exception to this general tendency has been *communist* regimes. These did, of course, provide political stability; indeed, it could be argued that in the contemporary world they provide the politically stable situations *par excellence*. But, of course, they were also viewed (correctly) as being inimical to American economic enterprise. *It is precisely this perception that is changing.* Communist regimes, particularly those within the Soviet orbit, have shown themselves increasingly to be reliable trade and investment partners; in the exact measure in which this is perceived to be the case, the political stability of these regimes comes to appear as an asset.

Empirically, the Soviets and their European satellites have demonstrated that they are very much interested in economic relations with American business. Empirically, they have turned out to be hard bargainers, but once they make an agreement, they keep it. Thus far, although American investments in these countries have been limited, they are invariably safe—or so it seems. There is no reason to think that this would change if the investments grew. In these countries there are no problems with a volatile public opinion, with anti-American intellectuals and political movements, with coups or terrorism, with aggressive labor unions. Inflation is controlled and tax regulations are simple. Once it can be assumed that communist countries are interested in long-range economic relations with American business, all these qualities become very attractive indeed. And, even better, no exercises in American "imperialism" are necessary to maintain these favorable conditions. In sum: *It is possible to do very good business with the communists.*

Admittedly, all these perceptions are based in the slim evidence of the last few years. The new view under discussion here makes some assumptions that cannot be empirically validated—particularly the assumption that the economic needs of the Soviets will continue to be what they are now, and the further assumption that a new generation of Soviet leaders will continue the present precarious balancing act between economic and ideological interests. Nobody (least of all the Sovietologists) can say how likely it is that these assumptions will hold. Can the Soviet economy (especially its agrarian sector) finally overcome its chronic inefficiencies? Can Soviet technology catch up with the West? Is an ideologically or militarily more aggressive leadership waiting in the wings? These assumptions, however, are about as good as any others held in connection with foreign economic undertakings—and they are almost certainly better than *any* assumptions about the future of that explosive area of erstwhile American "imperialism" known as the Third World.

But it is in Europe that this shift in perception may have the most far-reaching consequences. It is Europe, *not* the Third World, that has been the major focus of American "imperialism"—using that term nonpejoratively, simply indicating the confluence of economic and political-military interests. It has been axiomatic since World War II that Europe was essential to American interests, economic *and* political-military, and the very existence of what we now know as Western Europe is due to this axiom. It is not necessary to conclude that this axiom is about to be rejected *in toto* by the American economic elite. There will continue to be important American economic interests in Western Europe. But increasingly there are also important American economic interests in *Eastern* Europe. Sooner or later, I contend, the difference between these two areas will become a little fuzzy in this perspective. One may pinpoint the shift by putting it this way: Until now, a Sovietization of Western Europe, be it by direct Soviet actions or by means of internal communist movements, was deemed to be fundamentally contrary to American interests, economic as well as other; such a Sovietization was simply unthinkable. What I believe is happinging now is that *a Sovietization of Western Europe is becoming less unthinkable*. Put differently, in all likelihood there will continue to be important American economic interests in Western Europe; it is, I think, becoming less self-evident that these interests necessitate the preservation of democracy in Western Europe and the expensive deployment of American military power to that end.[2]

If one wanted to be ironic, one could say that American businessmen are beginning to get rid of their Marxist presuppositions. It is Marxism that has insisted on the inevitable linkage of American capitalism and American empire. But what if Marxism has been wrong all along? What if American imperial power comes to be seen as an economic disadvantage by the "ruling circles" of the American economy? The rudest shock would come to those European intellectuals (probably the majority) whose anti-Americanism has been coupled with the serene assurance that American power will continue to protect them from the Russians. It would be interesting to observe the reaction on the day when Western Europe wakes up to the fact that American "imperialism" has, indeed, gone home—and that it is left alone with the Russians, armed only with France's *force de frappe* and a lot of Swedish rhetoric.

If the above constitutes an emerging new intellectual-industrial complex in American foreign policy, who is on the other side? Certainly there continue to be people in the economic elite who view things differently, whether for ideological reasons (one can still say "free world" in business circles in this country without immediately losing the entire audience) or because of a different notion of economic interests. There still are intellectuals, in a rather beleaguered state, who perceive a connection between American power and freedom. There is, of course, the military (though I would be at a loss to evaluate its influence on foreign policy at this point—a new C. Wright Mills is needed for this task). And then there are various figures in the political establishment, among whom Henry Kissinger has occupied a dramatically central position. All too often he has been compared to Metternich. Whatever may be the usefulness of this comparison, it is important to remember that Metternich was eminently *successful*. The design of international order he created at the Congress of Vienna lasted for almost exactly one century—which, in terms of human history, must be reckoned as almost incredible success. Kissinger's restless efforts to keep together the disintegrating fabric of an international order in which American power is a key element seem unlikely to achieve comparable success.

All these elite groupings function in a context of democratic politics and public opinion which are presently in a state of considerable flux. Thus it is difficult to assess which viewpoint "has the troops" in terms of American politics. There continues to be a large segment of the American people that is highly susceptible to, let us say, imperial sentiments. The popular response to the *Mayaguez* incident and, more recently, to Patrick Moynihan's speeches at the United Nations may be cited as evidence. Undoubtedly, though, there is also a widespread weariness of foreign commitments, a fear of Vietnam-like episodes in the future, and considerable disillusionment with patriotic rhetoric about America's mission in the world. The new intellectual-industrial complex is in a position to respond to this mood in a peculiar way. If the proposition is to dismantle the American empire, the intellectuals make it seem morally right and the businessmen make it appear realistic. A combination of self-righteousness and hard-nosed realism is hard to beat in American politics.

To sum up the argument: What I have called here a new intellectual-industrial complex is a curious symbiosis of perceptions of the world which, I think, is beginning to have an influence on American foreign policy. It is only poorly described as isolationist; neither of its two component groups envisage the withdrawal of the United States from the world. Rather, to use Harlan Cleveland's provocative phrase, America is to be a partner in an emerging "planetary bargain"; the coinage to be used in this bargain is largely moral for one group, largely economic for the other; both would deemphasize the coinage of military and political power. If one were to use the terminology of Vilfredo Pareto, one could say that the methods of "foxes" are to be substituted for those of "lions."

The symbiosis is fragile. In this alliance between putative morality and alleged realism either side could fall apart. One can imagine various eventualities raising questions among the intellectuals about their moral assumptions; new threats to the survival of Israel must, alas, rank high on the list. The businessmen might come to doubt the realism of some of their own perceptions; what, for instance, if an economically irrational Bonapartism came to the fore in the post-Brezhnev Soviet leadership? Needless to say, neither American intellectuals nor

American businessmen have much control over the processes that might lead to such eventualities. The symbiosis, then, may not be permanent. All the same, I believe that its emergence at this important moment in world affairs is a fact to be taken account of, a fact with potentially far-reaching consequences even if it should turn out to be transitory.

American imperial power since World War II has been an often uneasy mixture of two purposes—the pursuit of American self-interest, as variously perceived, and the defense of the shrinking number of democratic societies. And whatever else American power may have been (all too often it was very depressing indeed, from any moral point of view), it was *also* the only significant shield of free societies in different parts of the world. What is being suggested here is that the two purposes may now come to be dissociated altogether—with considerable consequences for the future of freedom in the world. Despite all the talk about a multilateral world, the only immediately visible beneficiary of a dismantling of the American empire will be the Soviet Union. In that case, the main hope for the survival of free societies is that the Soviet empire may soon turn out to be as ramshackle as ours. It is a tenuous hope.

9

Intellectual Conservatism:

Two Paradoxes

The great majority of people in most human societies is conservative. The reasons for this are not at all mysterious. Most people are conservative in the sense that they take the basic structures of their society for granted and try to work out the problems of their own lives within these structures. In the words of Alfred Schutz, the social world is "taken for granted until further notice." To be sure, "notice" is sometimes given in a variety of ways—through an intensification of social conflicts, through economic or military disasters, through natural catastrophe, or (more rarely) by means of religious or quasi-religious enthusiasm. In such situations the basic structures of society may become problematic even to large masses of people and, at least for a time, their "natural" conservatism may be breached. This conservatism is typically unreflected, not given to theorizing, self-assured rather than defensive in tone. It has been wonderfully caught in Edmund Burke's image of peaceful cows contentedly munching their grass under the ancient trees. An altogether different kind of conservatism is that of intellectuals. It is highly reflective, productive of theories that sometimes attain cosmic scope, typically aggressive rather than self-assured. As Karl Mannheim has shown convincingly, such intellectual conservatism typically arises in defense of the status quo against theoretical and political challenges, that is, it is typically a response to the ideas and actions of others.

Contemporary intellectual conservatism in America has arisen in response to the triumphant onslaught of political and ideological liberalism. In its initial impulse a defense of the American status quo, it has been forced into a dissenting role against the new status quo established by victorious liberalism. Today this kind of conservatism occupies a minority position on the American scene. Its ideology is heterodox, its voice is one of dissent.

All this can be said *sine ira et studio*, in the mode of "value-free" objectivity appropriate to my craft of sociologist. But this is not really how I feel about these matters. I have a personal relation to conservatism, with dimensions both of ire and of zeal. For I, too, am a conservative, though my conservatism has been intellectually nurtured less by Burke than by Burckhardt and Weber, and emotionally inspired not so much by visions of Anglo-American cattle as by childhood stories of the vanished glories of Habsburg Austria. Time and again, especially in the last few years of epidemic hysteria, I have been reassured by the presence of a vocal intellectual conservatism on the American scene. And yet, the initial pleasure was recurrently replaced by acute disappointment. It seems to me that the reasons for this disappointment transcend my personal idiosyncrasies and therefore merit some reflection.

I have no doubts about the useful critical function of the intellectual conservatism best represented by a publication like *National Review*. If it had done no more than continuously prick holes in the magnificent balloon of the world view of the *New York Times,* this alone would justify its existence. It has done more. Conservative intellectuals have helped to redress our vision of the world, have reminded us of experiences and insights that the liberal establishment has liked to forget, have offered alternative ways of approaching the problems of our time. Yet, if one regards conservatism as more than a game played by intellectuals, one will not be satisfied by this critical utility. One will have hopes for political and moral leadership by a renascent conservatism, all the more so in a situation in which the utopian schemes of both liberalism and radicalism are increasingly revealed as bankrupt. The ideological coffers of the latter seem incapable of producing much more than dreary old formulas, be they reiterated by the tired voices of establishmentarian gurus or with shrill fervor by the radicalized offspring of these gurus. Almost every one of our problems, domestic as well as international, cries out desperately for new ideas, new formulations, new approaches. It is reasonable to expect that at least some of these would come from the right. If this is so, it would also seem reasonable to invest hope in a potential leadership role of intellectual conservatism. The disappointment is all the more acute because of this.

No doubt there are many external factors, sociological as well as political, which militate against such a role for intellectual conservatism. There are also some factors in the realm of ideas. I would like to single out two for discussion here. One is a paradox in the theoretical perspective of American conservatism, the other a paradox (not to say a flaw) in its moral stance.

The paradox in theoretical perspective is the result of the aforementioned development, in which intellectual conservatism came to be a dissenting movement in America. It is the paradox of an antiliberal conservatism in a liberal society.

This paradox becomes manifest regardless of whether one understands liberalism in its classical sense or in the sense it has in recent American politics. Historically, liberalism has been the ideology of rising bourgeoisie, first coming into view in the seventeenth century, maturing through the eighteenth, and bursting onto the European scene with apocalyptic thunder in 1789. In such a historical perspective liberalism represents the ideological presence of the continuing French Revolution. As conservatives have seen more clearly than anyone else, the various creeds of revolutionary socialism are organic offshoots from this underlying ideology of the modern age. Historically, the institutional embodiments of liberalism have been the bourgeoisie as a class, capitalism as an economic system, the national state and popular democracy in the political sphere. Thus, logically enough, the conservative reaction against the French Revolution and its continuing consequences was directed (with varying emphases, of course) against all of these manifestations. Seen through the sardonically perceptive eyes of, say, a Metternich, the bourgeoisie was the principal villain in the drama of modern disintegration. It was the bourgeoisie that brought about the capitalist economy, its ethic corroding the old foundations of a Christian order of public life. Closely allied to this "spirit of capitalism" were the other two principles of disorder—modern nationalism and modern mass democracy. It was against all of these that Metternich mounted a heroic action of rearguard defense. Nor is this way of looking at the modern world altogether obsolete today. It persists in the older conservative movements on the continent of Europe (one may think here of Spain, for example).

If one understands liberalism in this classical sense, one must say that America, as we know it today, has been the creation of liberalism. Indeed, America may well be described as *the* liberal society. This was seen with lucid clarity by de Tocqueville, and there is no reason to revise his formulations of the fact. It was the bourgeoisie that shaped America in the nineteenth century, that gave it its fundamental ethos, that indeed made it into a "middle-class society." To be sure, other options may have been open at an earlier stage of American history. One may argue concerning the dates at which they were definitively foreclosed. The latest date, beyond which there could no longer be the slightest doubt, was the defeat of the South in the Civil War. Since then, clearly and seemingly irrevocably, American society has been founded on the institutional artifacts of the bourgeoisie—an open class system, a capitalist economy, and a democratic polity. As could hardly be otherwise, the "American creed" reflected these institutional realities. In other words, liberalism became *the* ideology of the society.

If one wants to eschew this kind of historical perspective and understand liberalism only as the ideology so named since the 1930s, then, too, I believe, one must come to the conclusion that present-day America is a liberal society. It is certainly so in the overwhelming portion of its political spectrum. The two-party system functions within this central consensus. I think one can even argue that most of the party formations to the right *or* left of this center have not deviated decisively from it. Thus it is hard to find politically significant movements on the right that seriously contemplate dismantling the welfare apparatus initiated by the New Deal, and outside the politically marginal coteries of intellectuals it is hard to find people on the left who seriously envisage a socialist order in America. In other words, right and left in America generally mean positions either within or quite close to the central consensus of liberalism. This consensus, moreover, transcends formal politics. It is firmly grounded in the consciousness of the vast mass of Americans, that "vital center" to which successful politicians must appeal. Contrary to some prophets of doom, there is no indication as yet that this mass of people has changed its basic ideological views. And, of course, the same liberal consensus is ongoingly reaffirmed by the major opinion-shaping agencies in the society, from the educational system (particularly the public schools) to the media of mass communication.

Here, then, is the paradox: If conservatism has any root meaning, it is that of wanting to preserve the existing order of things. But the existing order of things in America is profoundly liberal, institutionally as well as ideologically. Thus the intellectual conservative in America, deeply critical of liberal ideology as he is, finds himself in the position of standing for the preservation of an order based on all those principles that offend him. If he has a classical (if you will, "European") view of conservatism, then his position is altogether quixotic, comparable to that of, say, running for senator from Massachusetts on a monarchist platform. If he has a more timely view of conservatism in terms of opposition to post–New Deal American liberalism, he still finds himself in the position of being for a status quo founded on the institutional and ideological products of precisely this liberalism. In either case, the position is paradoxical.

It seems to me that this paradox has given intellectual conservatism in America a certain air of negativism and even petulance reminiscent of the petulant exasperation of a self-consciously *kulturny* English teacher over the invincible barbarisms of his freshmen. It is, after all, difficult to maintain with serenity an image of oneself as a man plugging the hole in the dike with his little finger. It is doubly difficult if one wants to accomplish this feat elegantly; inevitably and distressingly, one begins to sweat. Of course, it is possible to withdraw in disgust from one's age. I believe that this is an intellectually and morally defensible option (and, God knows, often a tempting one), which, however, implies a withdrawal from political participation. To the extent that conservatives intend to be politically relevant, this option is closed to them, and so is the resolution of the paradox by withdrawal.

The second paradox is of a different order. It is a flaw in moral rather than theoretical perspective. The name I like to give to this is "selective humanism."

Conservatives have always been strong on morality. While their liberal antagonists have been dreaming of a society based on some sort of value-neutral rationality, conservatives have kept on insisting that social order must have a moral foundation to be viable. They have not always been right in the particular positions into which this has led them, but, on the whole, their sociological instincts have been sounder than those of the liberals. For example, it is possible to have different positions on the issue of prayers in the public schools, but it is sociologically evident that a society is headed for serious trouble if its educational system rigorously excludes all considerations of morality as "sectarian." For another example, one may hold a number of views on the relation of law and individual conscience, but conservatives have undoubtedly been the better sociologists for maintaining that any society will fall apart if obedience to law is left to continuous (and ipso facto unpredictable) individual decisions.

In recent years intellectual conservatives in America have performed an invaluable function in debunking the moral pretensions and myopias of liberalism. The conservative critique of, for example, the hypocrisy of the stance of upper-middle-class liberal intellectuals on the busing issue has been a breath of fresh air in a smog of murky rhetoric. The "moralism" of conservatives has, I think, been especially important in its perception of the human reality of communism. Again and again, in this particular matter, conservatives have credibly represented a tradition of humanistic concern in the face of the contortions of interpretation undertaken by liberal intellectuals. At the present time, I have found this profoundly refreshing in the public discussion of Communist China. One of the morally revolting spectacles of recent years has been the reception given to Maoist China in the liberal press, which has been hailing the new international prominence of this regime as a salvatory event, conveniently forgetting the hecatombs of murdered human beings upon which the regime has been founded. Mention of what can most accurately be described as the Chinese holocaust has suddenly become taboo in the utterances of "responsible" liberal journalists and "concerned" liberal scholars (both groups, one sadly suspects, having a particular "concern" for getting visas to Peking). It has become necessary to turn to the conservative remnant in the public media for honest reminders of these realities.

It would be exhilarating if this were the end of the story. Alas, it is not, for intellectual conservatives have had their own versions of the selective humanism for which they so justly castigate their opponents. True, they insist on calling Maoism the moral monstrosity it is. But they have been singularly silent about the mass murders perpetrated when the present Indonesian regime came to power. True, conservatives have continued to point up the terror and the tortures of the communist regimes in Europe, but they have been reticent concerning terror in Brazil or tortures in Greece. I am anxious not to be misunderstood on this point: I would insist myself that, since the demise of Nazism, the most enormous inhumanities have been those perpetrated in the name of communism. Nor would I object if someone points out that, say, compared to China, Greece under the colonels provides a modicum of humanitarian government. What I find morally intolerable is the general principle of applying different standards of what is humanly acceptable to communist and anticommunist regimes. To be sure, we must denounce "their" murderers. We must also denounce "ours." The former denunciation will not be credible without the latter.

This flaw in the moral vision of conservatism has been especially grave with regard to the war in Vietnam. Conservatives have been fully justified in showing up the moral bankruptcy of a supposedly "humanist" left that has been extolling the virtues of North Vietnam and of the Vietcong without ever mentioning the atrocities committed by its heroes as standard operating procedure. Conservatives have also been quite right in pinning down the less outrageous, but probably more consequential, inconsistencies in the liberal wing of the antiwar movement, such as the simultaneous beliefs that, somehow, the Vietcong represent the will of the people, and that the Saigon regime must be repudiated because its elections would not get by the Fair Ballot Association of Minnesota. What conservatives have tragically overlooked (or, worse, have sardonically caricaturized) has been the genuine moral outrage of large numbers of ideologically innocent Americans at the atrocious conduct of this war by our own forces—conduct all the more atrocious for being standard operating procedure, too. The devastation of large areas of the country designated as "free-fire zones," the merciless bombing and shelling of inhabited villages vaguely suspected of sheltering the enemy, the routine torture of prisoners, the deliberate "generation" of vast masses of refugees—all these have been part and parcel of the human reality of this war. I have repeatedly come across an interesting response to these facts in conversation with conservatives. Sometimes, of course, these facts are denied. This is uninteresting, except perhaps to psychologists. But if the facts are not denied, it happens every so often that my partner in such conversation will set his jaw more firmly, try to look tough (always a hard feat for intellectuals, right *or* left), and start talking about the hard necessities of power in the real world. Fine. I, too, have heard of *realpolitik*. But one cannot have it both ways. *Either* "everything goes" in the struggle for power in the real world, *or* there are limits beyond which moral outrage has a right to be heard. It is always the case that one side's atrocities are the *realpolitik* of the other.

Whatever some of its spectacular follies, the movement against the Vietnam war has been, I believe, one of the more cheering expressions of a genuinely American humanism in our time. Shorn of its follies, it represents a sign of hope for the future of the society. The failure to understand this has separated intellectual conservatives from one of the most promising moral impulses in the current American situation. The failure is one of moral judgment as well as of political vision. These two are not always connected. In this instance, I think, they are—with depressing implications for the future of American conservatism.

If these two paradoxes were endemic to intellectual conservatism, anyone who identifies with the latter position would be best advised to observe a mournful silence. I don't think that they are endemic. On the contrary, I believe that both paradoxes are capable of resolution, although I'm not exactly sanguine about the chances that many conservatives will agree with my approach.

The first paradox can be resolved by distinguishing more sharply between what one may call two levels of conservatism, the practical and the theoretical levels with which we started out on the present considerations. I count myself a conservative on both levels. On the practical level, I would like to preserve American society essentially in its present structures. I would like to solve its problems (including those that I regard as morally urgent, such as the problem of justice for its racial minorities) within those structures, and I have considerable confidence that this is possible. This position, unlike that of liberals, is *not* based on any quasi-religious glorification of these structures. Middle-class values are not the apex of man's moral history, capitalism is not the final marvel of economic ingenuity, and neither the national state nor mass democracy represents the ultimate political redemptions. All the same, in a world of relativities, these structures and even the less than overwhelmingly convincing ideas that legitimate them have proved themselves worthy of considerable respect. This respect is translated into positive political commitment when one looks at the empirically available alternatives. In itself it may make little sense (at least to me) to be ultimately committed to the bourgeois *Weltanschauung,* but it makes urgent sense to be committed to resistance against the forces that are seeking to replace the bourgeois universe by their own versions of utopia. In sum: It is possible to want to preserve the basic status quo of American society as a practical political goal, without necessarily sharing the entire legitimating apparatus of liberalism that appertains to this society.

At the risk of being misunderstood, I will introduce an analogy. Enough has been said to make clear that my sympathies for communism are close to nil. The communist societies of Eastern Europe, with which I have personal acquaintance, are profoundly unattractive to me. Yet I'm fairly certain that, if I were unfortunate enough to have to live in one of these societies today, I would not be striving for their revolutionary overthrow. Nor would this be simply because of a lack of personal courage (anyway, no man knows his courage until it is tested). I imagine that I would, in such a situation, make the same political judgment that I make here and now—namely that, because of the power of the Soviet Union and other realistic considerations, these societies are likely to remain communist for the rest of our lifetimes. I might then try to withdraw as far as I'm allowed from political participation. However, to the extent that I would be unable or perhaps reluctant to withdraw, I would try to work practically within the existing structures, to attempt to modify them as much as I can in terms of those moral and human values to which I owe allegiance. In other words, my objective political actions (to borrow from the Marxist vocabulary) would be within the structures of the status quo, and would thus be objectively conservatory in their effects. The analogy limps, for the simple reason that my dissent from communism is enormously greater than my dissent from American liberalism. But that, exactly, is my point: The practical logic holds *a fortiori* in the case of the latter.

I also count myself a conservative on the theoretical or philosophical level. If properly provoked, I can deliver myself of a conservative credo literally dripping with such medievalism as to get me excluded from faculty parties from here to eternity. In a world of relativities, I must come to terms with the fact that this credo is hopelessly out of date. Perhaps the last *really* worthwhile political enterprise in the twentieth century would have been to try and preserve the Austro-Hungarian monarchy. The cause, alas, is lost, and in any case I was born a quarter century too late for joining its banners. I have no practical alternative to political engagements with which I can only identify in a less than ultimate mode. This is regrettable ("If I had only been there to advise you, back around 1910!"), but it constitutes neither a logical nor a moral contradiction.

Needless to say, American intellectual conservatives do not, in any great numbers, share these peculiar ideological hang-ups of mine (the encounter between William Buckley and Otto von Habsburg, on "Firing Line" some time ago, made that graphically clear). However, their hang-ups and mine are not too dissimilar in terms of theoretical distance from the liberal consensus. It seems to me that intellectual conservatives with a variety of positions can make the same distinction between ultimate philosophical credo and practical political engagement. This distinction resolves the paradox, and at the same time converts the political stance of conservatives from nagging negativism to realistic political actions. It hardly needs emphasizing that these actions inevitably will lead to cooperative ventures with those exasperating liberals who dominate the "vital center" of American politics.

The second paradox can be resolved by a recollection that should not be overly difficult to those committed to an intellectual tradition of conservatism. It is the recollection that conservatism is not only a "perennial philosophy" but (*pace* Aldous Huxley) a perennial humanism. To be a conservative means above all to be aware of the historical dimension of the human condition. The knowledge of history is heavy with anguish. The moral utility of history, for this reason, is compassion. Unlike the enthusiasts for revolution and radical change, the conservative ought to be prudent about upsetting the fragile structures that protect men's lives from the terrors of chaos. His ought to be a prudence born of knowledgeable skepticism regarding all utopian promises, and born especially of a care to avoid the senseless suffering that most attempts to realize such promises have produced historically. The great radicalisms of the modern era have all claimed to love mankind; the conservative ought to cultivate affection for individual men in their concrete and irreplaceable particularity.

Such a conservatism of compassion is rooted in a long tradition of moral wisdom of both classical and biblical inspiration. It is not a tradition of weakness in action or of pacifism. At the same time, it excludes the kind of selective humanism mentioned above. Conversely, it remains open to the humane impulses of the time, wherever these may come from. In the eighteenth century Austria was the first country to abolish judicial torture and then capital punishment. The first happened under Maria Theresa, the second under Joseph II, both monarchs fully qualifying for the title of "despot" in the world view of later revolutionaries. A conservatism understanding itself in the context of this perennial humanism would not be capable of, for example, the often fanatical affirmation of capital punishment that characterizes conservatives in several countries. When an issue of *National Review* appeared with a picture of a hangman's noose on the cover (inside was an article regretting the passing of the death penality), there was in this a melancholy symmetry with the famous cover of the *New York Review of Books* depicting a Molotov cocktail. It is curious that there is not only a great similarity between different sorts of inhumanity, but also between the legitimations that intellectuals think up for the inhuman acts. In the perspective of perennial humanism, the conservative intellectual embracing the gallows looks amazingly like his leftist cousin hugging a bomb. The difference, it seems to me, is that the conservative has less excuse.

My reasons for wanting to resolve the second paradox are moral be-

fore they are political. There is a political aspect to this, too. Despite
its dark sides, our time has witnessed some remarkable and cheering
manifestations of humane compassion, and some of these have had political repercussions. It is not only morally regrettable, but might well
be politically self-defeating, if conservatism remains blind to these currents of revitalized humanism. There is something deeply offensive
about the conservative affinity for the hangman. It also don't look so
good. This was finally realized even by the Church of England, which
has had a long-lasting fondness for the death penalty comparable in
emotional intensity to its devotion to the Book of Common Prayer.
Some years ago, when the House of Lords had its great debate on the
issue, there was one big surprise. The Archbishop of Canterbury,
mirabile dictu, came out for abolition.

There are some good reasons to think that a conservative hour may
be beginning in America. Will it be possible for intellectual conservatives to grasp that hour? Whatever they do, the country is likely
to move to the right, and politicians are likely to respond to this movement. The question of who will provide the ideas and interpretations,
the intellectual arsenal, for this movement is of very great political importance. I hope that it will be, among others, intellectual conservatives with both practical and moral suppleness. It seems to me
that a resolution of the two paradoxes along the lines indicated will be
one condition for this. It further seems to me that the choice before intellectual conservatives in America is relatively simple: It is a choice
between meaningful political participation and sectarianism.

10

Reflections on Patriotism

The roots of patriotism are in childhood. At least in Western languages this is expressed in the terms that most commonly evoke patriotic sentiments—fatherland, motherland, homeland, native country. Patriotism refers basically to places, people, and things with which one is at home, and there are few later experiences that can match the sense of at-homeness experienced by the child. The world then is still a very new place, and most of it is strange, much of it terrifying. The familiar, the secure zones of the world have, for this reason, a particular sweetness about them. In later life this constellation of perceptions and feelings is lost or at least greatly weakened. It can be evoked anew, however, often by seemingly trivial stimuli—the sights and sounds of childhood, sometimes its smells or even the touch of objects from that period of biographical dawn. This is not to deny that individuals can leave their place of origin and find themselves at home elsewhere. Migration has been a common human experience from times immemorial. It is safe to say, however, that the very capacity to be at home in the world is formed in very early childhood, and it is likely that those who missed this experience then will have great difficulty achieving it later on, no matter where they migrate.

The broadest definition of patriotism would be *loving one's own*: This is my place, these are my people, and in this place and with these people I'm most myself. On this level of experience, in all probability, there are profound anthropological foundations to patriotism. Put differently, there is a "natural" patriotism which is rooted in the very constitution of man, and is thus cross-culturally and historically constant. In all cultures and periods of history of which we have knowledge, human beings have had these sentiments, have "loved their own," and have had moral notions attached to this experiential com-

This chapter originally appeared in *Worldview* (July, 1974). Copyright ʿ 1974 by The Council on Religion and International Affairs. Reprinted by permission.

plex. Thus, everywhere, there is some notion of treason—the moral offence of betraying "one's own." And on this fundamental level it is hard to disagree with the moral judgment. The affirmation of patriotism and the moral condemnation of its betrayal are constitutive of man (if you will, of "human nature"), and by the same token human society would not be possible without this moral basis (of modern theorists, it was probably Emile Durkheim who understood this most clearly).

As soon as one moves from this primal level of patriotic sentiment and morality to more complex levels, one enters a sphere of cultural and historical relativities. In other words, while the *core* of patriotic allegiance is, as it were, anthropologically given, its *outer limits* are historically relative and socially constructed. They are matters of agreed-upon definition: The people on this side of the river, who are descended from the great water-buffalo, are my people; the people on the other side, descended from some evidently inferior being, are not. If the aforementioned core patriotism is anthropologically given, this extended patriotism is sociologically basic; on such social definitions of who constitutes "one's own" hinge all elementary forms of human interaction—economic, sexual, political, and so on. The incest taboo was, in all probability, one of the most archaic institutions embodying this definition of limits, straddling the "natural" and the "artificial" elements of solidarity: I may not marry "my own," be it my sister with whom I have grown up since childhood, or my fifth cousin whom I have rarely met but with whom I share membership in the water-buffalo clan.

For much of human history the line between these two types of belonging, and the patriotic sentiments pertaining to them, was fluid and probably not very clearly perceived. The reason for this is very simple: Most people lived in small communities all their lives and had at least occasional face-to-face encounters with just about everyone classified as belonging to "their own." At least in principle, and probably in practice, all the individuals belonging to the water-buffalo clan were physically accessible to each other. Even the citizen of republican Rome who said that it is sweet and proper to die for one's fatherland (*patria*) was speaking of a somewhat overgrown village, most of whose inhabitants probably knew each other fairly well and who frequently met face to face. To a surprising degree this type of patriotism has survived into modern times; Benjamin Barber's recent study of Swiss politics[1] gives an eloquent account of the conflict between such an archaic patriotism and the abstract solidarities of a modern nation-state (one of the merits of Barber's work is that he rejects the facile characterizations of the former as "backward" or "reactionary").

Thus we may distinguish three types of patriotism, depending on the range of people perceived as "one's own"—those with whom the individual has shared a substantial portion of his life experiences; those with whom the individual can, at least in principle, enter into face-to-face relationships; and those with whom such relationships are not possible in their entirety, so that the individual can only perceive them as "his own" by virtue of an act of abstract thinking. For example, I belong with my sister in a way different from how I belong with my entire clan; this difference pales if compared with the way I belong, say, to the Swiss nation—most of whose citizens I have never met and *can* never meet, even if I live in Switzerland all my life. For our purposes, the distinction between the first and second type is not essential; we may subsume both types (following Barber's usage) under the heading *communal patriotism*. This may then be contrasted with *abstract patriotism*, that is, with perceptions and sentiments of belonging with people whom one has never met, never will meet, and at least in their aggregate cannot meet face to face. This comparison is not at all necessarily odious—while it is a mistake to hang pejorative labels on communal solidarities, it is equally a mistake to romanticize them.

Leaving aside the problems of members of the water-buffalo clan and denizens of remote Alpine valleys, every individual in a modern society is likely to have two different sets of patriotic allegiances—those that link him with others whose lives he has actually shared in concrete face-to-face experiences, and those that unite him with large numbers of people on the basis of an abstract categorization not produced by his actual life experience. The cognitive and emotional contents of the two statements "I'm a Red Hook Italian" and "I'm an American citizen" may serve by way of further illustration. This is not to say that the latter statement is less real, but that its reality is of a different order. Nor is it to say that one or the other form of patriotism is morally superior, only that the former is more "natural," in that it is more firmly rooted in the totality of the individual's biographical experience. For example, it is possible for an American citizen never to have set foot in the United States and not even to speak English (say, the child of Americans living in a foreign country), and yet to have a strong patriotic allegiance to the country of his citizenship. By contrast, to be a "Red Hook Italian" necessarily requires a sequence of biographical experiences which cannot be obtained by virtue of a legal document or any comparably abstract instrumentality.

Communal patriotism is clearly possible without abstract patriotism. Indeed, it has existed as such through most of human history. A more interesting question is whether an abstract patriotism can be viable without rootage in the patriotic sentiments of empirically available human communities. Edmund Burke thought that it cannot: Only if, as he put it, an individual feels loyalty to his "small platoon" can he then be loyal to any larger social entities. One of Burke's crucial criticisms of the revolutionary ideology of his time was that it glorified abstractions ("the people," "the nation," "humanity") as against the concrete communities in which men live, and he emphasized that such abstractions cannot survive unless they are rooted in much more concrete experiences of human community. He was probably right. One of the great themes of modern sociology has been the transition from communal to abstract solidarities—in the by-now classical terms of Ferdinand Toennies, from *Gemeinschaft* to *Gesellschaft*. A number of sociologists (among contemporaries we may mention Robert Nisbet) have expressed the view that this transition can never be complete: Unless *Gesellschaft* is "supported" by a network of *Gemeinschaft*-type relations, its institutions will soon become "hollow," devoid of reality, and therefore will not long survive. Put differently, the virtues of American citizenship are unlikely to survive or even be real to people unless they are grounded in the virtues of much smaller communities, virtues that are ongoingly realized in the face-to-face dealings of people with each other. Abstract patriotism is rooted, must be rooted, in communal patriotisms. This does not mean, however, that it can be logically deduced from the latter; it is possible for me to be a "Red Hook Italian" and have only a minimal stake in my American citizenship. Nor is it altogether obvious why I *should* have such a larger stake. An *argument* of some moral complexity may be necessary to convince me that I should regard as "my own," say, Californians of Swedish ancestry—as against my uncle, who lives around the corner on Union Street but who has never bothered to be naturalized. Again, this need not mean that such an argument would be fallacious. It does mean that abstractions are always a somewhat cerebral business, as against the concrete experience of being a (let us assume) cherished nephew.

Modernity is indeed characterized by the high degree of abstraction pertaining to its institutional order (the Dutch sociologist Anton Zij-derveld has aptly described the latter as "the abstract society"). Still, the tension between communal and abstract patriotism is by no means an exclusively modern phenomenon—a Jewish tentmaker from a provincial hamlet in Asia Minor could boast about coming from "no mean city" and at the same time announce (proudly, one surmises) his Roman citizenship. What is peculiarly modern is that the nation-state (itself a recent apparition on the stage of history) has become the major focus of patriotic sentiment. Indeed, the very idea of patriotism has come to be associated so closely with the nation-state that a considerable amount of reflection is required to grasp that patriotism has older and different roots.

By its very nature, the patriotism attached to the nation-state is highly abstract. This is true even in quite small countries. The individual can no more have face-to-face experience of four million fellow Swiss as of two hundred million fellow Americans. For this reason, modern patriotic identities are subject to considerable variability. This becomes particularly evident in the case of new nation-states. Sometimes from one day to another, a subject of the Habsburgs redefines himself as a Czechoslovak, or a Kikuyu as a Kenyan. In territories disputed by competing modern patriotisms, it often happens that members of the same family opt for different national identities. The parts of Central Europe once governed by the Habsburgs can serve as a rich laboratory for such family divisions. Older nation-states differ from newer ones, not so much in the degree of abstraction of their patriotism, but simply in the degree to which people have become habituated to it. In principle, it is no more "natural" for an individual to be French than to be Czechoslovak; it is just that France has been around longer as a nation-state, so that people have become accustomed to taking the abstraction as reality. But as recent "mininationalisms" are making increasingly clear, even the oldest nation-states are far from immune to the possibility that national identities can be redefined—as with the Breton, Basque, and Provençal movements in France.

National (or ethnic) identities can be constructed, reconstructed, disassembled—not exactly at will, but with a good deal of flexibility. The patriotic ideologies of nation-states, of course, are constrained to deny this. They must present the arbitrary constructions as necessary facticities, that is, as *given*. Patriotic allegiance to the particular nation-state is legitimated by virtue of a common culture and language as well as a common history. But any one of these can be highly fictitious. It is misleading to think that, as a rule, a common history produces a sense of national belonging. On the contrary, in many instances the common history is freely invented in order to legitimate the national construction. Modern educational systems, invariably under the control of nation-state governments, are the most important purveyors of these "myths of origins." African schoolchildren were made to write essays in French schools on "our ancestors, the Franks." Funny, perhaps, but no more absurd than the same essay being written by children in the former territories of the Count of Toulouse.

Nevertheless, the abstractions can be concretized in everyday experience. What is more, the longer the abstractions have been around, the more massive will be these concretizations. Language is probably the most important vehicle of this process; the French language is very much a reality of individual experience, and it is so today for the inhabitants of Toulouse no less than for those living in the lands of the old Kingdom of the Franks. Apart from language, there is a collage of specifically French experiences and French things, by now more or less common to all regions of the nation-state. If one wants to know what these are, there is an easy answer: *They are all those experiences and things that a Frenchman will miss when he goes abroad.* And they are anything but abstract: the peculiar mixture of order and sloppy chaos characteristic of French urban scenes; the elegant invectives exchanged by French motorists (centuries of malignant court-language put on wheels by Renault); the smell and touch of French bakeries; the more than a little tired theater of French eroticism.

To be sure, these concrete realities have little to do directly with the grand rhetoric of national patriotism. Yet there are important mediations between the two. Unless concrete, experiential associations can be evoked by the rhetoric, it will remain empty and unconvincing (except perhaps for the very short periods when most people can be inspired by pure ideas). No wonder patriotic rhetoric must always come back to homes, mothers, children playing in the streets—*French* homes, to be sure, and *French* children on *French* streets. It could well be that, if all the motives were known, more French soldiers fought at Verdun for the smell of French bread than for the great ideas of liberty, equality, and fraternity. Nor is such sacrifice for the sweet, familiar things of home necessarily an illusion. A personal reminiscence here: In my childhood, in the 1930s, I spent several summers in the South Tyrol (renamed Alto Adige by the Italians) when Mussolini's government was trying systematically to suppress the German language.

There were people then who said that they would rather die than give up their language, and some even said this about the colorful regional costumes (which were also banned by the government). It seems to me that one ought to think very seriously before dismissing such sentiments as irrational.

It is possible now to amplify what was said previously about the necessary rootage of abstract patriotism in communal patriotism. The character of this rootage is what we have called concretization. In other words, *the abstract notions of patriotism attached to the nation-state will be (and remain) plausible to individuals to the degree that they can be related to concrete everyday experiences in ordinary life.* This fact serves as a *limit* to the arbitrariness of abstract definitions of identity. But the limit is by no means rigid. Just as national identities can be invented, concrete experiences can be engineered. The longer such an engineering feat can be kept going, the greater will be its plausibility (Czechoslovakia, that is, is ahead of Kenya in this game of reality construction). Obviously there are many variables involved in each historical instance of this dynamic—amount of coercion, ideological currents, economic interests, availability of alternatives to the particular national identity being "engineered," and so on. All the same, there is a remarkable sociological and psychological continuity in all of this. After all, Frenchmen are not all *that* different from Kikuyus.

The patriotism of the nation-state is one of the most potent ideological forces in the world today. It is mainly among Western intellectuals that patriotism has of late acquired a bad name. This is not the place to explore the reasons why (an undertaking that would require another chapter of at least this length). In view of this almost pornographic status of patriotic sentiments today, however, it is appropriate to ask whether the ethical depreciation of patriotism has merit beyond the peculiar intellectual milieus in question.

An oversimplified answer to the question would be in terms of a differentiation between patriotism and nationalism—the former (in view, say, of our preceding considerations) may then be accorded ethical value, the latter not. Nationalism, in that case, could be defined as some sort of exaggerated patriotism, a quasi-religious dedication to the nation or nation-state. Perhaps such a distinction has some relevance, but current usage is quite confused and, in any case, the distinction is unlikely to be of much help in answering the ethical question. If one decides, on whatever grounds, that some cases of patriotism are ethically meritorious, one will be constrained to extend this approbation to some cases of nationalism, however defined. Perhaps the most that one can say to the distinction on the grounds of the Judaeo-Christian tradition is that any instances in which the nation is placed at the very top of the hierarchy of values should be deemed idolatry. There are cases in which such a judgment may be ethically significant (as it was, for example, in the case of Nazi Germany). Most of the time, however, one must deal with far more complex cases. Also, in a Judaeo-Christian perspective, the absolutization of *any* human institution, even of the family, may be deemed idolatrous—the nation is just one of the many possible candidates for the role of chief idol.

More likely, it will be necessary to explore each individual case separately for purposes of ethical valuation. There are great differences among nations, nation-states, and national ideologies. One must ask, in each case, just what they *represent* in terms of human realities and human values. This question applies both to the abstract (ipso facto heavily ideological) level of patriotic sentiments and to the concrete everyday experiences in which these are rooted. In other words, the question has relevance both to the great ideas of the French republic and to the smell of French bread.

On the level of everyday experiences, it seems possible to propose a general human right: *Every human being has the right to his own tradition.* Put differently, *no one may be deprived of his own childhood.* Thus the South Tyroleans were correct in perceiving their fundamental human rights being violated when the Italian government sought to rob them of their language, and of the sounds and sights of their childhood. The right to the language of one's origins probably makes the ethical point most clearly: Every language is an immensely valuable depository of human experiences, of joys, sorrows, and uniquely irreplaceable perceptions of the world. Those whose lives have been shaped by a language have a basic right to its possession and, if necessary, its defense. Conversely, there is an ethical and political obligation to protect the human values deposited in any language. *Mutatis mutandis,* the same thinking applies to other components of a tradition, including some that may seem trivial to an outsider, such as the sight of a group of Tyroleans, dressed in regional garb and carrying their ancient banners, marching down a familiar street to the stirring music of a *Trachtenkapelle.*

Like other human rights, this one is not absolute. There are traditions that embody the oppression and enslavement of others. There are even happy childhoods full of cruelty to others (contrary to current beliefs, happiness is not in itself a sign of virtue). It seems impossible to propose general criteria for this sort of ethical differentiation. Each case will have to be looked at separately.

Similarly, one must ask what values are represented by nation-states and their ideologies on the level of abstract patriotism. The French republic represented very different values from Nazi Germany, a fact that would only have been obscured by either the approbation or repudiation of *both* nationalisms. The United States represented different values when its armies poured into Europe in 1944 and when they fought in Vietnam. The goal of national integration has vastly different meanings in Western industrial societies and in the Third World. Again, no general ethical formulas seem possible here. There appears no alternative to a painstaking exploration of each individual case: To what degree have the Nazi past and the requirements of world peace made the ethical claims of German national unity obsolete? Does American patriotism have an *a priori* claim to the allegiance of every group within the country, including those who would reject the claim (such as some blacks, say, or Chicanos)? Was the goal of national integration worth the human costs of the Nigerian civil war? If so, does the same logic lead to a repudiation of the insurrection that led to the dismemberment of Pakistan? More generally: When is "Balkanization" a genuine evil and when is it evoked as a cover for oppression? What is being suggested here amounts to a procedure of *moral costs/benefits analysis*. Such a procedure does not exist at the present time. What is worse, few people are even interested in developing one. A further pursuit of this topic would go beyond our present scope.

It has often been pointed out that American patriotism is distinctive in that it refers to a very specific ideology, the one that Gunnar Myrdal aptly called the "American creed." This is, of course, a valid description, even though American patriotism is not quite as distinctive in this respect as some would have it. There are strong "creedal" components in other patriotisms, as in those of the Latin American countries, and most notably (an important commonality) in that of the Soviet Union. All the same, American patriotism is characterized by a peculiar linkage with a highly articulate political ideology, and it is assumed that every American will not only love his country but owe allegiance to its official ideology. This, of course, has led to the peculiar notion of "un-American" beliefs—contrary to current liberal opinion, a notion present from the beginnings of the American republic: A Tory believer in the divine right of kings was as much beyond the ideologically acceptable pale (even if the term "un-American" was not used then) as, say, a believer in the redemptive goal of socialist revolution later on in the history of the republic. It follows that any ethical valuation of American patriotism, at least on this level, will hinge on an assessment of the value and the continuing viability of this specific ideology. American patriotism will be plausible to those who affirm the basic propositions of the "American creed"; it will be repudiated by those to whom the "creed" has come to appear as a form of false consciousness. (*Mutatis mutandis*, the same holds for Soviet patriotism, a point of as much interest to Ukrainians or Uzbeks as to American blacks or Chicanos.)

It is all the more important to stress that even American patriotism is not exhausted by these ideological abstractions. If it were, one could only predict a dim future for it; few people can live by abstractions for very long. Again, a useful question to ask in this connection is what an American will miss abroad. The answer will invariably bring into view a particular cluster of American experiences and realities—from the particularities of the American language and of American comic sensibilities (how many Englishmen laugh at American jokes?) to the sights of a drugstore, the sounds of a high-school band, and the taste of hamburgers. It is out of such stuff that any subjectively real patriotism is fashioned—and it is a serious error of understanding to denigrate this. By comparison with these vivid realities, the abstractions of the "American creed" are rather pallid in most people's minds. An interesting question would concern the extent to which the "creed" has actually penetrated this level of everyday realities. One may think here of the ingrained egalitarianism of American manners, or of the exuberant surrealism of American humor. In that case, what the American misses abroad will at least implicitly contain certain elements of the "creed." Still, it is safe to assume that he will only rarely miss such overt expressions of the "creed" as recitations of the Oath of the Allegiance or Fourth of July festivities.

The concrete realities of much of what we think of today as the American way of life would, in all likelihood, survive a demise of the present political system. There would probably be high-school bands in the American People's Republic and subjects of the Principality of Brooklyn would eat hamburgers, even if jokes became more ironic in the former and manners more deferential in the latter (bowing from the waist in Flatbush?!). There would, in that case, be considerable continuity in the concrete contents of American patriotism (as there has been in Russian patriotism following the establishment of the communist state). It remains true, however, that the survival of the American political system is intrinsically linked with the further course and character of American patriotism. More specifically, American democracy will be vital to the degree that its basic propositions are linked to the patriotism inspired by the concrete experiences of American life. In other words, American democracy will be in bad shape on the day when most Americans are content to have the hamburgers without the "creed."

It is likely that we are nowhere near this point today. But the denigration of patriotism in important milieus of American intellectual and academic life is dangerous nonetheless. Intellectuals and academics are far less important in society than in their own opinion of themselves, but they occupy positions in which reality is defined for large numbers of other people. Even if most of these people are suspicious of the intellectuals' definitions of reality, there are political consequences to the ensuing vacuum of legitimations. Many American intellectuals have been eating the hamburgers while denigrating the "creed," and this is not only morally ambiguous (by all indications, they continue to enjoy the repast) but politically unhealthy. A revitalization of patriotism, and its relegitimation by the intellectual leadership, is important for the future viability of American democracy. To say this does not in itself prejudge the particular political coloration of such a resurgent patriotism; in principle, it could occur at just about any point in the political spectrum. It could well be left as well as liberal (indeed, it is already remarkable to what extent ideas and movements deemed as being "on the left" all over the world are of American origin). It could also be conservative or "on the right." One of the measures of the crisis of patriotism in intellectual circles today is that only the possibility of a rightist resurgence seems plausible to many in those circles. Such a realignment of the symbols of patriotic sentiment cannot happen overnight. It requires political as well as intellectual leadership, and one hardly needs to add that the political leadership with which the American republic has been blessed in recent years has done little toward that end, despite its unrestrained exhibition of patriotic symbolism.

The "American creed" has been largely the creation of political liberalism. This is a *Weltanschauung* that has to its credit impressive humane achievements, and the defensiveness of liberals in the face of their left critics over the last few years has little justification in the record (I should add that I say this without being a member of the liberal camp myself; I continue to be emphatically and unapologetically conservative in my own basic political stance). Any fair critique of liberalism should begin with an acknowledgment of its achievements in the sphere of human values and liberty. When it comes to the topic under discussion here, though, liberalism has always suffered from an excessive emphasis on abstract patriotism. This is a tendency that goes back to the roots of liberalism in Enlightenment thought; in some ways it is *the* Achilles heel of liberal political thought. This has made liberals peculiarly blind to the communal solidarities and particularisms on which, as we suggested earlier, the abstract edifice of modern institutions must necessarily rest. Without giving up their fundamental convictions, liberals should be able to cultivate a new sensitivity to the concrete communities that give meaning and a sense of being at home to most human beings—the realities of family, church, neighborhood, and ethnic group, to mention but the cardinal ones. It may be hoped that the black movement has given some useful lessons in this regard to its white liberal supporters. Also, liberals should be able to become more positively aware of the human values embodied in the concrete everyday experiences of social life. Put differently, they should be capable of overcoming the caricature of "Middle America" in their own minds. Perhaps the fiasco of the McGovern campaign has had some educational impact in this area (if it has not, the major blame attaches to Richard Nixon).

American society, as any other modern society, is an order of highly abstract institutions. These are legitimated by ideas that, most of the time, are quite remote from the everyday experiences of people—that is, from the loyalties and emotions of concrete patriotic sentiment. For this reason it is of great importance that there be *mediating structures* between the abstractions of the political system and the concrete lives of individuals. Public policy should vigorously protect these structures where they exist (for example, it should be public policy to foster the family, the church, and the neighborhood), and where they do not exist or have disappeared it should be a public concern to invent and bring into being new structures that can fulfill this mediating role. If this necessity is truly understood, what emerges is a new political program. It will be a program that cuts diagonally across the present ideological boundaries, a program neither left nor right in the conventional sense. The elaboration of its details could become one of the most exciting enterprises in the coming period of American history.

11

In Praise of Particularity:

The Concept of

Mediating Structures

From the beginning the American republic conceived of itself as a great experiment in the realization of liberty. This experiment has come to be conjoined, serendipitously, with another fact about America—its peculiar relationship to the process of modernization. Talcott Parsons has called America "the lead society." This is not an expression of nationalist megalomania, but rather a descriptive (if you will, a "value-free") statement to the effect that a number of modernizing forces have gone further in this country than anywhere else. It is in this double sense that I am prepared to use the term *"chosen"* for America. For better or for worse, we are the most modernized society in the contemporary world. And, audaciously, we continue to carry on the experiment of free institutions in this not necessarily enviable condition. Liberty is on the retreat today all over the world. I cannot pursue here the far-reaching, and sinister, implications of this for America's role on the international scene. But the institutions that embody liberty are also under great pressure domestically. My observations in what follows pertain to this domestic crisis. They are animated by the hope that, if we can resolve this crisis without abandoning the experiment, we may still serve as a lesson for the human race. Perhaps we are "chosen" to do this.

The following remarks are concerned with an attempt to link socio-

This chapter first appeared in *The Review of Politics* (July, 1976) and subsequently in Walter Nicgorski and Ronald Weber, eds., *An Almost Chosen People* (Notre Dame: University of Notre Dame Press, 1976).

logical theory and public policy. There is something vaguely disreputable even about saying this. Sociologists are supposed to come in two kinds. There is the larger group, which consists of people intimately related to computers and other mathematical gadgets; these people make costly studies of very specific areas of social life; they report on these studies in barbaric English; once in a while their findings have a bearing on some issue of public policy. Then there is a smaller group, consisting of people who are all in sociology by some sort of biographical mistake (they really should be in philosophy or literature); these people mostly write books about the theories of dead Germans; as far as public policy is concerned, this theorizing has no relevance at all—and a good thing it is. Broadly speaking, this was the generally perceived division of the species "sociologist" when I was a student in the 1950s; after a short interlude, this seems to be the general perception once more. For a brief period in the late 1960s this dichotomy was challenged: Sociological theory was called on to be politically relevant. Of those who responded to this clarion call, there are few left today; most of them have simply switched their allegiance from one set of dead Germans to another set of even deader ones; the rest, with some relief, have returned to the comforting mysteries of quantitative techniques.

Occasionally I get the feeling that I'm the last convert to the message that sociological theorists should become politically relevant. (Lest this remark be misinterpreted as betraying delusions of grandeur, let me hasten to add that the feeling is one of pure paranoia.) Like many others, I was sucked into political relevance by my opposition to the Vietnam war, which turned my attention—first political, only later social-scientific—to the Third World. In consequence, for several years the focus of my work was problems of modernization and development; while some of this work was quite theoretical, it was not possible (nor did I want it to be possible) to divorce the theoretical problems from the urgent political questions. Actually, I was surprised myself when I discovered that my sociological theorizing was, in places, relevant indeed to questions of development policy. I did not follow the much-traveled route from this discovery into Marxist scholasticism. Neither did I, at this late stage, transform myself into the kind of person who can talk to a computer. What I did do was to turn my attention back to this country. If sociological theory can be relevant to public policy in Third World countries, who knows, it may have a comparable relevance in America.

Let me be a little more specific. One funny thing that happened to me in the Third World was that I developed a strong sympathy with tribalism. This was all the more surprising as it was contrary to my own values as well as my own biography—I have always been deracinated, cosmopolitan, and totally unattracted to what Marx so aptly called the idiocy of village life. But, while I have no desire personally to find some all-embracing *Gemeinschaft* as a refuge from the rootlessness of modernity, I gained an enormous respect for the positive human values of such intact premodern communities as still exist in the Third World—communities of kinship, tribe, locality, and region—and the frequently moving efforts to preserve these communities under the violent pressures of modernization. Conversely, I gained a better understanding of the price exacted by modernity. I have no wish to romanticize tribalism. Rather, I think that an appreciation of the human significance of tribalism (taking that term in its broadest possible sense) can be of great help in *a critique of modernity* (and please note that a critique is *not* an attack, *not* a blanket rejection). Such a critique spans the theoretical and the political levels. My present work on mediating structures comes out of these concerns (at the moment I'm engaged in elaborating the public-policy implications of the basic concept, in collaboration with Richard Neuhaus, in a project funded by the American Enterprise Institute).

What are mediating structures? The concept has vast implications, but it can be defined simply: Mediating structures are those institutions which stand between the individual in his private sphere and the large institutions of the public sphere. The concept is by no means new; indeed, a good case can be made that it is a central theme of the sociological tradition. What might be new, however, is the translation of the concept into a paradigm for public policy, in the specific conditions of American politics today. A *locus classicus* of the concept is on the last pages of Emile Durkheim's *Suicide*, where he describes the "tempest" of modernization, sweeping away what he calls the "little aggregations" in which people existed through most of human history, leaving only the state on the one hand and a mass of individuals, "like so many liquid molecules," on the other hand. Similar analyses can be found in the classical German sociologists (Ferdinand Toennies, Max Weber, Georg Simmel), and in this country in the works of Charles Cooley, Thorstein Veblen, and the writers of the Chicago School. Talcott Parsons and Robert Nisbet have made important contributions to this conceptualization in recent American sociology. If one wants to

pursue the concept beyond the sociological tradition, one may go back
to earlier sources, which interestingly are both on the right and the left
of the political-ideological spectrum. One may refer to Edmund Burke
(insisting on the importance of "small platoons" as the foundation for
all wider loyalties), Alexis de Tocqueville (finding in voluntary associations one of the keys to the vitality of American democracy), and Otto
von Gierke (with his fixation on the alleged virtues of medieval guilds).
At the same time, one may refer to sources on the left, within Marxism, and even more clearly in the anarcho-syndicalist tradition. But it
is not my intention here to give a history-of-ideas treatment. Instead,
let me explicate the concept, necessarily in very brief form, as I understand it in my own sociological theorizing.

Modernization brings about a novel dichotomization of social life.
The dichotomy is between the huge and immensely powerful institutions of the public sphere (the state, the large economic agglome-
rates that we now know as corporations and labor unions, and the
ever-growing bureaucracies that administer sectors of society not properly political or economic, such as education or the organized professions) and the private sphere, which is a curious interstitial area "left
over," as it were, by the large institutions and indeed (in the words of
Arnold Gehlen) marked by "underinstitutionalization." Put more
simply, the dichotomy is between the megastructures and private life.
These two spheres of modern society are experienced by the individual
in very different ways. The megastructures are remote, often hard to
understand or downright unreal, impersonal, and ipso facto unsatisfactory as sources for individual meaning and identity. In the classical
Marxian term, the megastructures are "alienating." By contrast, private life is experienced as the single most important area for the discovery and actualization of meaning and identity. While, of course, the
megastructures impose limits and controls on private life, they also
leave the individual (at least in Western societies) a remarkable degree
of freedom in shaping his private life. The latter is under-
institutionalized in the precise degree to which the individual is left to
his own devices in a wide range of activities that are crucial to the formation of a meaningful identity, from expressing his religious preference to settling on a sexual life style. This is heady stuff. It is also asking a lot of the individual; in effect, it is asking him to create his own
private world *de novo*, with few and unreliable institutional supports
in this audacious assignment. In the well-known Durkheimian term,
private life is always under the shadow of *anomie*. Modernization

therefore breeds alienation and anomie, which is another way of saying that modernity has a built-in crisis which, once set in motion, is very difficult to resolve.

As long as the individual can indeed find meaning and identity in his private life, he can manage to put up with the meaningless and dis-identifying world of the megastructures. For many people the formula for this adjustment goes something like this: "I put in my time on the job between nine and five, I pay my taxes, I don't upset any applecarts in my union—and then I go home, where I can really be myself." In other words, as long as private life is *not* anomic, the alienations of the megastructures are at least tolerable. The situation becomes intolerable if "home," that refuge of stability and value in an alien world, ceases to be such a refuge—when, say, my wife leaves me, my children take on life styles that are strange and unacceptable to me, my church becomes incomprehensible, my neighborhood becomes a place of danger, and so on. The very underinstitutionalization of private life, however, makes it likely that my home will indeed be threatened by these or similar anomic disintegrations. Conversely, the best defenses against the threat are those institutions, however weakened, which still give a measure of stability to private life. These are, precisely, the mediating institutions, notably those of family, church, voluntary association, neighborhood, and subculture.

The mediating structures, then, are essential if private life is to remain "home." This does not mean that they have to continue in their traditional forms. It is possible that there may be new forms of family, church, or subculture, and that these may become the institutional anchorage for individual meaning and identity, always provided that they acquire the necessary degree of stability, that they can be relied upon. It is equally important to see that the mediating structures are *also* essential for the megastructures, and especially for those that constitute the political order in a modern society. Why? The reasons are actually quite simple. No society, modern or otherwise, can survive without what Durkheim called a "collective conscience," that is, without moral values that have general authority. The megastructures, because of their remoteness and sheer vastness, are unsuitable for the generation and maintenance of such a general morality. Bureaucrats are the poorest of *moralistes*. The megastructures, and especially the state, must depend for, let us say, "moral sustenance" on institutions or social formations that are "below" them. They must do so, to be exact, unless coercion is to replace moral authority as the basis of political order.

But neither can a general morality rest upon the unstable and unreliable efforts of atomized individuals engaged in private experiments of "life styling." The social contract cannot be renegotiated every day by millions of individual "consenting adults," not unless society is to lapse into intermittent chaos. To be sure, there are ways in which the megastructures, especially the political ones, can modify their own institutional organization so as to be less remote, less alienating—by the various modalities of democratic accountability, openness to grass-roots initiatives, by decentralization or debureaucratization. Such modifications are, indeed, recurring goals of the democratic ideal. It is unlikely, all the same, that these modifications will ever be adequate substitutes for those structures that mediate between the political order and the home life of individuals; if they became such substitutes, the democratic ideal, certainly in its American version, would be in great trouble.

Let me sum up the argument thus far. The progressive disintegration of mediating structures constitutes a double crisis, on the level of individual life and also on a political level. Without mediating structures, private life comes to be engulfed in a deepening anomie. Without mediating structures, the political order is drawn into the same anomie by being deprived of the moral foundation upon which it rests. Since the political order, unlike the individual, cannot commit suicide or go insane (though it might be argued that there are political analogues to suicide and insanity), it is confronted with the necessity of substituting coercion for moral consent. One does not have to be a sociological theorist to perceive that this substitution has, if nothing else, the one great virtue of simplification. It seems to me that this is a major psychological clue to the otherwise incomprehensible attraction of totalitarian movements and regimes: Totalitarianism promises to resolve the dichotomy of private and public; it keeps the promise in a perverse way, by so politicizing the private that it is absorbed in the public.

This is not the place to pursue these questions of political psychology. But I want to turn to a different, if related, question. How do the major political ideologies relate to mediating structures?

The broad tradition of liberal ideology, all the way back to the Enlightenment, has an especially close relationship to the process of modernization. Indeed, the argument can be made that this tradition embodies the myth of modernity more than any other. It is not surprising, then, that it has been singularly blind to the importance and at times even the very existence of mediating structures. Liberalism is, above all, a faith in rationality. Its designs for society are highly rational, abstract, universalistic. Burke, in criticizing the programs of the French revolutionaries, aptly called them "geometrical." Liberalism, of course, has undergone profound transformations since then, in France as elsewhere. In America, as has often been pointed out, liberalism underwent a remarkable conversion in this century, basically from faith in the market to faith in government (paradoxically, those adhering to the older version of the liberal creed now call themselves conservatives). Yet the underlying faith in the powers of rationality has remained unchanged. While before the anonymous forces of the market (Adam Smith's "invisible hand") were supposed to make human affairs come out in accord with rationality, now the planning and controls of government are expected to achieve that salvific result. It is precisely the mediating structures that stand in the way of this "geometry." They are "irrational" (that is, based on emotion and value, not on functional utility), concrete, highly particularistic, and ipso facto resistant to the rationales of either market or government. In terms of contemporary American liberalism, the sundry "irrationalities" of human life are firmly assigned to the private sphere (where liberals are sincerely committed to protecting them under the rubric of individual rights). As far as public policy is concerned, "geometry" continues to reign. No better up-to-date illustration of this can be found than the liberally inspired designs for racial integration in places like Boston or Louisville, abstract "geometries" imposed without regard for the fabric of communities in which people live their daily lives. These designs bear an uncomfortable resemblance to those concocted by liberal social scientists engaged in "nation building" in Vietnam. Those, too, were abstract "geometries" with no relation to the living fabric of society—and, significantly, there was the same mania for quantification.

The left tradition of political ideology (which, *in nuce*, is the tradition of socialist thought) has been more clear-sighted in this matter. It is no accident that alienation occupies the place it does in Marxist thought. I would contend that the protest against the abstractions of modernity is at the heart of the socialist ideal: Socialism is a faith in renewed community. The weakness of the left perception is that it ascribes alienation to capitalism alone and thus fails to see that the abolition of capitalism brings on new alienations of even greater potency, namely, the alienations of the socialist state, a political formation that (at any rate to date) has shown itself to be endemically totalitarian. The contemporary American left fully shares this weakness. It perceives the alienating power of those megastructures that are linked to capitalism (the currently favorite target is the multinational corporation); it is totally blind to the realities of the socialist regimes it admires (usually these are varieties of oriental despotism masquerading as Marxist); in its disdain for the irrationalities of mediating structures (family, church, and so on), it stands squarely in the liberal tradition of the Enlightenment. The New Left of the mid-1960s, especially in its linkages with the anarcho-syndicalist elements of the counterculture, showed some promise of overcoming this weakness. In all likelihood, this kind of New Left thinking is now a matter of the past.

Classical European conservatism, as exemplified by Burke, was vibrantly aware of the importance of mediating structures. *Its* weakness was an inability to perceive the irreversible realities of modernization, a clinging to premodern imagery, and in consequence an inability to generate viable policies for a modern society. As far as contemporary America is concerned, this classical conservatism has little if any relevance (*pace* the ritual invocations of Burke's name in places like *National Review*). Contemporary American conservatism is Old Testament liberalism. Its quarrel with the latter-day liberal covenant of the New Deal is interesting, even important, but of little help with regard to the point at issue. Contemporary American conservatives do indeed perceive the alienations of big government; they are blind to the alienations of big business; their faith in the allegedly benign rationality of market forces is a wonder to behold. Even so, it must be said in fairness that it is in these circles, along with the circles of what remains of the New Left and the counterculture, that one finds some measure of understanding of mediating structures.

This rapid survey of the ideological spectrum thus leads to a negative result: Nowhere on this spectrum is the concept of mediating structures really at home. But a positive conclusion may be drawn from this. Precisely for this reason is the concept politically promising. *It cuts across the ideological divides.* At a moment of history when many people, in all the different political camps, feel that the old ideologies have become sterile and that new starting points are needed, this cutting-across quality of the concept of mediating structures makes it politically interesting. This becomes clear, I think, as one passes from general considerations to concrete policy implications. One finds that these implications jump back and forth between conventionally right-wing and left-wing positions. In other words, the concept slices reality up in new ways.

In the project I'm working on with Richard Neuhaus, we have formulated two overall policy propositions, both based on the understanding outlined above of the importance of mediating institutions in society. One: *Public policy should protect and foster mediating structures.* Two: *Wherever possible, public policy should utilize the mediating structures as its agents.* The two propositions could be called, respectively, minimalist and maximalist. Minimally, the message to government is: leave these institutions alone. Maximally, the message is: see where you can actually use these institutions. The two, of course, are not necessarily contradictory. One may apply to some policy areas, the other to different areas. On the whole, the minimal injunction is more palatable to those on the right, the maximal one to those farther left (one could put this observation cynically by saying that, with appropriate modifications, the concept could be written into either the Republican or the Democratic platform), though this bifurcation does not always hold.

The empirical presupposition of the minimalist proposition is that many programs of public policy have actively hurt mediating structures, to the great detriment of the society. The remedy is that public policy should cease and desist. This injunction in itself represents an amplification of the liberal value of civil liberties and rights. It suggests that the protections of the latter should extend to certain communities and communal institutions as well as to individuals.

A few concrete examples: public policy should desist from forcing welfare mothers to go to work and turn their children over to day-care centers. This, of course, is but a particularly obnoxious aspect of much broader welfare policies that have been detrimental to family stability among the poor, a point that has been amply documented, especially for the black community. Public policy, and especially the courts, should reverse the recent interpretation of the First Amendment as signifying the legal establishment of a secularist creed at the expense of the historic religious traditions of the society. The Supreme Court decision on prayer in the public schools was a high point of this secularist wave, but by no means an end point. There is now a case in the courts of New York that challenges the right of religious social-work agencies to employ religious criteria in assigning children for adoption; if resolved in favor of the plaintiffs, the case would result in a massive assault on the liberty and integrity of religious communities. Largely under the heading of fighting corruption and/or inefficiency, public policy tends to favor public social-work agencies over private ones. Alliances of professional organizations and government agencies impose standards on private agencies that, very often, have no real function other than driving these agencies out of business. This is but part of a general animus against voluntary associations, be they working in welfare, health or education. Our proposition is that voluntarism should be encouraged, not hampered, by public policy. Mention has already been made of the assault on neighborhoods in the name of racial integration. Of course racial justice should be very high on the agenda of public policy in this country. There are many ways in which public policy can promote this goal, not only by proscriptive legislation but through positive programs (especially in employment, housing, and education); many of these programs, in all likelihood, will have little relation to mediating structures. But the current court-enforced busing programs are, almost without exception, an exercise in profound sociological folly. Unless reversed, these policies will have severely detrimental effects on urban life (including the goal of racial justice). Public policy, especially in the area of education, has tended to be indifferent if not hostile to the racial, ethnic, and religious diversity of American society. The black movement has been first in sharply challenging this leveling (and ipso facto anomie-generating) tendency. The same challenge has now been taken up by Hispanics, American Indians and various groups involved in the revival of white ethnicity. No doubt there are dangers in this (including the danger of cultural and political Balkanization recurrently brought up by liberal critics). Nevertheless there is good reason to welcome this new awareness of the vital role of subcultures in the, let us say, moral constitution of this country. Without abandoning the rights of the individual apart from any subculture, public policy should protect, not seek to destroy, the living subcultures from which people derive meaning and identity. Bilingualism in education is one interesting issue in this context.

The maximalist proposition, needless to say, is the much riskier one. The biggest risk was well put by one critic of our project, when he suggested that one of the worst things that could happen was great government enthusiasm for this proposition. Eventually there might even be a Secretary for Mediating Structures in the cabinet—and that might well be the end of mediating structures. Agents of public policy are subject to public controls. Are there ways of having public policy uti-

lize mediating structures without destroying them in the process? I
have no definitely reassuring answer to this question, and it troubles
me. Still, I think that there are possibilities to be explored here.

Probably the most auspicious model for the maximalist proposition
is the voucher concept in education. Various versions of this concept
have been discussed, and there is now going on some very modest experimentation along its lines. It is a model for the following reasons. It
does not represent a retreat from public involvement in this particular
area of social life; it only represents a retreat from one exclusive mod-
ality through which public involvement has hitherto been expressed. It
empowers people to make decisions who have no decision-making
power in this area now (more specifically, it gives lower-income families the power to make the same decisions on the education of their
children that higher-income families have already). It respects the pluralism of American life. It may also be, alas, a model for the furious
opposition it has aroused from an odd alliance of vested interests: the
bureaucratic establishment of public education and the teachers'
unions, both of whom have an interest (in the case of the unions, possibly, a perceived rather than a real one) in maintaining the status quo of
educational monopoly, liberals worried about cultural Balkanization,
and militant secularists opposed to any form of public support of religious institutions. The voucher concept, as applied to education,
touches on every one of the mediating structures enumerated: family,
church, voluntary association, neighborhood, and subculture. For this
reason, one of the questions we are thinking about is how in other
areas of public policy, besides education, analogues to the voucher concept might be designed. But this is not the only direction along which
one may think in exploring the maximalist proposition. Some other examples go like this. The concepts of family income maintenance
and/or children's allowances. Tax incentives for voluntary efforts (religiously sponsored as well as other) in attacking various social problems. Decentralization and community control of some functions of
municipal government (including law enforcement and health deliv-
ery). Zoning and housing policies that work with rather than against
existing communities and/or life styles (always with the proviso that
such policies are not racially exclusive and do not infringe on the rights
of individuals).

To list these examples is to acknowledge the immense complexity of
these issues of public policy. I am well aware of this. The concept of
mediating structures is no panacea, but rather the starting point for

very careful, prudent explorations. Yet it was necessary here to become very concrete, in order to show the direct line that goes from very broad considerations of sociological theory to the highly specific problems that occupy people in the day-by-day business of public policy.

Let me come to the close. The history of freedom in the modern world has for a long time been marked by the often conflicting claims of universalism and particularity. The main thrust of modernity has always been universalizing, and nothing in the foregoing seeks to deny the liberating effects of this universalism for countless human beings. However, as with most human endeavors, universalism pushed to an extreme becomes destructive. The "liquid molecules" of individuals caught in a chaotic private world, and the leveling tyranny of the totalitarian state, are the twin consequences of universalism gone berserk. It is time, I believe, to return to a praise of particularity, especially in America. The prospects for freedom, and indeed for anything that could be called political decency, are very dim on the contemporary scene. Our time continues to be viewed by some as an age of liberation; increasingly it appears, in fact, as an age of spreading oppression and deepening misery. America is one of the very few places left in which there is at least a fighting chance for innovations and experiments within the framework of free institutions. There is also a specifically American tradition of balancing universalism and particularity, of pluralism, of combining the power of the modern state with the energies of voluntary associations. The concept of mediating structures, as applied to public policy in this country, may be one way of revitalizing an American political heritage that seems all the more precious as, every day, it seems more in peril.

III

TRANSCENDING
MODERNITY

12

Prologue: Bestrangement in Stockholm

Storytelling is supposed to be good for theology, or so we have been instructed of late. Some of the arguments for this view make a good deal of sense, as long as the stories focus on something other than the individual telling them. So I will tell a story. It tells how one may worship God in a language one does not understand, and its lesson is the importance of ordaining women to the priesthood.

On a recent visit to Sweden, I was advised to attend an experimental liturgy being celebrated in the cathedral of Stockholm in connection with a diocesan clergy conference. My spontaneous association of experimental liturgies is with the assorted horrors of what, broadly speaking, one may call the California sensibility. But I went anyway, partly because I had nothing else to do that morning, partly because in a place of pervasive secularity even perverted religiosity promises some spiritual relief. The experiment turned out to be rather tame (though it seemed to agitate the bishop, who was sitting in the row ahead of mine). There were a couple of priests with guitars who led the congregation in the singing of some folksy sounding songs (Country Northern?), and there was a very youthful jazz combo self-consciously assembled behind the altar in blue jeans. All in all, it was the sort of thing that would have been avant-garde among American Methodists in the 1950s. Following this exercise in daring innovation there was a communion service. That, as far as I could tell (I don't understand Swedish), was in accordance with standard Lutheran practice. Liturgically, then, the whole affair was anything but startling. But its interest for me lay elsewhere.

For one thing, I almost always profit from participating in wor-

This chapter originally appeared in *The Christian Century* (November 12, 1975). Copyright ©
1975 by Christian Century Foundation. Reprinted by permission.

ship when I don't understand the words. It is not an experience I have very often, so it is possible that the relative rarity of it strengthens the effect. Be this as it may, there occurs that peculiar ambiguity of the familiar and the strange which Bertold Brecht, in the context of the theater, called *Verfremdung* (definitely *not* to be translated as "alienation"; I would suggest "bestrangement"): The meaning of the presentation is enforced by being cast in unexpected forms. Protestants have paid a high price for putting the mass into the vernacular (Catholics are now beginning to pay it); the familiar language makes the message more intelligible, but it also trivializes. Conversely, every liturgical language that is alien points to the otherness and to the ineradicable unutterability of God. I wonder whether it was not just this kind of "bestrangement" that astonished the multitude on Pentecost day those many years ago in Jerusalem. Here, then, the words of the Lord's Supper came to me in Swedish. Of course I knew what they were; I could follow the service, word by word. Yet each word was weightier than it would have been in English or (for me) in German. Finally, I think, that is the weight of the Incarnation—He who is utterly beyond forms taking human form among us—and our language (the human form *par excellence)* trying to grasp the miracle and, inevitably, hovering between proclamation and babbling.

But there was a double *Verfremdung* that morning in Stockholm, for me if not for anyone else there. There were the women priests, perhaps one-fourth of the assembled clergy. At first I didn't realize that they were women. Milling around the cathedral all the clergy wore what I understand to be full-dress uniform for such occasions, a long frock coat with many buttons, all in black, topped either by a Roman collar or the double bib called *Baeffchen* in Germany. The men wore black trousers under this, the women black skirts, and the difference was not immediately obvious. I first saw a young male priest in this getup, with shoulder-length hair announcing his modernity. Then I saw a second priest with long hair, was about to add him to the hippie contingent, took another look, and saw that this one was a woman. Only then I became aware of the distribution of the sexes in the congregation.

At the altar, of course, everyone was dressed in the same priestly garb. There were three cocelebrants, two men and a woman. The woman was rather small, quite young, with a wistful expression on her face. She reminded me a little of Giulietta Massina in *La Strada.* She divided the distribution of the elements with one of the men; he distributed the bread, she the wine. I went up to the altar with all these people in their long black frock coats, unwitting (or perhaps witting) witnesses to the proposition that the communion of saints reunites us with our nineteenth-century grandfathers (not to mention first-century Galileans, Parthians, Medes, and Elamites). She tilted the cup into my mouth and said, very precisely: *"Christi blod!"* I returned to my pew, past the bishop (was he still annoyed by the guitars?), and the pre-Vatican II phrase was in my mind, joyously: *"Ite, missa est."* Only later I reflected about the appropriateness, for an American of German mother tongue, to respond in Latin to a word of grace spoken in Swedish.

God, who is beyond all worlds, came into this world in human form. The form was most particular: He came as a Jew, and as a man. Presumably this Jewish man spoke Aramaic, but every other language would be equally close or equally remote in the face of that unspeakable event. We babble about it in all our languages, and over and over again the transcendence of the event manifests itself in our linguistic breakdowns. We cannot contain the event by insisting on the Jewishness of its form (Peter tried that) or on its masculinity. The Gentile Christian testifies to the transcendence of the incarnate God, as does the woman priest. The presence of women at the altar symbolizes in yet another way the unspeakable mystery that is at the center of our faith. And *that* is the reason why the ordination of women is important.

Let me conclude my story. It is *not* the story of a conversion. I have never questioned the ordination of women. Neither have I become *(Gott behuete)* a belated convert to theological feminism. Along with some others I have recently insisted that the world must not set the agenda for the church. On the other hand, what happens in the world (even if it's among the Assyrians) can be occasion for the church to reflect on its own agenda. All religious symbols are contingent, penultimate, fragile in their plausibility. Sometimes, I think, there are very good reasons to hold on tenaciously to old symbols (I have great sympathy for the Raskolniki and their "superstitious" resistance to the modernizing tyranny of the Russian monarchs). At other times innovative symbolizations may greatly enhance religious understanding (it is salutary to remember that, at one time, the icons of Byzantium were startling novelties). The question about any symbolic representation of the faith is not whether it is old or new, "backward" or avant-garde, but whether it brings us any closer to the transcendent reality to which it refers.

13

Religion in

a Revolutionary Society

Surely in beginning my discussion with the question of religion in a revolutionary society, I have accepted for myself a formidable assignment—no less than the overall consideration of the place of religion in contemporary America. I have some reservations about applying the adjective "revolutionary" to American society, but, nevertheless, the term does refer to something very real in that society—namely, its quality of rapid and far-reaching change—and for this reason I describe our present society, not just that of 1776, as revolutionary.

This quality of change makes my assignment all the more difficult. It is a source of constant embarrassment to all commentators and forecasters. Just look what happened to the most celebrated recent diagnoses of our situation. Harvey Cox published his best-selling beatification of the new urbanism just before everyone agreed that American cities had become unfit for civilized habitation. The proclamation of the death of God hit the cover of *Time* magazine just before the onset of a massive resurgence of flamboyant supernaturalism. And just as Daniel Bell had so impressively proclaimed the coming of post-industrial society, an energy crisis arrived to make one think that we will be lucky if we manage to stay around as an *industrial* society. Perhaps the only advice one can give to the sociological prophet is to write his book quickly, and then go into hiding—or, alternatively, to be very, very careful. This means, among other things, that I cannot spare my reader a certain number of pedantic distinctions, qualifications, and less-than-inspiring formulations.

This chapter originally appeared in *America's Continuing Revolution.* Copyright ' 1973, 1974, and 1975 by the American Enterprise Institute. Reprinted by permission.

The consideration before me involves some sort of answer to the question, "Where are we at?" To try for this answer, it will help to find a date in the past with which to compare the present moment. If one wants to make sweeping statements, one will likely pick a date far back in history, like 1776, or the time of the Reformation, or even the late Ice Age (as Andrew Greeley did recently, his thesis being that "the basic human religious needs and the basic religious functions have not changed very notably since the late Ice Age," the credibility of which thesis clearly hinges on one's understanding of "basic"). Taking seriously my own warning to be careful, I propose to take a much more recent date: 1955. This happens to be the year in which an important book on American religion was published, Will Herberg's *Protestant—Catholic—Jew.*[1] More important, though, the mid-1950s were the years just before a number of significant ruptures in the course of American religion and of American society generally (ruptures, incidentally, which no one foresaw). It is a convenient date with which to compare the present moment. In attempting to meet my assignment, therefore, I will concentrate on two questions: *What was the situation of American religion in 1955? What has happened to it since then?*

Since this period has of late become the subject of intensive nostalgia, I should add that my choice of date is nonnostalgically motivated. I was wonderfully young at the time, and I am all too susceptible to reminiscing about my youth in a rosy glow of memories. I am quite sure that I and my contemporaries had no notion *then* of living in a particularly rosy time. It is probably inevitable that we look back on the time of our youth as some sort of Golden Age. I imagine that this was the case with individuals who were young during the Black Death or the invasions of Genghis Khan. There is a temptation to project one's own decline since then to the society at large. The temptation is to be resisted now.

In other words, the comparison between 1955 and now is not necessarily odious. But before I start comparing, I must elaborate one essential distinction, that between *denominational religion* and *civil religion.*

Denominational religion in America refers to what most people mean when they speak of religion—the bodies of Christian and Jewish tradition as these are enshrined in the major religious organizations in this country. Denominational religion is the religion of the churches. The plural, *churches,* is very important: There are many churches in

America, and for a long time now they have existed side by side under conditions of legal equality. Indeed, Richard Niebuhr suggested that the very term "denomination" be defined on the basis of this pluralism. A denomination is a church that, at least for all practical purposes, has come to accept coexistence with other churches. This coexistence was brought about in America by unique historical circumstances which were not intended by anyone and which at first were accepted with great reluctance. Later on, a virtue was made out of the necessity, as religious tolerance became part and parcel of the national ideology as well as of the basic laws of the American republic. (Let me say in passing that I regard religious tolerance as a virtue indeed. It is all the more interesting to recognize that its original attainment was unintended. I incline to the view that most moral achievements in history have this character of serendipity. Or, if I may put it in Lutheran language, virtue comes from undeserved grace.)

Civil religion in America refers to a somewhat vaguer entity, an amalgam of beliefs and norms that are deemed to be fundamental to the American political order. In the last few years the idea of an American civil religion has been much discussed in terms proposed in an influential essay on the topic by Robert Bellah, but both the idea and the phrase antedate this essay.[2] Herberg, for instance, discussed very much the same idea using a slightly different terminology. The general assumption here is that the American polity not only bases itself on a set of commonly held values (this is true of any human society), but that these values add up to something that can plausibly be called a religion. The contents of this religion are some basic convictions about human destiny and human rights as expressed in American democratic institutions. Gunnar Myrdal, in his classic study of the Negro in America, aptly called all this "the American creed." The proposition that all men are created equal is a first article of this creed.

An obvious question concerns the relationship between these two religious entities. Different answers have been given to this question, and I can claim no particular competence in the historical scholarship necessary to adjudicate among them. Thus, to take an example of recent scholarly debate, I cannot say whether the civil religion of the American republic should be seen in an essential continuity with the Puritan concept of the covenant, or whether it should be understood as the result of a decisive rupture with Puritanism brought about by the Deist element among the Founding Fathers. Be this as it may, it is clear that the two religious entities have had profound relations with

each other from the beginning. Nor is there any doubt that crucial in-
gredients of the civil religion derive directly from the Protestant mainstream of American church life, to the extent that to this day the civil
religion carries an unmistakably Protestant flavor (a point always seen
more clearly by non-Protestants than by Protestants, for people are always more likely to notice unfamiliar flavors). For instance, the codifi-
cation of the rights of the individual conscience in the American political creed loudly betrays its Protestant roots, even when (perhaps especially when) it is couched in denominationally neutral language.

It is important to understand how the civil religion relates to the
pluralism of denominations. In one sense the civil religion is based on a
principle of religious tolerance. Except for some isolated cases (Tom
Paine was one), spokesmen of the civil religion were not only friendly
to the major churches but insisted that the latter were vital to the moral
health of the nation. In another sense, however, the civil religion
marks the *limits* of tolerance, and indeed of pluralism. While it accepts
a broad diversity of religious beliefs in the society, it limits diversity
when it comes to its *own* beliefs. The lines between acceptable and unacceptable diversity have frequently shifted in the course of time, but to
this day the category "un-American" points to the fact that there are
clearly unacceptable deviations from the common civil creed. Belief in
the divine right of kings, for example, was as clearly beyond the lines of
official acceptability in an earlier period of American history as belief
in redemption through socialist revolution came to be later on.

Unlike some of the democratic ideologies of Europe and Latin
America, democracy in the United States was not inimical to the
churches. The separation between church and state in the American
Constitution did not, until very recently, imply that the state must be
antiseptically clean of all religious qualities—only that the state must
not give unfair advantage to one denomination over another. In other
words, the assumptions underlying the separation of church and state
were pluralist rather than secularist. It is no accident that there is no
adequate American translation of the French term *laïque,* and that
(again, until very recently) there was no widespread demand that the
American polity should become a "lay state" in the French sense. Indeed, a good case can be made that church/state relations in this country had the character of a "pluralistic establishment": Officially accredited denominations were allowed to share equally in a variety of
privileges bestowed by the state. Exemption from taxation and opportunity for chaplaincy in public institutions are cases in point. Just

which groups were to be regarded as officially accredited, of course, was subject to redefinition.

To put it differently, the beneficiaries of the "pluralistic establishment" have been an expanding group ever since the system was inaugurated. First were added various less-than-respectable Protestant bodies (such as the Quakers), then Catholics and Jews, and finally groups completely outside what is commonly called the Judaeo-Christian tradition. The struggle of the Mormons to obtain "accreditation" marked an interesting case in this process. Recent court decisions on what (if my memory serves me correctly) were actually called "the religious rights of atheists," as well as recent litigation by Black Muslims, mark the degree of expansion of the system to date.

Historically, then, denominational religion and civil religion have not been antagonistic entities in America. Their relationship has rather been a symbiotic one. The denominations enjoyed a variety of benefits in a "pluralistic establishment," the existence of which was not only fostered by the state but solemnly legitimated by the civil religion to which the state adhered. Conversely, the civil religion drew specific contents and (in all likelihood) general credibility from the ongoing life of the denominations. Nevertheless, each entity has had a distinct history, with different forces impinging on the one or the other. Any assessment of the contemporary situation must allow for this distinction.

The Denominational Bull Market

Keeping this distinction in mind, let us go back to the period around 1955: What was the situation at that time?

As far as denominational religion was concerned, the market was bullish indeed. These were the years of what was then called a "religious revival." All the statistical indicators of organized religion were pointing up. Church membership reached historically unprecedented heights. Most significant (or so it seemed then), it was younger people, especially young married couples, who became active in the churches in large numbers. The offspring of these people crowded the Sunday schools, creating a veritable boom in religious education. Church attendance was up, and so was financial giving to the churches. Much of this money was profitably invested, and the denominational coffers

were full as never before. Understandably, the denominational functionaries thought in terms of expansion. "Church extension" was the
phrase constantly on their lips. There was an impressive boom in
church building, especially in the new middle-class suburbs. The seminaries were filled with young men getting ready to swell the ranks of
the clergy. Perhaps they were not "the brightest and the best" among
their peers, but they were competent enough to fulfill the increasingly
complex tasks required of the clerical profession in this situation. In
the bustling suburban "church plants" (a common term at the time)
this clerical profession often meant a bewildering agglomeration of
roles, adding to the traditional religious ones such new roles as that of
business administrator, educational supervisor, family counselor, and
public relations expert.

The "religious revival" affected most of the denominations in the
Protestant camp, and it affected Catholics and Jews as well. It seemed
as if everyone were becoming active in his respective "religious preference." (By the way, an etymological study of this term derived from
the consumer market would be worth making some day.) It was important, therefore, that all of this took place in a context of (apparently) solidifying ecumenism and interfaith amity. The Protestants
within the mainline denominations were going through something of
an ecumenical orgy. There were several church mergers, the most significant of these (long in preparation) being the union between the
Congregationalists and the Evangelical and Reformed church to become the United Church of Christ. The formation of this body in 1957
was widely heralded as a landmark in the movement toward Christian
unity. Quite apart from these organizational mergers, there was a ple-
thora of agencies concerned full time with interdenominational relations, ranging from the still young National Council of Churches to
state and local councils. While some of these agencies engaged in theological discussion, most of their work was severely practical. An important task was the one formerly called "comity" and recently re-
baptized as "church planning." Especially on the local level this meant
that church expansion was based on research and on agreements
among the denominations not to engage in irrational competition with
each other—and particularly not to steal each other's prospective
members. The religious market, in other words, was increasingly par-
celled out among cartel-like planning bodies (and no antitrust laws
stood in the way of these conspiracies to restrain free competition). Be-

yond all these formal processes of collaboration, there was a broad variety of informal acts of *rapprochement*—intercommunion, exchange of pulpits, interdenominational ministries in special areas, and so on.

It should be emphasized that most of this occurred within the mainstream denominations, which had a predominantly middle-class constituency. The more fundamentalist groups, with their lower-middle-class and working-class members, stood apart, undergoing at the same time quite dramatic growth of their own. It seems that the apartness of these groups was not much noticed and even less regretted by the ecumenists: The presence of the Greek Orthodox in the National Council was noted with pleasure, the absence of the Pentecostalists was of little concern. More noticed was the new relationship to Catholics and Jews. While the Roman Catholic church still moved slowly in those pre-Vatican II days, there was little doubt that the old hostility between the two major Christian confessions was a matter of the past. And both Protestants and Catholics habitually expressed goodwill toward Judaism and the Jewish community, not only through such organizations as the National Conference of Christians and Jews but, more important, in local churches and synagogues throughout the country. Significantly, the major Protestant denominations increasingly took for granted that practicing Catholics and Jews were not fair game for evangelistic activity, thus at least informally including them in ecumenical "comity."

In retrospect it has come to seem plausible that at least some of this religious boom was deceptive. Even then there were quite a few individuals who questioned how religious the "religious revival" really was. Several factors contributing to it had very little to do with religious motives proper—high social mobility, with large numbers of people moving into the middle class and believing that the old nexus between bourgeois respectability and church membership still held; high geographical mobility, with migrants finding in the churches a convenient symbol of continuity in their lives; the postwar baby boom, with parents feeling vaguely that Sunday schools could provide some sort of moral instruction that they themselves felt incompetent to give (there are data showing that frequently it was the children who dragged their parents after them into the churches, rather than the other way around). As a result of these factors, there was a good deal of what might be called *invisible secularization*. In the midst of all this boisterous activity the deepening erosion of religious content in the churches was widely overlooked.

The "religious revival" in the denominations was paralleled by an equally impressive flowering of the civil religion. These, after all, were the Eisenhower years, aptly characterized by William Lee Miller, in a famous article in *The Reporter* magazine as "Piety along the Potomac." Indeed, it was Eisenhower himself who made statements that could be taken as crystalline expressions of the mid-1950s version of the civil religion, such as this one: "Our government makes no sense unless it is founded in a deeply felt religious faith—and I don't care what it is." The political relevance of this faith, deeply felt and at the same time seemingly devoid of content, was expressed in another Eisenhower statement: "America is great because she is good." One may call this patriotic religion or religious patriotism. Either way, the content was America—its political and social institutions, its history, its moral values, and not least its mission in the world.

The rhetoric of the national government during these years was full of such religiopolitical formulations. Except for a small minority of anti-Eisenhower intellectuals, the country found this rhetoric in accord with its mood. Despite some shocks (notably the McCarthyite hysteria and the less-than-victorious ending of the Korean conflict), the mood was still one of national self-confidence, if not complacency. There was still the afterglow, as it were, of America's great victory in World War II—a most credible conjunction of greatness and goodness. The postwar American empire was going well, with American soldiers mounting the battlements of freedom from Korea to Berlin. The cold war, if anything, deepened the affirmation of the virtues of the American way of life as against the communist adversary. (Not the least of the latter's evils was its ideology of "godless materialism.") The economy was going well, the dollar was king, and American businessmen as well as tourists circled the globe as emissaries from Eldorado. Indeed, many of its intellectuals were celebrating America (even if, as it later turned out, some of the celebration was subsidized by the CIA).

I do not want to exaggerate. I am not suggesting that there were no tensions, no doubts, in this mood. But compared to what happened later, this period impresses one in retrospect by the apparent unbrokenness—intactness—of the American creed. Just as the imperial cult of classical Rome was sustained by the unquestioned veneration of the familial shrines in innumerable households, so the American civil religion drew its strength from the daily matter-of-course enactment of the virtues of the American way of life by innumerable individual citizens. I would not like to be misunderstood here: I am *not* saying that

there was more morality in the 1950s than there is today; I *am* saying
that such morality as was practiced was taken for granted in a different
way. The American virtues, and the virtue of America as a society,
were still upheld in the mind of the country as self-evident truths. I
suppose that this assurance might well be characterized as innocence.
To a remarkable degree, this rather grandiose self-image of Americans
was reflected in the way they were viewed by foreigners—not least by
the two major enemy nations of World War II.

Religion and Comfort

If that was the situation in 1955, what has happened since?

To summarize the change, I shall take the liberty of making reference to my first book, a sociological critique of American Protestantism
published in 1961.[3] In this book, when describing the notion that the
world is essentially what it is supposed to be, I used the phrase "the
okay world." I argued that religion in middle-class America served to
maintain this sense of the world being "okay." I still think this was a
fair description. The change since then can be conveniently summed up
by saying that more and more people have come to the conclusion that
their world is *not* "okay," and religion has lost much of its ability to
persuade them that it is.

In denominational religion the changes have differed greatly by
class. The Protestant groups drawing most of their membership from
below the upper middle class have continued to grow, some of them in
a dramatic way. They have largely remained untouched by the crises
and self-doubts that have lacerated their higher-class brethen. Their
theological fundamentalism has been modified here and there and their
organizational style has been modernized, but as far as an outside observer can judge, their self-confidence as upholders of Evangelical
truth has remained largely unbroken. The picture is quite different in
the mainstream denominations.

By the mid-1960s the "religious revival" was clearly over. All
the statistical indicators started ebbing or even pointing down
—membership, attendance, financial giving, and (logically
church expansion. As budgets became leaner, the denominational and
interdenominational organizations were forced to cut down on program as well as staff. Seminary enrollments stayed high, but there was

widespread suspicion that the automatic exemption of seminary students from the draft had much to do with this (a suspicion that appears to be borne out in what is happening in the seminaries now). The market for denominational religion, in short, was becoming bearish. Not surprisingly, its amicable management through ecumenical cartels seemed less and less attractive. There appeared a marked reluctance to engage in further mergers, characterized by some observers (perhaps euphemistically) as "a resurgence of denominational spirit." The organizational mood became one of retrenchment.

More deeply, the 1960s were characterized in mainstream Protestantism by what can best be described in Gilbert Murray's phrase as a "failure of nerve." The best-known theological movements seemed to vie with each other in the eagerness with which they sought to divest the churches of their traditional contents and to replace these with a variety of secular gospels—existentialism, psychoanalysis, revolutionary liberation, or avant-garde sensitivity. The "death-of-God" theology was the grotesque climax of this theological self-disembowelment. At the same time the church functionaries, increasingly panicky about the fate of their organizations, tended to jump on whatever cultural or political bandwagon was proclaimed by the so-called opinion leaders as the latest revelation of the *Zeitgeist*. As was to be expected, all these efforts "to make the church more relevant to modern society" had the effect of aggravating rather than alleviating the religious recession. Those church members who still felt loyalty to the traditional content of their faith were bewildered if not repelled by all this, and those whose membership was motivated by secular considerations to begin with often felt that such commodities as "personal growth" or "raised consciousness" could be obtained just as well (and less expensively) outside the churches. The major consequence (unintended, needless to say) of Vatican II seems to have been to spread the aforementioned Protestant miseries through the Catholic community; the "failure of nerve" has become ecumenical, too. At the same time, American Judaism and the American Jewish community in general have been driven by a variety of causes into a much more particularistic and defensive posture than was the case when Herberg announced the arrival of a "tripartite" American faith.

Just as there was good reason to doubt that the "religious revival" of the 1950s was caused by some sort of mass conversion, so it is unlikely that the subsequent decline is to be explained by sudden spiritual transformations. My own tendency is to think that secularization has been a long-lasting and fairly even process, and that nothing drastic happened to the American religious consciousness either after World War II or in the most recent decade. What happened, I think, is that the mundane social forces that made for the "religious revival" subsequently weakened. Most important, the linkage between middle-class status and church membership weakened (something that took place in England in the wake of World War I). In consequence, the previously invisible secularization became much more visible. If you like, secularization came out of the closet. The inability of the churches to confront the emerging skeleton with a modicum of dignity almost certainly contributed to its devastating effect.

The changes that have taken place in the civil religion, I think, resulted partly from these changes in denominational religion (inevitable in view of the symbiotic relation between the two), and partly from extraneous developments in the society. To some degree, it can be said, the American polity has become more *laïque* in recent years, and I suspect that this is largely due to the more openly acknowledged secularism of that portion of the college-educated upper middle class that finances what it considers good causes—in this instance, the cause of pushing secularist cases through the courts. The Supreme Court proscription of prayer in the public schools was the most spectacular of these cases. It was an exercise in extraordinary sociological blindness, though it appears that those who advocated it have learned absolutely nothing from the outcry that ensued. The same *laïque* trend may be seen in the rigid resistance to any allocation of tax funds to church schools, in threats to the tax-exempt status of religious institutions, and in current discussion of various forms of chaplaincy. More important, a militant secularism today comes dangerously close to denying the right of the churches to attempt influencing public policy in accordance with religious morality. The abortion issue illustrates this most clearly. I doubt whether the tendency of the courts to go along with the secularists has profound reasons. Most likely it can be explained simply in terms of the parties attended by federal judges and the magazines read by their wives. (I assure you that I intend no disrespect to our judiciary—actually one of our more cheering institutions—but I am too much of a sociologist to believe that its decisions are made in some judicial heaven sublimely detached from the sociocultural ambience of its members.)

There has thus come to be a threat to the old symbiosis between denominational and civil religion in America. And a more dramatic threat has come from much larger events in the society. It has often been said in the last few years that the legitimacy of the American political order faces the gravest crisis since the Civil War. Even after making proper allowance for the propensity of professional social critics to exaggerate, the diagnosis stands up under scrutiny. To be sure, there are important class and regional differences: What is perceived as doomsday by readers of the *New York Review of Books* may seem a less than overwhelming nuisance to the reader of a small-town newspaper in Kansas, and there is hard evidence to the effect that there continue to be large masses of people whose "okay world" has *not* been fundamentally shaken. Yet few people have remained untouched by the political and moral questioning induced by the headline events of the last decade—the continuing racial crisis, the seemingly endless fiasco of the imperial adventure in Indochina, the eruption of chaos on campus, and finally the shock of the Watergate revelations. I doubt if these events, singly or even in combination, are ultimate causes of the crisis of the American political creed; I think it is more plausible to see this crisis rooted in much more basic tensions and discontents of modern society, of "revolutionary" society, and to understand the events as *occasions* for the underlying difficulties to become manifest.

Obviously I cannot develop this point here. Suffice it to say that the survival in the twentieth century of a political order conceived in the eighteenth is not something about which I am sanguine (though, let me hasten to add, I fervently believe in the continuing effort to keep this eighteenth-century vision alive). We have been passing through a process that sociologists rather ominously describe as *delegitimation*—that is, a weakening of the values and assumptions on which a political order is based. We have been lucky, I think, that this malaise of the political system has not so far been accompanied by severe dislocations in the economy; I can only express the hope that our luck continues to hold.

It may then be said that the civil religion has been affected by a double secularization. It has been affected by the secularizing processes in the proper sense of the word, the same processes that have come to the fore in the area of denominational religion. But it has also undergone a "secularization," that is, a weakening in the plausibility of its own creed, quite apart from the relation of this creed to the several churches. Put simply, the phrase "under God," as lately introduced into the Oath of Allegiance, has become implausible to many people. But even without this phrase the propositions about America contained in the oath have come to sound hollow in many ears. *That* is the measure of our crisis.

An Eternal Return

However prudent one may want to be with regard to the tricky business of prediction, it is almost inevitable in a consideration such as this to look toward the future. What are some plausible scenarios?

As we look at the future of denominational religion in America, a crucial consideration will be how one views the further course of secularization. In the last few years I have come to believe that many observers of the religious scene (myself among them) have overestimated both the degree and the irreversibility of secularization. There are a number of indications, to paraphrase Mark Twain, that the news about the demise of religion has been exaggerated. Also, there are signs of a vigorous resurgence of religion in quarters where one would have least expected it (as, for instance, among the college-age children of the most orthodox secularists). All this need not mean that we are on the brink of a new Reformation (though I doubt if people thought they were on the brink of a Reformation at the beginning of the sixteenth century either), but it seems increasingly likely to me that there are limits to secularization. I am not saying this because of any philosophical or theological beliefs about the truth of the religious view of reality, although I believe in this truth. Rather, I am impressed by the intrinsic inability of secularized world views to answer the deeper questions of the human condition, questions of *whence, whither,* and *why.* These seem to be ineradicable and they are answered only in the most banal ways by the *ersatz* religions of secularism. Perhaps, finally, the reversibility of the process of secularization is probable because of the pervasive boredom of a world without gods.

This does not necessarily mean that a return to religion would also mean a return to the churches. It is perfectly possible that future religious resurgences will create new institutional forms and that the existing institutions will be left behind as museum pieces of a bygone era. There are two propositions, though, of which I am fairly certain. First, any important religious movements in America will emerge out of the

Judaeo-Christian tradition rather than from esoterica imported from the Orient. And second, the likelihood that such revitalizing movements remain within the existing churches will increase as the churches return to the traditional contents of their faith and give up self-defeating attempts to transform their traditions in accordance with the myth of "modern man."

The scenarios for the American civil religion hinge most obviously on one's prognoses for American society at large. Only the most foolhardy would pretend to certainty on this score. But one thing is reasonably certain: No political order can stand a long process of delegitimation such as the one we have been going through of late. There is only a limited number of possible outcomes to such a crisis of legitimacy. One, perhaps the most obvious, is that the society will move into a period of general decline, marked both by intensifying disturbance within and a shrinkage of its power in the world outside. Not much imagination is required to see what such a decline would mean internationally. A second possible outcome is a termination of the crisis by force, by the imposition of the traditional virtues by the power of the state. It hardly needs stressing that democracy and freedom, as we have known them, would not survive such an "Augustan age" in America. The third possibility is a revitalization of the American creed from within, a new effort to breathe the spirit of conviction into the fragile edifice of our political institutions. This possibility depends above all on political and intellectual leadership, of which there is little evidence at the moment. The future of the American experiment depends upon a quick end to this particular scarcity and upon the emergence of an altogether new unity of political will, moral conviction, and historical imagination—in order to preserve the society descending from our Revolution.

14

A Sociological View of the
Secularization of Theology

Considerable public attention in this country has in past years been focused on a movement in Protestant theology variously described as "radical," "secular," or just plain "new." This attention has gone far beyond the confines of organized religion proper, even attracting comment from such venerable theological journals as *Time, Newsweek,* and *The New Yorker.* The newsworthiness of the movement was enhanced by its connection with several other developments of wide public interest, such as the civil rights movement, in which there was also a "radical" involvement by religious figures; the so-called youth problem, which supposedly involves widespread disillusion with societal values, religious and other; and the long-lasting news field day provided by the Vatican Council. By now, such bywords of the "secular" theologians as "death of God" or "post-Christian era" are old hat topics of discussion at businessmen's Bible breakfasts and in book reviews in the provincial press. To the extent that public issues in our society are largely determined by the mass media, it is possible to say that the "new" theology is established as a public issue.

The spectacle afforded by the movement is strange. Indeed, it has all the characteristics of a man-bites-dog story. The phrase "secular theology" itself strikes with intriguing dissonance, while phrases such as "atheist theology" or "religionless Christianity" seem to come from a script for the theater of the absurd. The strangeness of the spectacle does not disappear on closer scrutiny. Professional theologians declare that their discipline must begin with the presupposition that there is no God. Clergymen, even bishops, charged with the performance of pub-

This chapter originally appeared in *Journal for the Scientific Study of Religion,* vol. VI, no. 1 (1967).

lic worship proclaim the senselessness of prayer. Salaried employees of religious organizations state that these organizations are destined to fade away—and the sooner, the better. To an outside observer, say a Muslim scholar of Western religion, all this might well appear as a bizarre manifestation of intellectual derangement or institutional suicide. An observer familiar with the background of these ideas can, of course, show that they did not spring from nowhere, but this still does not explain why they have attained their peculiar virulence at this time, nor how they can so plausibly present themselves as the wave of the future. A sociological view of the matter (more specifically, a view in terms of the sociology of knowledge) can add something to our understanding of what is happening. Before we attempt this, a closer look at the ideational content of the phenomenon will be necessary.

The Ideational Content

While the roots of these ideas are in earlier developments, particularly in post-World War II controversies within German Protestant theology, their explosion into public view may conveniently be placed in 1963, when John Robinson's *Honest to God* was first published in England. The book immediately produced a violent public controversy there, which was repeated in other countries as the book was translated. In this country, not surprisingly, the book rapidly achieved bestseller status, and the attention paid to this controversy by the mass media attained the crescendo appropriate to the style of our cultural life. Since then, a number of American figures have either associated themselves, or been associated by others, with Robinson's overall theological stance—notably William Hamilton, Paul Van Buren, Gabriel Vahanian, Thomas Altizer, and Harvey Cox. Paul Tillich, to what one heard was his dismay, is widely regarded as a sort of elder statesman. The movement continues to be definitely Protestant, but it has found an echo both among *aggiornamento*-minded Catholics and among liberal Jews. It is safe to assume that the movement represents something much more significant than a curiosity of the Protestant imagination.

The various figures associated with the movement differ considerably in their precise positions and in the level of theoretical sophistication. All the same, it is possible to identify a central characteristic common to all of them—namely, a denial, in various degrees and on different grounds, of the objective validity of the supernatural affirmations of the Christian tradition. Put differently, the movement generally shows a shift from a transcendental to an immanent perspective, and from an objective to a subjective understanding of religion. Generally, traditional affirmations referring to otherworldly entities or events are "translated" to refer to concerns of this world, and traditional affirmations about the nature of something "out there" (to use a phrase of Robinson's) are "translated" to become statements about the nature of man or his temporal situation. For example, the resurrection is no longer understood as a cosmic event, but as a symbol of human existential or psychological processes; Christian eschatology ceases to refer to the interventions of a transcendent God, but becomes an ethical perspective on current political affairs.

It is important to understand that this general characteristic of the "new" theology is anything but new. Rather, it stands in a certain continuity with classical Protestant liberalism at least as far back as Schleiermacher's "translation" of the Lutheran *"Christus pro me"* into a concept of "religious experience." It is instructive in this connection to read Adolf Harnack's great manifesto of Protestant liberalism, *Das Wesen des Christentums,* first published in 1900, and imagine what *Time* might say about it if it had just been written by a "radical" seminary professor. The immediate European antecedents of the new theology are commonly given as Rudolf Bultmann and Dietrich Bonhoeffer. In the latter case, it takes great selectivity to find legitimations for the current positions in Bonhoeffer's writings (mostly in the fragmentary and, by their very nature, ambiguous writings of the underground period, particularly the correspondence from prison). In the case of Bultmann, however, the connection with classical liberalism is not hard to see. The Anglo-American theologians cannot even claim newness with respect to the degree of their "radicalness." If Bultmann is not already radical enough, there are such figures of contemporary German-speaking theology as Friedrich Gogarten and Fritz Buri, not to mention, once more, Tillich's daring "correlations" between the Christian tradition and modern secular thought. In addition to some of the conceptual tools, of which more in a moment, what is new here is, above all, the resonance of these ideas in a mass public. This fact by itself leads to the suspicion that there is a sociological dimension to the phenomenon.

In addition to the central characteristic indicated before, the secular theologians share a common presupposition that the traditional religious affirmations are no longer tenable, either because they do not meet certain modern philosophical or scientific criteria of validity, or because they are contrary to an alleged modern world view that is somehow binding on everybody. In some cases it is not quite clear which of these two reasons (logically quite different) is the decisive one. Must the traditional affirmations be given up because we now know that they are false, or because we simply cannot put them over any more? Because of this confusion, the presupposition that the tradition is now untenable often hovers uneasily between questions of epistemology and of evangelistic tactics. Be this as it may, the conclusion typically comes out as a statement that "we cannot any longer. . ." maintain this or that element of the tradition, or cannot perhaps even maintain the tradition itself. This conclusion could, of course, result in the rejection of the theological enterprise as such or of the ecclesiastical institutions that embody the tradition—and we know that there are individuals who do just that.

The interesting thing about the secular theologians, however, is that they do *not* draw this conclusion. Not only do they continue to operate as theologians, but most of them do so within the context of traditional ecclesiastical institutions. That this creates a certain amount of practical strain is obvious and needs no elaboration here. The strain, however, is also theoretical. The problem of translation, consequently, is one of great urgency. In other words, if the situation is interpreted in such a way that "we cannot any longer," then a way must be found to deal with the tradition so that "we can again"—that is, can again exist as ecclesiastically involved theologians. It should be stressed as emphatically as possible that putting the problem in these terms *in no way* questions the sincerity of such an intellectual operation. On the contrary, the desire for sincerity is probably one of the strongest driving forces in this whole movement. The issue is not whether such an operation is sincere, but what theoretical procedures are required for it. In other words, given the problem of translation, where are the grammars?

Classical Protestant liberalism used various forms of philosophical rationalism or positivism to solve the same problem, as well as the newly refined tools of historical scholarship. To some extent these methods are still used, both in the demolition and in the reconstruction phases of the translation enterprise. New conceptual tools have been added, derived from existentialism, psychoanalysis, sociology, and linguistic analysis (probably in declining order of importance). With the exception of the last, which understandably plays a greater part in the English branch of the movement and which in this country has been particularly employed by Van Buren, these conceptual machineries permeate the entire ideational complex and often overlap in both of the above-mentioned phases.[1]

It is important to see that these conceptual mechanisms have two applications. They may be used by some writers in the movement on a high level of theoretical sophistication, and yet have an ideological correlate on a lower level of popular consciousness. Take the application of existentialism to our problem, for example. Concepts derived from existential philosophy, particularly Heidegger's, are the standard operating procedures of Bultmann's particular translation exercise—to wit, his famous program of "demythologization." With system and consistency, the entire transcendental frame of reference of the Christian tradition is demolished, that is, consigned to the mythological world view that "we cannot any longer" maintain. (His one lapse in consistency, as was immediately pointed out by some of his critics, was the retention of an acting God.) The major items so treated are then translated into terms that make sense within the frame of reference of an existentialist anthropology—a procedure, of course, of the most radical detranscendentalization and subjectivization imaginable. Thus transcendental ontology becomes immanent anthropology, and *Heilsgeschichte* becomes a kind of biography, the biography of the individual in terms of whose *Existenz* the reinterpreted tradition is still supposed to make sense. A similar procedure, employed with immense erudition and ingenuity, is at the center of Tillich's translation enterprise, and it is reiterated in one way or another (though rarely with the same intellectual force) by most of the figures in this movement.

The sometimes awe-inspiring eggheadedness of the existentialist vocabulary must not be allowed to obscure the "pop" correlates of the movement. For example, existentialist *Angst* and alienation are not limited to seminary professors who have read Heidegger. To a remarkable degree, these experiences seem to be shared by suburban housewives. As a result, the translations undertaken by the seminary professors can be popularly applied by ministers with suburban housewives in their clientele. To use a Weberian term, there appears to be an "elective affinity" between certain ideas of Heidegger and the mentality of certain suburban housewives. The explanation of this, as we shall try to show presently, is to be sought *not* in a philosophical analysis of Heidegger, but in a sociology-of-knowledge perspective on the quasi-Heideggerian housewives.

Ideas derived from psychoanalysis (psychologism, as I have said, would probably be a better term) play a prominent part in the translation procedures. The traditional religious affirmations are understood as symbols of (largely unconscious) psychological states and, as such, declared to have continuing positive significance. The optimistic twist to Freud's original understanding of religion that this entails is, in any case, consonant with (to pervert a phrase of Harry Stack Sullivan) the benevolent transformation that Freudianism underwent in America. Since psychoanalytically derived ideas are by now widely diffused in American society, almost instant relevance is guaranteed by an interpretation and, equally important, to an application of religion in these terms. At least part of the appeal of Tillich's theology may be explained by its ingenious combination of the conceptual mechanisms of existentialism and psychologism, both of them being ideational complexes that are, so to speak, "in the air" culturally. But, without in the least trying to denigrate Tillich's intellectual achievement in itself—for which one may have the highest respect, even if one totally disagrees with it—it should be emphasized that essentially similar procedures are employed on greatly inferior levels of sophistication. There, too, quasi-existentialist malaise is interpreted in psychologistic terms, psychotherapeutic measures are advocated to cope with the matter among people already predisposed to accept the diagnosis, and religion comes in as a "symbolization" in both the diagnostic and the therapeutic phases of the operation. There, is therefore, a very important link between Tillich and, say, Norman Vincent Peale—*not,* needless to say, in their statures as religious thinkers, but in the common relevance of their thinking in a psychologically inclined population. Here, of course, the subjectivization of the traditional religious contents appears in pure form. Robinson's "Daddy on a cloud" has become a psychological datum, the "up there" is relocated "deep down within" human consciousness, and, in a truly impressive theoretical *salto mortale*, this very dissolution of theology into psychology is hailed as a vindication of religion.

Conceptual machinery derived from sociology can also be applied both diagnostically and therapeutically in the translation enterprise, and perhaps this is the point where I should acknowledge my own past share in both applications, with the added comment that these days I much prefer the diagnostic to the therapeutic role. Sociology can demonstrate easily enough that large segments of traditional religious lore have become irrelevant (that is, subjectively meaningless and/or practically inapplicable) to the man in the street. The conclusion may then be drawn that the remedy lies in reinterpreting the tradition so that it *will* be relevant (that is, subjectively meaningful and practically applicable). Harvey Cox's recommendation to the churches to "speak politically" is a good recent example of this. Here, particularly, the point should be stressed again that our analysis has *no bearing whatever* on the sincerity and intrinsic worth of such political activities. The point is, quite simply, that theology and ecclesiastical practice accommodate themselves to the reality presuppositions of the man in the street. The events and moral issues of Mississippi and Vietnam became real to the man in the street. The traditional religious affirmations about God, world, and man are very largely unreal. The sociologically derived programs for theology and church give cognitive as well as practical priority to the reality presuppositions of the man in the street over those of the religious tradition. Those with an inclination toward linguistic analysis as now fashionable in Anglo-American philosophy can perform essentially the same operation with different conceptual tools, for here, too, the reality of the man in the street is accorded a privileged cognitive status. There are some problems of application in both translation procedures, since, after all, there are significant variations within the species "man in the street." What is real and relevant to the young social worker is not necessarily so to the corporation executive. The general character of translation therefore, will vary in accordance with the target audience addressed by the translators.

Whatever the particular conceptual machinery employed, the reinterpretation of the Christian tradition by the secular theologians entails an accommodation between the tradition and what is, correctly or not, taken to be modern consciousness. Nor is there any question as to where something must give way in this process, as between the two entities to be accommodated. Almost invariably the tradition is made to conform to the cognitive and normative standard of the alleged modern consciousness. Our movement thus replicates to an amazing degree, in form if not in content, Feuerbach's famous program of reducing theology to anthropology.

The Infrastructure of the Movement

We have already indicated some of the practical consequences drawn from these theological developments. It would be naive sociologically to think that there are not also practical, specifically social, roots for the theological developments. In other words, there is a sociologically graspable *Sitz im Leben,* a nontheoretical infrastructure, from which the theological ideas in question have sprung. Their self-avowed starting point is the disintegration of Christendom as a general and assumed universe of discourse in Western culture. This disintegration, however, is itself an effect of broad historical forces that have created the modern world. Put differently, secularization in both society and consciousness is itself a phenomenon that must be explained. The usual explanations in terms of the growth of a rational and scientific world view (which is where Bultmann begins and where he is pretty generally followed by our secular theologians) are for this reason unsatisfactory, whatever their merits in particular cases. We strongly suspect that no explanation that remains only within the framework of the history of ideas is likely to serve as an adequate means to understand the phenomenon of secularization. The weakness of any such "idealistic" explanations is actually illustrated very well by the secular theologians as a case in point. Their general procedure is to relativize the religious tradition by means of certain modern ideas. It does not occur to them, on the whole, that these modern ideas, which serve as their criteria of validity or relevance, can themselves be relativized.

Let us grant Bultmann, for example, that people using electricity and radios generally find the miracles of the New Testament less than credible. Let us also leave aside here the question as to why, despite electricity and radios, these people still manage to find a place in their world view for luxuriant irrationalities of a nonreligious nature. Let us even grant Bultmann (what should not be granted to him at all) that all these electricity- and radio-users share with him a scientific world view. But just this fact, if it were a fact, would cry out for explanation! And what equally cries out for explanation is the fact that Bultmann, and with him the entire movement, takes for granted the epistomological superiority of the electricity- and radio-users over the New Testament writers—to the point where the theoretical possibility that there may be a nonscientific reality that has been lost to modern man is not even considered. In other words, secularized consciousness is taken for granted, not just as an empirical datum but as an unquestioned standard of cognitive validity. Otherwise, the possibility that there may be a cognitive need for modern consciousness to be *re*mythologized would at least make an appearance in the theological argument, if only for the purpose of rejecting it, not on tactical, but on epistemological grounds.

It is at this point that a sociology-of-knowledge perspective begins to be useful. The question as to who is ultimately right in his knowledge of the world—Bultmann, the electricity-using man in the street, or St. Paul—is, of course, bracketed in this perspective. What is asserted, though, is that all three exist and think in their own unquestioned worlds, that are themselves grounded in specific social infrastructures. Just as the religious tradition was grounded in such a specific infrastructure, *so also* are the ideas employed to relativize the tradition. The general blindness of the relativizing theologians to the relativity of their own debunking apparatus points directly to the need for analyzing the infrastructure of their own ideas.

Obviously, it is impossible here to discuss various possible explanations of the origins of secularization either in terms of the history of ideas or in sociohistorical terms. We readily admit a certain partiality to the notion, frequently expressed by the theological figures who interest us here, that decisive impulses toward secularization may be found in biblical religion itself. This notion, to our knowledge, was first elaborated systematically in Max Weber's understanding of the "disenchantment of the world," though, especially if one thinks in Weberian terms, it is well to keep in mind that this process was unintended and thus profoundly ironical. Nor is it our intent to quarrel with the various theories that explain the transformation of modern consciousness in terms of economic, technological, and social-structural terms. It is readily evident that so complex a phenomenon will have to be analyzed in multicausal terms, and it is evident, at least to me, that "ideal" and "material" factors will be found to interact dialectically in the historical chain of causes. However, there is one causal factor that is rarely emphasized in this connection and which we would consider to be decisive in the formation of an infrastructure capable of giving rise to modern secularized consciousness—namely, the pluralization of social worlds.

Christendom developed in a situation in which the great majority of people lived within the same overall social structure, as given in the feudal system, and the same overall world view, as maintained by the church as sole reality-defining institution. This is not to say that medieval society was monolithic or in a state of perfect equilibrium. There were strains within the social structure, as shown by the peasant uprisings, and there were challenges to the monopoly of the church, as expressed in the various heretical movements. All the same, Christendom provided both a social-structural and a cognitive unity that was lost, probably irretrievably, upon its dissolution at the beginning of the modern age. By the same token, the social world of Christendom was contained in a way that ours cannot possibly be. This, again, does not mean that there was no awareness of other worlds. There was always the world of Islam before the gates and the world of Judaism within the actual confines of the *res christiana*. These discrepant worlds, however, were only rarely capable of becoming threats to the unquestioned reality of the Christian world. The one was kept away at the point of the sword, the other carefully segregated, often enough also with the sword.

Our own situation, by contrast, is one in which discrepant worlds coexist within the same society, contemporaneously challenging each other's cognitive and normative claims. We cannot discuss here the various factors that have gone into this—the ideological schisms unleashed by the Renaissance, Reformation, and Enlightenment; the opening up of strange lands (and ideas!) in the great voyages of discovery; the growth of highly differentiated and mobile social structures through urbanization and industrialization; the transformations of "knowledge" brought on by the invention of printing and, later, by mass literacy; the recent impact of the mass media of communication; and so on. We can only stress the net result of this pluralization of worlds—that it has become very difficult to maintain, or, for that matter, to establish *de novo,* any monopoly in the definition of reality. Instead, our situation is characterized by a market of world views, simultaneously in competition with each other. In this situation the maintenance of any certitudes that go much beyond the empirical necessities of the society and the individual to function is very difficult indeed. Inasmuch as religion essentially rests upon superempirical certitudes, the pluralistic situation is a secularizing one and, ipso facto, plunges religion into a crisis of credibility. The particular theological movement that interests us here must be understood, then, as emerging from a situation in which the traditional religious certitudes have become progressively less credible, not necessarily because modern man has some intrinsically superior access to the truth, but because he exists in a sociocultural situation which itself undermines religious certitude.

We have so far avoided formulating our perspective in systematic sociology-of-knowledge terms, so as not to offend prematurely with the proverbial barbarity of the specialist's jargon. At this point, however, there must be at least some explication of the systematic features of the perspective. In this context, this must unavoidably be done in somewhat of an axiomatic manner. Let us first reformulate the above description of the background of our phenomenon in more systematic terms: The movement under consideration presupposes a *deobjectivation* of the traditional religious contents, which in turn presupposes a disintegration of the traditional *plausibility structure* of these contents. What does this mean?

Deobjectivation

Human consciousness emerges out of practical activity. Its contents, pretheoretical as well as theoretical, remain related to this activity in diverse ways. This does not mean that theoretical consciousness, or "ideas," are to be understood as mere epiphenomena or as dependent variables determined in a one-sided causation by nontheoretical, non-"ideal" processes. Rather, theories and ideas continually interact with the human activity from which they spring. In other words, the relationship between consciousness and activity is a dialectical one—activity produces ideas, which in turn produce new forms of activity. The more or less permanent constellations of activity that we know as "societies" are, therefore, in an ongoing dialectical relationship with the "worlds" that form the cognitive and normative meaning coordinates of individual existence. Religious worlds, as much as any others, are thus produced by an infrastructure of social activity and, in turn, act back upon this infrastructure.

The socially produced world attains and retains the status of objective reality in the consciousness of its inhabitants in the course of common, continuing social activity. Conversely, the status of objective reality will be lost if the common social activity that served as its infrastructure disintegrates. It is very important to remember that these social processes of reality-confirmation and reality-disconfirmation apply to contents that, by whatever criteria of validity, the scientific observer regards as true, as well as to those he regards as false. Thus the objective reality of astrological forces is confirmed by the same social processes that, in another society, confirm the objective reality of the scientific world view. The sociologist, of course, is not in a position to judge between the rival cognitive claims of astrology and modern science; he can only point out that each will be taken for granted in the specific situations where everyday social experience confirms it. Human theories and ideas, then, require specific infrastructures of confirmatory social interaction if they are to retain what William James aptly called their "accent of reality." If such infrastructures are strong and enduring, then the theoretical constructions grounded in them take on an objective reality close to that of natural phenomena—they are taken for granted with the same unquestioned certitude given to the "facts of life" encountered in the physical universe. Again, this holds for religious ideation as much as for any other. It is as "natural" to be Catholic in a Catholic milieu as to be a Muslim in Arabia. What is more, we have good reason to doubt an individual's "Catholic consciousness" if he is transplanted to Arabia, and to doubt a Muslim's religious certitudes in the reverse case.

The social infrastructure of a particular ideational complex, along with various concomitant maintenance procedures, practical as well as theoretical, constitute its plausibility structure, that is, set the conditions within which the ideas in question have a chance of remaining plausible. Within the plausibility structure, the individual encounters others who confirm, by their attitudes and assumptions, that the particular ideational complex is to be taken for granted as reality. Among these others there may be authority figures, officially accredited reality-definers, who will from time to time engage in especially solemn confirmations, frequently by means of terrifying and awe-inspiring ceremonies. If the individual should, for one reason or another, develop doubts about the officially defined verities, the plausibility structure will usually provide various mechanisms of "mental hygiene" for the eradication of doubts. Put simply, the plausibility structure is to be understood as a collection of people, procedures, and mental processes geared to the task of keeping a specific definition of reality going. It does not require great sociological sophistication to see that such a social and social-psychological matrix is a condition *sine qua non* of all religious ideation. It is precisely for this reason that religion is a communal or collective enterprise. At the risk of offending theological sensitivities, we can state this fact simply by appropriating the sentence,

Extra ecclesiam nulla salus, with the slight modification that *salus* in our context does not refer to a superempirical destiny of the individual, but to the plausibility of the religious contents represented by any particular *ecclesia* within this empirically available consciousness.

Strongly integrated plausibility structures will produce firm objectivations, and will be capable of supporting world views and ideas with a firm status of objective reality within the consciousness of their adherents. As soon as plausibility structures begin to disintegrate, this status of objective reality begins to totter. Uncertainty, doubts, questions, make their appearance. What was previously "known" becomes, at best, "believed." In a further step, it is an "opinion," or even a "feeling." In other words, the particular contents of consciousness that used to be taken for granted as "knowledge" are progressively de-objectivated. In the case of religious contents, the process can be readily understood by contrasting the state of, say, "living in a Christian world" with a desperate "leap of faith" into a Christian position, and, finally, with having some sort of a Christian label attached to one's "religious preference" or "religious interest." These last two phrases, which need no explanation in an American setting, express with admirable succinctness what has taken place in the deobjectivation of the religious tradition.

The excursion into general sociology-of-knowledge theory has, we hope, been useful. It should be clearer now in what way a sociology-of-knowledge perspective may be applied to the situation that interests us here. The recent history of Western religion makes a great deal more sense in this perspective, into which it has been placed only rarely, if at all. To my knowledge, the closest to it may be found in the work of some contemporary German sociologists, notably Arnold Gehlen, who coined the term "subjectivization" for a broad range of modern cultural phenomena, and Helmut Schelsky, who applied Gehlen's notions to the sociology of religion. In any case, we would contend that our present religious situation can be understood much more readily if we apply to it the aforementioned concept of deobjectivation. The general background of the movement under consideration here is the reality loss of the religious tradition in the consciousness of increasing numbers of people, something that is not to be ascribed to some mysterious intellectual fall from grace, but to specific and empirically available social developments. The secularization of consciousness and the pluralization of society must be understood together, as two facets of the same general and dialectical process. The important fact that this process has now burst beyond the confines of the Western world and, as a result of modernization, has become a worldwide phenomenon cannot be considered here, but should at least be kept in mind.

Defense or Accommodation?

The problem that poses itself as a result of the process of de-objectivation is simple—how to perpetuate an institution, whose reality presuppositions are no longer socially taken for granted. The problem has an obvious practical side, which produces the headaches of all those responsible for the economic and general well-being of organized religion. There is an equally obvious theoretical problem of how to legitimize the continuing social existence of the institution and its tradition, in the absence of the massive reality confirmation that previously sustained them. This, of course, is where the headaches of the theologians come in, or more accurately, of those theologians who continue to operate as legitimating functionaries of the institution. The manner in which our particular group of secular theologians has responded to the problem will be further clarified, we think, if we ask ourselves what options are possible in our situation in the first place.

There are two fundamental options, with variations within each—defense and accommodation. The institution may take on a defensive posture vis-à-vis the secularizing-pluralizing process, continue to affirm the old objectivities, and, as far as possible, go on with its own life and thought despite the regrettable developments on the "outside." Or the institution may accommodate itself to this "outside" in a variety of practical and theoretical compromises. Both options have been tried. Both entail considerable practical and theoretical difficulties.

The main practical difficulty of the defense posture is one of "social engineering." If one is to go on proclaiming the old objectivities in a social milieu that refuses to accept them, one must maintain or construct some sort of subsociety within which there can be a viable plausibility structure for the traditional affirmations. What is more, this subsociety must be carefully and continuously protected against the pluralistic turbulence outside its gates. Put a little rudely, one must maintain a ghetto. This is not easy under any circumstances. It becomes very difficult in a modern society with mass literacy and mass communications, unless the subsociety can exercise totalitarian control over its territory and population. The theoretical difficulties are directly related to this. One can repeat the old legitimations as if nothing had happened in which case one risks, sooner or later, a complete collapse of plausibility. Or one may carry on a ceaseless theoretical warfare, a kind of permanent apologetic, in which case one risks, sooner or later, contamination by the very reality one is trying to keep out.

The extreme example of this choice is the closed world of certain sects which exist as deviant reality-enclaves within the surrounding social world, with which they maintain only the minimal relations required for economic and political survival. The old-line Amish settlements or the Hasidic communities in New York may serve as illustrations. Less extreme cases are more common. The most important example is the Catholic church, which until very recently has confronted the modern world almost everywhere in a posture of determined defensiveness and, as a result, has had to spend a good deal of its institutional energy on the maintenance of Catholic subsocieties. It is hardly fanciful to suggest that the social engineering difficulties just indicated account in large measure for the *aggiornamento* now in process, setting loose disintegrating forces that, we suspect, the official promoters of the *aggiornamento* will find hard to control.

Within Protestantism and Judaism, orthodoxy and neoorthodoxy everywhere have had to go hand in hand with an energetic reconstruction of social milieus that could serve as plausibility structures for the reaffirmed objectivities of old. Thus, it is not so much a theological as a sociological imperative that led from the Barthian return to the tradition to the so-called rediscovery of the church. To put it a little rudely again, one needs a pretty strong church as a social-psychological support if one is to believe what the Barthians want one to believe. We strongly suspect, incidentally, that the long dominance of neoorthodoxy in European Protestantism had much to do with political situations on the "outside" that made subsocietal self-enclosure morally appealing, and that the postwar decline in this domination is directly related to the loss of this essentially nonreligious appeal. In sum, orthodox or neoorthodox positions in our situation inevitably tend toward sectarian social forms for their maintenance, which will be successful to the degree that people can be motivated to be sectarians—a stand that is contingent upon many, mostly nonreligious, factors beyond the control of ecclesiastical authorities.

The accommodation posture is obviously the more "modern" one. But it, too, has its great difficulties, which can be summed up in the simple question, "Just how far should one go?" Usually the answer is first given in tactical terms, just as the entire accommodation process typically begins with an effort to solve the tactical problem—that is, the problem of getting one's message across to a recalcitrant clientele. One then goes as far as one has to for the pastoral or evangelistic purpose at hand. The difficulty with such a procedure is that there is a built-in "escalation" factor. The clientele is likely to become more, not less, recalcitrant in the secularizing-pluralizing situation, and one is consequently obligated to ever-deepening concessions to the reality presuppositions of the people one wants to keep or win. The difficulty attains a new dimension, however, as these presuppositions begin to infect the thinking of the tacticians themselves—again, an almost inevitable outcome under the circumstances. The question is then no longer, "Just how far should one go?" but, "How far must *I* go to continue believing myself?" When this point is reached, the floodgates are opened to a veritable onslaught of relativizing challenges to the tradition. In sum, the intrinsic problem of the accommodation option is that, once taken, it has the powerful tendency to escalate to the point where the plausibility of the tradition collapses, so to speak, from within.

The fierce opposition to concessions of even a minor sort among ultraorthodox elements in the religious institutions may thus be said to rest upon a rather sound sociological instinct, which is frequently absent in their more "open-minded" opponents. Therefore, quite apart from one's own intellectual and moral sympathies, one cannot deny a good measure of sociological sense to the authorities that squelched the modernist movement in the Catholic church a half-century ago, or, for that matter, to the conservatives in the church today who fear that the *aggiornamento* will open up a Pandora's box of ecclesiastical and theological troubles. The history of a couple of centuries of Protestant accommodation can hardly be reassuring to them.

The Choice of the Secular Theologians

But it is high time that we return to our secular theologians. How is one to understand their place in the general situation that we have tried to describe? Historically, as already mentioned, the "new" movement stands in a continuity with classical Protestant liberalism. While its theological propositions are hardly more radical than at least some made long ago by the generations of Ritschl and Harnack, their overall posture seems more radical precisely because the disintegration of the plausibility structures has greatly accelerated since the period of the classical liberals. Whatever one may think of the newness of the "new" theology, it stands at an extreme pole of the defense-accommodation continuum of theological postures—so extreme that it is hard to imagine any further steps in that direction short of the final self-liquidation of the ecclesiastical-theological enterprise as such.

Accommodation with the secular theologians has become total. The reality presuppositions of our age have become the only valid criteria for the handling of tradition. From the viewpoint of the conservative apologetician, the secular theologians have surrendered to the enemy. The more moderate liberal position may be characterized as a bargaining procedure with secularized consciousness: "We'll give you the Virgin Birth, but we'll keep the Resurrection"; "You can have the Jesus of history, but we'll hold on to the Christ of the apostolic faith"; and so on. The secular theology disdains such negotiation. It surrenders all. Indeed, it goes farther in its abandonment of the tradition than most people who do not identify themselves with it. For example, the secular theologians show a greater willingness to abandon belief in a life after death than does the unchurched man in the street, who commonly retains some lingering hopes in this matter. And, at least in America, it seems that theologians today have a greater propensity to proclaim themselves as atheists than the average, theologically untrained skeptic. The whole thing reminds one strongly of the old story of the drunkard who carefully walked in the gutter so that he could not possibly fall into it. The transformation of transcendence into immanence, and the change from objectivity to subjectivity, is completed. The paradoxical result is that one can now feel safe from the secularizing and subjectivizing forces threatening the tradition. The worst, so to speak, has already happened—one has preempted it to oneself.

It is important, we think, to understand that this posture can be very liberating. Apart from the general rewards of feeling oneself to be "with it," there is the liberation of "going all the way," being done once and for all with the agonies of compromise. Indeed, this liberating quality, we suspect, is psychologically very much the same as that which comes from the opposite movement of the "leap of faith." All "radical" decisions have this much in common psychologically: To quote the punchline of a classic American joke, one is rid, once and for all, of "all those choices." In this case the choices include, at least, a good many theological ones. Every theologian must ask himself the question, vis-à-vis his tradition, "What do I believe?" And the answer, "Nothing!", can be as alleviating as the answer, "Everything!"

To think, however, that the fundamental problem of the *institution* can be solved in this manner is, obviously, mistaken. The practical and theoretical difficulties raised by secular theology for the churches are almost too apparent to elaborate. Practically, secular theology leads to programs of nonreligious activity that, almost by definition, are very hard to distinguish from similar programs launched under lay auspices. For example, it is not easy to retain any sort of marginal differentiation between psychotherapeutic or political-action programs sponsored by the churches or by purely secular organizations. The thought that one might just as well dispense with the "Christian" label is hardly avoidable sooner or later. There is thus a built-in self-defeating factor in all such programs of "secular Christianity". Very much the same problem arises on the level of theorizing. After all, a theoretical mind can usually stand only a certain amount of paradox. The particular paradox of engaging in the discipline of divinity while denying the divine is hardly likely to recommend itself to many people for very long.

Conclusions

Sociological prediction is dangerous business, as everyone knows who has tried it. We would not like to engage in it here. Yet some projections into the future are hard to avoid in an analysis such as this. If one projects a continuation of the movement under consideration here to the point where it becomes the dominant ideology within the Protestant community, one would also have to project that this community is on the brink of dissolution as an institution. This is not very likely, certainly not in America. There are powerful social functions carried on by the institutional complex of American Protestantism. Most of these, to be sure, are of an essentially nonreligious character, but there are strong reasons for maintaining at least a semblance of continuity with the traditional institutional legitimations. While in many ways American Protestantism is already secularized both in its social functionality and in its consciousness, there is no need to proclaim this from the rooftops as a theological verity. At the same time, the aforementioned difficulties for any sort of orthodoxy within our situation would certainly not lead one to expect a vigorous resurgence of antimodernism, unless, indeed, we are fated to undergo convulsions similar in intensity to those that brought the Barthian movement into a position of dominance in Europe in the 1930s. What is now happening in the Catholic community seems to support this. If one is to make a prediction, then probably the safest would be that there will be no reversal in the secularization and deobjectivation processes, but that the extreme legitimations of these will be considerably blunted as they are diffused through the community and become respectable. The probable fate of the secular theology, once its appeal as the *dernier cri* in religion has passed, would then be its absorption into the legitimating apparatus of the institution (which, incidentally, is exactly what happened with classical liberalism). We strongly suspect that this process of neutralization is already taking place as these "challenging new insights" are integrated in various ecclesiastical programs. In this process there is nothing to prevent the "death of God" from becoming but another program emphasis, which, if properly administered, need not result in undue disturbances in the ongoing life of the institution.

A few slightly less than scientific words in conclusion. The foregoing analysis has moved with some care within a sociological frame of reference. It goes without saying that this imposes certain limits on one's view of these matters. The most important limit is that any question about the ultimate truth or error of the theological positions under consideration must be rigidly excluded from the analysis. When it comes to such questions of truth or error, the most that sociology can do is to make one aware of the sociohistorical relativity of one's own cognitive presuppositions—an awareness that I, for one, would strongly recommend to the secular theologians. But I will take the liberty here of at least one little step beyond the proper limits of sociological inquiry.

If anyone should think that the previous analysis camouflages some strong position of certitude, I can only assure him that nothing could be farther from the truth. I cannot, I am afraid, lay claim to any certitudes, positive *or* negative, in the fundamental questions of religion. I can only claim a persistent and, at times at least, passionate concern for these questions. In speaking of deobjectivation and its consequences, therefore, I speak of something that involves myself. But perhaps it is precisely for this reason that I am somewhat less than amicably disposed toward those who claim to have reached the end of a road on which I still regard myself as traveling, regardless of whether they do so by proclaiming the "death of God" or His "undeniable" presence.

It seems to me that the essence of religion has been the confrontation with an *other,* believed to exist as a reality in the universe external to and vastly different from man—something that is indeed "out there," as Robinson puts it. The fundamental religious proposition, therefore, is that man is not alone in reality. Whether this is or is not part of the socially objectivated world view of a particular society is as irrelevant to its possible validity as, for instance, the absence from the world view of Zulu society of any notion of quantum theory is irrelevant to the validity of the quantum theory. The theological enterprise reduces itself to absurdity if it engages itself with the fundamental proposition of religion on any terms other than those of its validity. Is man alone in reality: Yes or no? If one is certain that the answer is "Yes," then, it seems to me, one could do better things with one's time than theology. In this respect one could learn from Marx. When he was certain that, with Feuerbach, the critique of religion was finished, he did not bother with it any more, but went on to concern himself with other things. But if one is *not* so certain that the religious proposition of an *other* confronting man in reality is only a gigantic illusion, then one can hardly dismiss the question about the validity of the proposition as irrelevant. In one way or another, inside or outside the traditional religious institutions, one will want to continue pursuing the question.

15

A Call for Authority in the Christian Community

There seems to be a sense of waiting in the American churches today. Everywhere one encounters the question, "What next?," sometimes asked in puzzlement, sometimes with deep apprehension. The question refers to a number of different levels. On the broadest level, of course, it is the question that every thoughtful person must ask himself about American society today. I doubt whether Christians have any greater wisdom on this that is not to be found elsewhere. Christians share with others in America the same moral anguish, are haunted by the same apocalyptic visions, struggle to glimpse signs of hope in the murky mess of our public life. But the question "What next?" also refers to specifically Christian concerns. On the level of theological thought, there also seems to be a pause. Nothing much is happening right now, one is told by observers of the theological scene; the theological excitements of yesteryear seem to have petered out, and no one has a very strong idea as to where the next focus of lively debate will be. On a deeper level the question "What next?" is one of faith—more accurately, perhaps, of the quest for faith. It is the question of those who have struggled long with tribulations and with doubt, who are rather exhausted by it all, and who yet wait for the morning when their stubborn hunches will be gloriously changed into certainties. On that last level the question is an ancient one indeed, reaching us over the centuries as one is calling us from Se'ir—"Watchman, what of the night? Watchman, what of the night?"

I cannot give confident answers on any of these levels. I'm neither a political nor a theological prophet, and certainly not one of those watchmen that God sends on occasion to tell us, in His name, what time it is in our night of waiting. I too must be a questioner, not an answer giver. What I will try to do here, however, is to comment on the situation from which this question comes, and (albeit with considerable trepidation) to suggest a new stance that, I think, is called for as Christians seek some answers.

Inevitably such comment will have a personal quality. In other words, I cannot play the part of the social scientist making detached and dispassionate statements about the situation. Or perhaps I should say that I *could* play this part very comfortably, but that I have the sneaking suspicion that this is not what is called for. I may be allowed then to begin with a personal reference. In 1961 my book *The Noise of Solemn Assemblies* was published.[1] At the time it made a considerable amount of noise of its own and I still meet people in some Protestant circles who identify me as its author in ego-sapping ignorance of my more recent literary productions. I don't think this book was terribly important in itself; it was part of a broad wave of sharp criticism from within that went through mainline Protestantism in the late 1950s and early 1960s. But (for reasons that, I'm sure, have something to do with original sin) one's own books serve as landmarks as one tries to figure out a portion of lived-through history. Thus, in thinking of my subject for this chapter, I thought of this particular book and naturally found myself asking, "What has happened since then?," and further, "Is there some continuity between what I felt I had to say then and what I would say now?"

What *has* happened since then? I think that most people, if they think back to 1961, will agree that the Christian community in America was in a vastly different situation from the one it is in today. The years that have elapsed since then have been ones of deepening crisis both for American society and for the American churches. At that time both seemed to have about them a quality of *intactness*, which some of us today may find difficult to recapture emotionally. Then, the critic appeared to be banging against the locked gates of majestically self-confident institutional edifices. Today he is more like a man storming through doors torn wide open by an earthquake. The ground on which we are standing has been profoundly shaken, and most of us feel it in our bones.

Different things have to be said at different times. At one time it may be necessary to remind Israel of God's judgment, at another time to speak tenderly to Jerusalem and to comfort God's people. Also, different things may have to be said in different places. This is a very big country. What has been heard *ad nauseam* in one place may still be the latest news in another. Nevertheless, as I was following the line of thought just mentioned I came to a conclusion that I find both surprising and somehow comforting—namely, *that, in essence, the same thing must be said today that I felt necessary to say then.*

The conclusion surprised me for two reasons. The first is that my own theological views have changed considerably since 1961, so that, for example, I can no longer use the stern, quasi-Barthian language with which I still felt comfortable at that time. But the more important reason for my surprise is the vastly changed situation of which I just spoke. Can it make sense to deliver, in essence, the same message to a house full of noisy celebration and to a house in which everyone is sitting under the table, waiting for the next rock to come flying in? I will suggest that, indeed, it does make sense. What is more, I will suggest that the same essential message that was once heard as an attack can at a later date be heard as comfort.

In 1961, and certainly all through the 1950s, there was, to be sure, a certain malaise in American Protestantism. It is probably safe to say, though, that it was limited to relatively small circles within the churches. Even there, in retrospect, it was a pretty mild affair, compared with the orgies of self-doubt and self-denigration that were to follow. The overall picture that confronted the critical observer was that of a secure, well-established, and generally self-satisfied "culture Protestantism." It was in this situation that a number of people, myself included, felt it necessary to protest that there was something very wrong with such an "establishment"—*not* because American culture or American society were peculiarly rotten (I did not believe this then and I do not believe it now), but because the Christian community must not identify itself fully with *any* sociocultural context. There are, to be sure, different views of the manner in which Christianity should relate to the historical situations in which it is embodied as a community. But it seems to me that there is always a need for sharp warnings when this relationship takes the form of comfortable, unproblematic identification. At such times, I think, it is necessary to recall that Christianity always stands over and beyond any particular culture, and that this transcendence involves judgment as well as grace.

The situation could not be more different today. Mainline Protestantism is marked by a widespread demoralization that (quite properly, I think) has been called a general failure of nerve. Its expressions range from masochistic self-laceration to hysterical defensiveness, but hardly anyone has remained untouched by it. If it has been suggested rather nastily that the institutional efforts to cope with the crisis are like rearranging the deck chairs on the *Titanic,* then it may be added that some of the critics of the institution have in effect been saying that we should blow up the ship before it even gets to the iceberg. Also, we are in good company now. The Catholics, who back in 1961 still seemed to be sitting pretty on their Rock of Peter, are now looking for plausible lifeboats with the rest of us. Panic seems to have crept up even on Southern Baptists and Missouri Lutherans. As to the rest of society, a convincing case could be made that, compared with some other institutions (the university, for example), the church is really not in such bad shape.

Christians, like other men, are creatures of habit. A man whose hat has been blown away by the wind will look for another hat to put in its place. A "culture Protestantism" whose culture has, or seems to have, been blown away promptly starts looking for a replacement. I think that many in our churches today can be described as being *in search of a culture with which to identify.* The liaison with American culture has gone sour, for whatever reasons. The solution seems to be the search for another culture with which a more satisfactory arrangement could be undertaken. I hope you will not think me facetious if, in this connection, I cite a passage by Johann Nestroy, the nineteenth-century Austrian comic playwright. It goes something like this: "There are some men who are shattered when their mistress leaves them. These are little souls. Then there are others, bigger souls, who quickly compensate for their loss by finding a replacement. The really great souls have the replacement ready before the loss has occurred." In this sense, it seems that we have no shortage of great souls.

There is today an anxious search for cultures other than that of so-called Middle America, for new cultural partners with which to enter into some form of Christian union. The list is long—the youth culture, the counterculture, black culture, various romanticized versions of Third World cultures, and the vision of a future culture that is expected to ensue from this or that revolutionary liberation. Theologians seem to be vying with each other to produce the formulas that will render these unions legitimate. It is all the more important to perceive the fundamental continuity between the earlier "culture Protestantism" and what is going on now. For once this continuity has been perceived, it suddenly becomes clear why the same essential message must be addressed today to the new "culture Protestants" *in spe.* Once more, I think, it is necessary to affirm the transcendence and the authority of Christianity over and beyond any cultural constellation in history, present or future, "established" or still striving for "establishment." It is necessary to do this now as it was then—*not* because American culture is peculiarly good, but because every conceivable alternative to it is itself transcended and judged in the Christian perspective.

To those who revel in the first love of this of that newly found sociocultural identification this affirmation will appear as an attack. In this they are no different from those who, in 1961, did not wish to be disturbed in their then-happy marriage with American culture. But there are others—Nestroy's little souls, perhaps, or could it be the poor in spirit?—who feel bereft of old securities and yet cannot console themselves with new ones. I will not speak of these in the third person, because I count myself as one of them. For those of us, then, who are at sea and unsure of our home in history, the affirmation of Christian transcendence comes as a word of great comfort. It tells us to be calm, to stop our frantic search for cultural and ideological refuges. It tells us that there is no abiding refuge in this world except one, but this one we do not have to search for, because it has been here all the time.

If there is any stance that has marked the Christian community in recent years, it is that of *listening*. In one sense, of course, Christians ought always to be listening. If we are commanded to love others, we must listen to them. But the stance that concerns me here has involved listening of a very specific kind, namely, listening for the redemptive word on the part of those who feel that they don't have it. More specifically, it has involved listening to an entity known as "modern man," in the expectation that thence will come the redemptive word.

There is, of course, a considerable history behind this stance. And, I hasten to add, there are aspects of this history that I value very positively. The idea that Christian thought ought to engage in an attentive dialogue with intellectual and cultural currents outside the Christian community presumably goes back all the way to the patristic age, and, in its most important modern form, to the age of classical Protestant liberalism. As to the idea that the entity "modern man" poses peculiar problems to Christian thought, it can easily be traced back at least to the eighteenth century. However, what has been involved in the listening stance in recent years is much more specific.

A major presupposition has been the alleged secularized consciousness of "modern man." It is presupposed that people in the modern West share a new and widely diffused consciousness (to wit, "modern consciousness"), and that this consciousness tends to preclude, or perhaps (in the more radical versions of this view) precludes absolutely, the traditional way in which religion has looked at the world. This presupposition is an empirical one, that is, it claims to say what "modern consciousness" actually is like. Commonly, the presupposition is coupled with a positive value judgment. It is not only stated as a fact that "modern consciousness" is secularized, but it is further claimed or assumed that this secularity is cognitively superior to whatever forms of consciousness preceded it. In other words, "modern consciousness" is not only diagnosed, but given three cheers into the bargain.

The problem of contemporary consciousness and its relation to religion is exceedingly complex. I have elsewhere dealt with it at great length in terms of the sociology of modern religion, and I could not possibly repeat these discussions here. I can only make the following observations (of necessity, without arguing them through): The empirical presupposition about the secularity of "modern consciousness," if taken as a hypothesis (as it should be), has a good deal of evidence in its favor. It is likely that a structure of consciousness has developed in the modern West that is distinctive and that tends away from traditional religious *Weltanschauungen*. At the same time, both the distinctiveness and the secularity of this consciousness have almost certainly been exaggerated. Also, it has been tacitly assumed that this secularization of consciousness is progressive and irreversible—a dubious assumption, as is becoming clearer all the time. More important, though, the jump from the empirical to the normative treatment of "modern consciousness" (that is, from the diagnosis to the three cheers) constitutes a lapse of logic of considerable crudity. After all, whatever "modern man" may in fact think, how can one be so sure that he is right? Could it not be that "modern consciousness," far from being the pinnacle of man's cognitive history, may rather be the result of an impoverishment in man's grasp of reality?

In the frame of reference of social science or historical scholarship, "modern man" and "modern consciousness" represent useful constructs. The debate about these constructs continues, and many issues in the debate are as yet unresolved. In the frame of reference of Christian thought, however, these same constructs have all too often become idols. "Modern man" and "modern consciousness" have not only been posited as facts, but have become golden calves around which a depressing number of Christian thinkers have staged an ongoing dance celebration. Since, alas, no one is quite sure just what are the authentic incarnations of these mythic entities, their celebration has been constantly changing. Every couple of years or so, a new ideology has been celebrated as *the* authentic expression of "modern consciousness," or a new cultural style or social movement as the definitive avatar of "modern man." This spectacle has been going on for over twenty years (roughly, I would say, since Bultmann's "demythologization" program became a focus of theological attention in America). More recently it has become more frantic, as the sense of crisis has been deepening in the American churches.

It is this particular listening stance that I would see in terms of a demoralized "culture Protestantism" in search of a new home. The search takes place on the level of theory as well as of praxis. On the theoretical level the search is expressed by embracing this or that contemporary intellectual position as the decisive voice of modernity with which Christians ought to enter into "dialogue"—such as existentialism, various psychoanalytic doctrines, cybernetics, Marxism, and so on. On the practical level the search leads to passionate identifications with a shifting series of cultural and sociopolitical phenomena—from modern urbanism to the "sensitivity" of the youth culture, the New Left to the ecology movement. "Dialogue" is often a misleading term to describe the ensuing relationships. In many cases it would be more apt to speak of "conversion" (and I need hardly add that I *don't* mean anybody's conversion to Christianity).

I would like to make it clear once more that I'm *not* saying that Christians ought not to listen to others' ideas, or to take seriously what happens in their cultural milieu, or to participate in the political struggles of the times. What troubles me is not the stance of listening as such, but that of listening with uncritical adulation if not idolatrous intent—of listening, if you will, with wide-eyed and open-mouthed wonder. Let me explicate what I mean by way of a timely example, that of the so-called counterculture.

This is a phenomenon both new and complex, and it is probably premature (certain fashionable oracles to the contrary) to attempt a definitive evaluation. I strongly suspect that, as with almost all human creations that merit the title "culture," this one will have to be evaluated eventually in other than black-and-white terms. Personally, I find some of this culture's features quite attractive (such as its pacifism, its racial tolerance, and its protest against certain pathologies of the Puritan ethic), some others simply a matter of aesthetic preference (such as its tastes in music and its peculiar fixation on bodily flora), and others quite repugnant (such as its dogmatic hedonism, its incapacity to make moral distinctions, and its collectivistic "horde" mentality). I'm sure that all these valuations are debatable, that they should be debated, and that Christians will want to do so from a Christian point of view. To say this, though, is a long cry from hailing the counterculture as a, perhaps *the,* great redemptive force of our age, as is now being done in quite a few places. The Protestant campus ministry is one such place (not everywhere, of course, but all too frequently). I understand that Christian ministry to any group will seek what Brunner used to call the *Anknuepfungspunkt,* the "point of contact" between the Christian message and the human concerns of the group. I'm less ready to understand the easy transition from ministering to the Canaanites and worshiping with them at the shrines of the *ba'alim.* I may add here that the last image is used deliberately. There are striking parallels between the sacred sexuality of the counterculture and that of the ancient Near East, and it strikes me as a measure of widespread theological bankruptcy that so few have seen this.

It seems to me that, quite simply, it is time to say "Enough!" to the dance around the golden calves of modernity. For over twenty years now we have been fascinated by the question, "What does modern man have to say to the church?" I wouldn't be too hesitant to answer, "Probably not much more than he has said so far!" We can be assured that new sociocultural constellations will appear in our lifetime, that probably some of them will be diametrically opposed to the presently prominent ones, and that there will be those who will hail them as redemptive events. We may be confronted by gurus of a new polytheism or by a triumphantly successful ideology of the New Right, by mind-blowing new life styles originating on the surface of the moon, or by movements of fanatical asceticism among the young. Will we, in each case, have to go through the same dreary cycle of wild enthusiasm and sober second thoughts? I'm enough of a sociologist to whisper "probably yes," but enough of a moralist to hope that (at least within the Christian community) there will be some who will disprove my sociology. It is they who, I hope, will turn to a much more significant question. To wit: *"What does the church have to say to modern man?"*

Before I make some comments on the stance implied in this question, I would like to say something about the context in which the church may find itself in the future. I have mentioned before that the notions about the progressiveness and irreversibility of secularization have become doubtful. A number of recent works in the sociology of religion (I will only cite here those of Andrew Greeley in this country and of David Martin in England) have greatly added to this doubt (at least in my case). This does *not* mean that those of us, social scientists and others, who have analyzed the recent history of religion under the aspect of secularization have been wrong in this analysis (though we may perhaps have exaggerated the *extent* of secularization). Where some of us (myself included) may have erred, however, is in projecting the indefinite continuation of present trends in the future. Not only was this projection logically unwarranted, but there is increasing positive evidence against it. I'm referring here to the resurgence of seemingly powerful religious impulses in sociocultural ambiences where one would least expect this in terms of the notion of progressive secularization, particularly among the young and in the college-educated upper middle class. To the extent that there, if anywhere, must be the habitat of "modern man," it seems that the latter's incapacity for religion and even for "mythological world views" has been somewhat exaggerated.

It would be foolhardy to make firm predictions on the basis of incomplete evidence and in a rapidly changing situation. It continues to be possible that the present upsurge of religiosity may turn out to be only a temporary disturbance in the global trend of progressive secularization. If so, Christians and others with religious *Weltanschauungen* will find themselves increasingly in a minority status (something that is not necessarily alarming, although it has consequences that must be faced). I must admit, though, that this scenario has come to seem increasingly implausible to me. I have been impressed, especially in America, by a widespread and apparently deepening hunger for religious answers among people of many different sorts. But another reason why progressive secularization seems more and more doubtful lies in the very demoralization discussed before. This demoralization, of course, is not limited to the religious communities but reflects a profound crisis of belief and values in the overall society. Old convictions have been shattered, institutions are tottering, there is a widespread sense of what sociologists call anomie—a feeling of rootlessness, of disorientation, and of the basic meanings of life being threatened. Individuals can live in such a condition, unhappy though it is, for a long time. Societies probably cannot (though the phrase "a long time" means something different for a society and an individual). If historical

experience is taken into account, societies afflicted with widespread anomie have either perished or have regenerated themselves through a renascence of their fundamental values. For reasons that are probably
deeply rooted in the constitution of man, such renascences have usually
had a powerful religious dimension.

It is considerations like these that, in my opinion, make it possible to
envisage a possibly powerful reversal of the secularization process. It is
clear that such a scenario hinges on many factors unrelated to what religious institutions may or may not do; mainly, it hinges on the general
fate of the society at large. No one can say what forms, either in ideas
or in social expression, such a religious resurgence might take. It might
conceivably occur *outside* the religious institutions as presently existing. Granted this scenario, however, I have two hunches about it, the
second of which is very strong. First, I'm inclined to the view that any
strong renascence of religion in American society will be *Christian,*
even if it should not be located in the ambience of the historic Christian
churches. It may well include the Jewish community, perhaps even in
a very close relationship. I have difficulty, on the other hand, imagining a prominent place in such a renascence for the currently fashionable Oriental cults. The latter are too much in contradiction to fundamental themes of American culture, not least to the central theme of a
national covenant with history that constitutes a fundamental nexus
between this culture and the Judaeo-Christian tradition. It seems more
plausible to me to view the current attraction of Oriental religiosity as
the direct result of disillusion with fundamental American values—and, *therefore,* to believe that this attraction would fade in the
precise measure that there would be a revitalization of American values and a new confidence in the moral viability of American society.

My second hunch about this scenario comes close to being a certainty: *If* there is going to be renascence of religion, its bearers will *not* be
the people who have been falling all over each other to be "relevant to
modern man." To the extent that modernity and secularization have
been closely linked phenomena in Western history, any movement of
countersecularization would imply a repudiation of "modern man" as
hitherto conceived. This is true even today, in the aforementioned religious manifestations in the youth culture and elsewhere. More important, strong eruptions of religious faith have always been marked by
the appearance of people with firm, unapologetic, often un-
compromising convictions—that is, by types the very opposite from

those presently engaged in the various "relevance" operations. Put simply: Ages of faith are not marked by "dialogue," but by *proclamation*.

"What does the church have to say to modern man?"

It is self-evident to me that this question cannot be answered in terms of the respective plausibility of this or that scenario. For the church to say X because it expects a new era of religiosity would be as reprehensible as the church saying Y because it thinks secularization to be irreversible. I assume that what the Christian community says to the world should be based on criteria of truth, *not* of sociocultural market research or public relations. Further, it is self-evident to me that what the church has to say, in any age, is always *essentially* the same. What the church is all about is that one old story of God's dealings with man, the story that spans the Exodus and Easter morning. When all is said and done, the Christian community consists of those people who keep on telling this story to each other, some of whom climb up on various boxes to tell the story to others. This is not to deny the ever-new ways in which the story falls on human ears, the different ways in which it may be told, or the vast variety of questions that may be addressed to the storytellers. The point is simply that the essence of the Christian message will remain the same if we imagine its communication to take place in catacombs or in the cathedrals of a new religious culture.

But there are different accents in which the message is delivered. It may be delivered in tones of quiet conviction or of intransigent fanaticism, in the dull context of what is culturally taken for granted, or haltingly and apologetically, or in the wonder of astonishing rediscovery. It is the combination of such accents that makes up the stance of the Christian community in any historical situation. It is in this sense that, I believe, a new stance is called for in our situation. Deliberately, and despite the danger of misunderstanding, I would like to call this *a stance of authority*.

Let me try and minimize the danger of being misunderstood: I'm certainly not calling for an attitude of arrogance or of "authoritarianism." I don't mean to be misunderstood either as an advocate of theological or ecclesiastical conservatism; I am neither. Nor would I want the term "authority" to carry the breath-stopping weight of New Testament *exousia;* very few among us today would have the courage to make such a claim. Perhaps the best way to explain what I have in mind is by saying that authority, in the sense I intend, is the opposite of the demoralization and the "failure of nerve" mentioned before. *It is the authority of those who have come to terms with their own experience and who are convinced that, in however imperfect a measure, they have grasped some important truths about the human condition.*

I'm fully aware that there are situations in which such authority is hard to come by. Specifically, I think I understand rather well the processes by which secularization has undermined firm religious belief in recent history and has brought about a profound crisis of credibility for the Judaeo-Christian tradition in the West. Yet, unless much of what I have said before is grossly mistaken, the situation in which the Christian community finds itself today is more favorable to such a regaining of confidence than the situation of only a few years ago. Then it seemed that the religious tradition was put in question by the massive certitudes of the modern world; today very few of these certitudes have escaped credibility crises of their own. It is not unreasonable to draw from this a lesson of skepticism regarding the challenges to faith of these erstwhile certitudes. The more bizarre exaggerations of religious accommodation to the modern spirit (I may mention the so-called death of God theology in this connection) provide a useful lesson, too—the one known to logicians as the reduction to absurdity. After all these doubts, sacrifices of both faith *and* intellect, and spiritual contortions, the time may have come for a simple but profoundly liberating insight, namely, that we may have known more and better than we gave ourselves credit for.

Today, especially in America, we are surrounded by hysterias of different sorts—the hysteria of those who have lost their old certitudes and the hysteria of those who, often with blind fanaticism, have committed themselves to new ones. It seems to me that Christians are in a very good position to remain free of either. I'm not suggesting that Christians are the blessed possessors of an unshakable certitude all their own, magically immune to the turmoil of the times. But after the tumbling down of all this ideological statuary, there is a good chance for a pause of recollection. Christians have much to recollect. I'm confident that, if they will only do so, the sharp illuminations of reality provided by the tradition will carry renewed conviction.

Although I have not dealt directly with a concern for the institutional structures of the church, I would like to affirm the importance of this concern. Every enduring human enterprise must exist in institutional structures, and the enterprise of the Christian community is no exception. What is more, anyone concerned for the institutional structures of the American church must ipso facto concern himself with the existing denominations and their relations to each other. I would even express the rather unfashionable opinion that there are occasions when bureaucratic organizations may be vehicles of grace.

All the same, I would also affirm that the concern for the institutional structures of the church will be vain *unless* there is also a new conviction and a new authority in the Christian community. There will almost certainly have to be structural changes (though, I suspect, they will turn out to be less drastic than many now hope or fear). There will have to be sustained thought as to the proper response of Christians to the agonizing travail of American society. It seems to me, though, that these tasks will only be meaningful to the extent that the Christian community regains its "nerve," and succeeds in achieving a new stance of confidence in itself and its message.

Intellectuals like to anticipate "historic moments," and some of my observations suggest that the Christian community in America might be on the eve of such a "historic moment." Caution and skepticism are very much in order with regard to such anticipations. All history is in the hands of God, and it seems that God is parsimonious in the enactment of "historic moments." Those who anticipate the latter with breathless impatience may grow old in the process. Even worse, those who thought that one such moment had actually come upon them may have to recognize later that they made a terrible mistake. If there is a sense of waiting in the American churches today, it may be said on a deeper level that the Christian community is *always* called to wait. Yet there *are* those moments in which God's presence in history manifests itself in lightning. I suppose that, as Christians, we always hope that we may experience such a moment at least once in our lifetime. Our waiting is marked by this hope. Presumably the best we can do is to wait in a stance that will permit us to see the lightning when it flashes across the horizon.

16

Cakes for the Queen of Heaven: 2,500 Years of Religious Ecstasy

The word that came to Jeremiah from the Lord: . . . "Thus says the Lord of hosts, the God of Israel, . . . For if you truly amend your ways and your doings, if you truly execute justice one with another, if you do not oppress the alien, the fatherless or the widow, or shed innocent blood in this place, and if you do not go after other gods to your own hurt, then I will let you dwell in this place. . . .

"As for you, do not pray for this people, . . . for I do not hear you. Do you not see what they are doing in the cities of Judah and in the streets of Jerusalem? The children gather wood, the fathers kindle fire, and the women knead dough, to make cakes for the queen of heaven; and they pour out drink offerings to other gods, to provoke me to anger. Is it I whom they provoke? says the Lord. Is it not themselves, to their own confusion? . . . Behold, my anger and my wrath will be poured out on this place, upon man and beast, upon the trees of the field and the fruit of the ground; it will burn and not be quenched" (Jer. 7:1 – 20).

Whatever the precise date of this passage from Jeremiah's prophecies—and, as is usually the case, biblical scholars disagree—the general historical context is clear: More than a century earlier the northern kingdom of Israel had been almost entirely annihilated by the Assyrians. Since this terrible event the little southern kingdom of Judah had been leading a precarious existence between the great powers in Mesopotamia and Egypt. From the beginning of his public activity, Jeremiah had been warning his compatriots against a great danger, a

This chapter originally appeared in *The Christian Century* (December 25, 1974). Copyright ʿ 1974 by Christian Century Foundation. Reprinted by permission.

strong and terrible enemy, that was to come from the north—the same direction from which the Assyrians had come.

Breaching the Covenant-Contract

It was this enemy that was to be the instrument of divine punishment of the sinful people of Israel. Over a hundred years before, the prophets of the north—especially Hosea—had spoken in just these terms about the Assyrians: Yahweh, the God of Israel, worked mysteriously through the forces of history, even through nations that had never heard of him, nations violently hostile to him. Even the Assyrians, a ferocious and merciless nation, could serve as the rod with which Yahweh would strike the people that had become unfaithful to the covenant. Unlike other gods, Yahweh was bound neither to a place nor to a people. His temple could just as well be in one place as in another. His relation to Israel was a contractual one rather than one of kinship. Yahweh had *chosen* Israel. He had bound himself to Israel in the covenant, but if Israel broke the terms of that contract, he was then free to repudiate the relationship. Now, once more, Jeremiah proclaimed these old truths about Yahweh, and the proclamation was given added weight by the frightful example of what had happened in the north.

Curiously, the sins denounced in the passage from Jeremiah (sins that constitute a breach of contract on the part of the people of Israel) are a mixture of social and religious offenses. There are easily recognized violations of social justice—failures to abide by the law, oppression of the weaker elements in society, the shedding of innocent blood. But these sociological sins are closely linked with the religious ones—the "going after other gods." This linkage is startling to modern ears. We are, to be sure, accustomed to the moral denunciation of social injustice, be it in religious or secular terms. A *New York Times* editorial writer would readily find himself at home in Jeremiah's catalogue of social evils. But we are not at all accustomed to seeing such evils linked with the failure to worship properly (in large part, of course, because we have only the haziest notion about worship, proper *or* improper). The linkage between social ethics and worship was also startling in the context of the ancient Near East—but not for the reason it startles us today. There was nothing hazy about worship in the ancient Near East; the individual was constantly surrounded by cult and ritual. Nor were the gods a remote or implausible hypothesis; on the contrary, they were tangibly close and real. It was not at all surprising for an Israelite prophet to assume that worship was of great importance. Rather, the unexpected thing was the assertion that the worship of Yahweh was directly and inevitably linked to the treatment of the lower classes of society. Not that this assertion was original to Jeremiah; he was merely reiterating an understanding of the covenant that harked back to very early times in the religious history of Israel.

"Cheap Grace" in the Temple of Astarte

What, then, was the improper worship that Jeremiah was talking about? Our passage indicates that a rather ecumenical array of gods was involved. The reference to kindling fires (for sacrifice) and pouring libations could, and probably did, refer to any number of divinities. But I think that the most interesting of the lot was that queen of heaven, for whom the women of Jerusalem made cakes (which, by the way, bore her image and were offered to her in a sacrificial cult). Who was she?

She was a very old divinity indeed, even then, and she had borne many names. In Mesopotamia she was known as Ishtar, in Syria-Palestine as Ashtoret. She reached Egypt as Ashtartu and in southern Arabia she appeared as a male god named Athtar. All these names have their root in a Semitic verb that denotes irrigation; everywhere she is associated with the waters that give fertility to the land. There are indications of similar goddesses from other parts of the Mediterranean world and from India. The Greeks called her Astarte and identified her with their own Aphrodite.

Astarte (I'll use the familiar Hellenized version of her name) was a key figure in the cult of sacred sexuality that was central to the religious life of the ancient Semites. Its basic assumptions were quite simple and, it seems, enormously attractive: Humanity was part and parcel of a divine cosmos. The rhythms of nature, particularly the sequences of the seasons and the movements of the stars, were suffused with divine forces. Using later religious terminology, we might say that the rhythms of nature were means of grace or sacraments. These same divine forces were also to be found within human beings, notably in their sexual and agricultural activity (the two were closely linked—the same creative powers gave fertility to the human womb and to the land). The cult of sacred sexuality put one in touch with the divine forces in the cosmos and within oneself. That cult, logically enough, tended everywhere toward the orgiastic. The temples of Astarte had attached to them priestesses or sacred prostitutes (the Hebrew Bible calls them *kedeshot*, "holy women"; the Greeks called them "hierodules," or "servants of the holy"), who offered sexual relations not for pleasure (though that might have been an occasional fringe benefit) but as a sacrament. (To defend the cult against the charge of sexism, I might add that some of its establishments also had male priests with similar functions.) In addition to its institution of sacred prostitution, the cult had a number of special occasions (harvest festivals and the like) on which normal sexual prohibitions were suspended and, according to the accounts we have, a good time was had by all.

It would be a mistake to attribute the great attraction of the cult of sacred sexuality *only* to the occasions of sexual release it provided, though this probably played a part. One might observe in this connection that, as human cultures go, that of the ancient Semites was not particularly "repressive" of the sexual impulse; there were plenty of *non*sacred prostitutes around, and the temples of Astarte did not have a monopoly in the brothel business. I think, rather, that we can grasp the attraction only if we pay attention to what I have called the sacramental character of sacred sexuality. The human being's fundamental religious quest is to establish contact with divine forces and beings that transcend him. The cult of sacred sexuality provided this contact in a way that was both easy and pleasurable. The gods were as close as one's own genitalia; to establish contact with them, when all was said mythologically and all was done ritually, one only had to do what, after all, one wanted to do anyway. It is hard to think of a more perfect example of what, many centuries later, Christians would call "cheap grace." At the same time, the cult provided *ecstasy*. In the throes of the orgiastic sacrament, the individual stepped outside his normal self and the humdrum restraints of ordinary life. He became one with the cosmos, with the gods, and ipso facto with his own true nature. He ate the apple and he became divine; what, in the biblical perspective, was the original seduction was also the most archaic experience of "consciousness expansion."

All divinities have a terrible aspect. But Astarte commonly appeared in a most comfortable form. According to an old Babylonian hymn used in her worship,

> . . . Ishtar is clothed with pleasure and love.
> She is laden with vitality, charm, and voluptuousness.
> In lips she is sweet; life is in her mouth.
> At her appearance rejoicing becomes full. . . .

The same hymn announces that Astarte "is sought after among the gods." No wonder! The Israelites, men and women both, succumbed to her psychedelic charm again and again. Nothing seemed to diminish her fascination. Toward the end of Jeremiah's ministry, when he lived in Egypt among the refugees from devastated Judah, once more we find him complaining about the women making cakes for the queen of heaven—despite that fact that, as God says through the mouth of the prophet, they "have seen all the evil that I brought upon Jerusalem and upon all the cities of Judah" (Jer. 44:2). And, more than half a millennium later, when Paul came to Corinth to preach the gospel, the city was famous for its great temple of Aphrodite, with its battalions of "hierodules" who, we might say, stood in a valid "apostolic succession" to the *kedeshot* of Jeremiah's time. The temptation of "cheap grace" spans the centuries; we may surmise that the Corinthian Christians were tempted for very much the old reasons.

Voluptuous Ecstasy or Stern Demands

But let me go back once more to ancient Israel: From the earliest layers of the biblical traditions to the most recent ones, the spokesmen of the God of the covenant violently repudiated the cult of sacred sexuality in all its forms. *Why?* First, it was *not* because these traditions were sexually "repressive," or "uptight," or averse to the satisfaction of "libidinal needs." On the contrary, ancient Israel was fairly relaxed about sexual matters, and until very late in its development it had no ideals of asceticism. The prophets were anything but "Puritans." They were denouncing not sex, but *sacred* sex. It is as if they said: "Go ahead, have your sexual pleasure—*but don't make a religion out of it.*" Also, in denouncing Astarte and the other gods of this kind of cult, they did *not* do so because they doubted the existence of these deities (though perhaps some of them did so doubt). The prophets were anything but adherents of a "modern scientific world view." Even Paul, writing at a much later time when Judaism had indeed become a fully "monotheistic" religion, could say in a quite open way: "For although there may be so-called gods in heaven or on earth—as indeed there are many 'gods' and many 'lords'—yet for us there is one God, the Father, from whom are all things and for whom we exist, and one Lord, Jesus Christ" (I Cor. 8:5–6).

The sacred sexuality complex was repudiated by those who spoke for Yahweh because it violated their central understanding of both God and humanity. The basic presupposition of sacred sexuality was the unity of the cosmos with the divine. It was precisely this unity that Yahwism violently rejected. Yahweh was the God who had *created* the heavens and the earth. As creator, he stood over and against the cosmos. He was not one with it; therefore, there was no way by which contact with him could be established by fusing the self with the inner processes of the cosmos. Put differently, ancient Israel polarized God and world in a hitherto unheard-of manner. By the same token, ancient Israel enormously radicalized the experience of transcendence. All gods are transcendent, in the sense of having their being beyond the borders of ordinary human life. Indeed, in this sense transcendence may be taken as a constitutive characteristic of all human religions. The God of Israel, however, was *utterly* transcendent. His power extended to every corner of the cosmos, but it *confronted* the cosmos rather than being immanent within it. Above all, Israel encountered its God as a God of history, through the mighty acts that were the foundation of the covenant.

This understanding of God was not an abstract, philosophical one. It came out of the very core of Israel's religious experience, and it had far-reaching moral implications. The covenant imposed cultic obligations on Israel, and the prophets were by no means anticultic (to think so is a very modern, indeed very Protestant misunderstanding). But these cultic obligations were inextricably linked with moral imperatives. Unlike the cult of sacred sexuality, the cult of Yahweh did not lead to otherworldy ecstasy; rather, it directed people back into the world, where their task was to do God's will in human affairs. Worship here was inevitably linked with the whole gamut of moral concerns in society—with social justice, with the right relations between nations and classes, with the protection of the weak. Unlike Astarte's, Yahweh's lips were anything but sweet; more often than not, his lips pronounced judgment. Unlike Astarte, Yahweh was not clothed with pleasure and voluptuousness; rather, his garb was righteousness. If Astarte's "grace" was cheap and comfortable, Yahweh's "grace" had to be dearly bought with moral effort and discipline.

Thus the opposition between the two religious possibilities was sharp and irreconcilable. It was *either* the voluptuous ecstasy of the one, *or* the stern demands of the other. Yahweh was a jealous God. Most important, the cultic betrayal of the covenant was inevitably linked with its moral betrayal: Those who offer cakes to the queen of heaven are the same ones who oppress the weak and who shed the blood of the innocent. Despite the vast gulfs of experience that lie between ourselves and Jeremiah's contemporaries, it should not be too difficult to see why: A religion of pleasure is not likely to be conducive to the often far-from-pleasurable efforts required by social concern; there is not much voluptuousness in taking care of widows and orphans.

Transcendence: Contraband Goods?

Inevitably there comes the question, *What does all this have to do with us today?* What should we care, after all, about who worshiped what in the Near East 2,500 years ago? Surely we have more urgent matters to worry about. Well, maybe. It seems to me, however, that these old stories speak to us in a surprisingly timely way, once we penetrate to their inner content through the enveloping layers of culturally alien materials.

To be sure, our spiritual situation today is very different from Jeremiah's. It is not only that we have behind us over two millennia of Jewish and Christian history, during which not one but several radical transformations of religious experience and consciousness took place. Our own situation is deeply marked by the phenomenon we know as secularization. Put simply, this means that trancendence of *any* sort has become progressively less real to many people. The gods which surrounded archaic man on all sides have receded. The cosmos, once permeated with divine beings and forces, has become empty, cold, a mathematical design. This, of course, is what is meant by the "modern scientific world view." Transcendence has been, shall we say, declared "inoperative" by the major agencies that "officially" define reality—the universities, the school system, the medical system, the communications media, and to some extent even the courts. Those who may be described as the "official reality-definers"—loosely speaking, the intellectuals and world-be intellectuals—are, throughout the Western world at least, overwhelmingly attached to that "modern scientific world view" which proscribes transcendence. In our society, as in others, these agencies together constitute what I like to call a "reality police." The "reality policemen"—teachers, psychiatrists, commentators, and so on—watch over the cognitive boundaries of the culture. In their perspective, transcendence in *any* of its historical forms is viewed as contraband goods. A contemporary who hears the voice of Yahweh, I daresay, would be just as suspect in that perspective as one who experiences the voluptuous ecstasies of Astarte. Such aberrations are promptly excommunicated intellectually (the psychiatrists have at hand a full-blown "syllabus of errors" for this purpose, as do language analysts and other assorted ideologists of the cognitive status quo), and the individual who refuses to recant may have to face "repressive" treatments of various degrees of severity (from losing his job to electroshock).

I strongly suspect that there is something close to an instinct for transcendence in human beings. We can learn something from Freud here: "Repressed" drives have a way of coming back, often in grossly distorted and bizarre forms. This is precisely what has been happening as a result of secularization and its agencies of "censorship." Very likely it has been happening all along, though some of the manifestations have been stronger or at least more visible in recent years. The gods are very old and very powerful; they are not easily "repressed." What is more, the "modern scientific world view" that was supposed to replace them has turned out to be a rather boring business for many people. The cosmos as a mathematical design may be inspiring to some physicists; the vision gives metaphysical cold feet to many others. Secularization has both demystified and trivialized reality.

It was G. K. Chesterton, as I recall, who observed that modernity has given ultimate authority to the world view of a slightly sleepy businessman right after lunch. Such a world view is not only unexciting; it also fails to do justice to some of the root experiences of human life, notably the experiences of mystery and of pain. If one looks at the matter in this way, it is hardly surprising that transcendence has refused to go away quietly and definitively. It continues a vigorous "underground" existence in many places; the gods, as it were, come in plain brown envelopes. In other places it continues to defend itself in institutions that, from the viewpoint of the "official" world view, are obsolete remnants of an earlier age. Sometimes, to the surprise of the ideological establishment, transcendence erupts in unexpected and cataclysmic ways. This is a useful approach to an understanding of what has been happening on the religious scene in the past few years.

Let me bring up Freud once more: "Repressed" material will erupt most violently where the "censorship" has been strongest. For this reason, the more colorful eruptions of transcendence have occurred *not* in the bosom of "reactionary" religious institutions but rather in those places where secularization has been most "repressively" established. In America, this means largely the college-educated upper middle class. The new Pentecostalism is spreading among progressive Roman Catholics and Episcopalians—*not* among Southern Baptists or Adventists. Black masses are celebrated in affluent suburbs—*not* in the areas of the working class. And it is the children of the most orthodox secularists, the offspring of thoroughly enlightened modern homes, who parade through the streets chanting Sanskrit hymns.

The Resurgence of Sacred Sexuality

One aspect of this recent religious upsurge is of immediate relevance: There has also been a resurgence of sacred sexuality. Perhaps nothing in human history ever vanishes completely—a disturbing or consoling notion, depending on the degree of one's faith in progress, but there it is: Astarte is alive and well, and if she lives anywhere, I suppose, it is in California.

The new sacred sexuality takes many forms. It appears in heavily secularized garb in various therapeutic cults, most of them offshoots of movements within the psychoanalytic camp—from Wilhelm Reich to the more sedate branches of the "new sensitivity." In the counterculture it revealed its religious thrust almost everywhere, linked as it was to psychedelic experimentation and an intense interest in the occult. Norman O. Brown has perhaps been the most influential spokesman of this overtly religious celebration of sexuality. Finally, sacred sexuality is directly embodied in subcultural religious movements and sects, most of them of Oriental inspiration. But this is only to look at the original "locations" of the phenomenon. By now it has been diffused widely through upper-middle-class culture in this country, most strongly on the West Coast but elsewhere as well. To an extent, it has become the ideology of the "sexual revolution."

In view of this variety of forms, it is useful to pay attention to the common core of these phenomena. Perhaps the most illuminating proposition in all of this is the injunction "to get in touch with one's body" (incidentally, a *moral* injunction, often put forth with considerable sternness). What does this imply? First, it implies some superficial beliefs about the place of sexuality in human experience (we might regard these as being in the antechamber of the temple of sacred sexuality proper): The belief that sexuality is a key, perhaps even *the* key, component of the quality of being human (in this, of course, lies the pervasive heritage of Freud); the belief that modern Western culture, and especially American culture, has unduly suppressed sexuality (this is the anti-Puritan aspect of the proposition), and that, as a result, not only are we sexually frustrated (and that frustration carries all sorts of physical and psychological pathologies in its wake), but our entire relation to our own bodies as well as the bodies of others has become distorted. We are afraid of the body, we are afraid to let go physically, to touch one another, to enjoy physical pleasure fully (and not just sexual pleasure in the narrower sense). "To get in touch with one's body" is an imperative of regained health, beyond that of deepened humanity. Sexual liberation is thus linked to liberation in a more basic way; it becomes a method of achieving a freer humanity, individually and perhaps even politically.

This much we could call "secularized Astartism." It is not the end of the story. The core proposition is expanded today by many into a fully religious view of the world—if you will, into Astartism *de*-secularized. Once more, "to get in touch with one's body" is to establish contact with the fundamental rhythms of the cosmos. The "new sensitivity" toward the body is linked with "expanded consciousness"—expanding, that is, toward the divine. The status quo is defined as an alienation between ourselves and the life-giving forces of nature; the projected salvation consists in overcoming that alienation and returning to the divine forces that are immanent in nature.

Some of the writings of the ecology movement have expressed this viewpoint eloquently, but it can also be found elsewhere (and, needless

to say, it can be found in the writings of "with-it" Christian theologians). It is interesting, by the way, that the blame for this alleged
alienation is commonly put on biblical religion and on the Judaeo-
Christian tradition as a whole—an insight with which it is impossible
to disagree. In this form of the proposition, we are once again in the
realm of authentic sacred sexuality. The liberation of the body is once
more linked to the ecstasies in which the divine womb of the cosmos is
reentered. The wheel has come full circle.

If you think that I'm now working up toward a prophetic denunciation of the new sacred sexuality, I must disappoint you. I'm no
Jeremiah, the last thing in the world I want to be is a prophet, and
there are worse things in our time than Astarte Rediviva. Also, let me
say emphatically that I hold no brief for Puritanism or for sexual "repression." I'm quite tolerant of even the excesses of the "sexual revolution" (my main objection to it is that it is antierotic, but that is another
topic), and I suspect that on balance it has done more good than harm.
There is one thing, however, that I have in common with the Israelite
prophetic tradition in this area: It is not sexuality, but *sacred* sexuality, which bothers me in religious terms. In an age in which we are
so much at the mercy of the "repressive triviality" of the secularists, I
incline toward an irenic attitude with regard to all, or nearly all, reaffirmations of transcendence: I would much prefer to live in a temple
of Astarte than in a global Skinner Box, and I'll take the poetry of William Blake over the dreary platitudes of positivist philosophers any
day.

The Vital Link Between Worship and Morality

Nevertheless, I cannot leave it at that—and no one can who has any
stake in that vision of the human condition that comes down to us from
ancient Israel. For both religious and ethical reasons I cannot leave it
there, and, in quite traditional fashion, I see once again the linkage between cult and ethics. Religiously, I believe that Jeremiah was right in
his faith in the utterly transcendent God who created heaven and
earth, who moves history, and who bids us do his work in the world.
We may cherish all the wonders of creation—as our passage has it,
"man and beast . . . the trees of the field and the fruit of the ground."
All these are good, indeed they are sweet (as the lips of love are sweet),

but they are *not* God, who stands over them in infinite majesty and who at times, as in our passage, stands over them in judgment. To say this is not to indulge in narrow intolerance. But one must be true to one's own experience; that means saying No as well as Yes. Now as then, it is not possible to worship *both* the God who created the world *and* a world itself perceived as divine.

But for ethical reasons also I cannot leave it with an attitude of total tolerance. There is still a vital connection between what we worship and what our morality is. Now as then, the world is full of injustice and misery. The God of the covenant demands of us that we work in this world, that we strive to combat injustice and to alleviate misery. A religion of pleasure, no matter what the intentions of its advocates, can only inhibit the efforts that are required by this moral demand. And, if I'm to be honest, at this point of my reflections my tolerance wears very thin indeed: In a world of mass murder and mass starvation, of unprecedented terror, odious tyrannies, and the threat of nuclear holocausts, there is something obscene about an order of priorities that starts off with bigger and better orgasms.

Let me conclude with what I regard as the root insight of Jeremiah's perspective: The transcendence of God and the wordly mission of humanity are not in contradiction. On the contrary, the worship of the God who is utterly beyond the world is deeply, inextricably linked with the most passionate engagement in the moral struggles of this world. Nor is the refusal to worship the creation instead of the Creator a denial of the good things of life. On the contrary, it is precisely in the celebration of the world as creation, and *not* in its worship as something divine, that we taste its hauntingly vulnerable sweetness.

17

The Devil and the Pornography

of the Modern Mind

He is very old and he comes from far away. Probably of Iranian origins (Ahriman, ruler in the dominion of darkness), he appears in the Bible as Satan, God's antagonist, seducer and liar. He has had many names—Beelzebub, Abaddon, Diabolos, Lucifer, Deoful—down to the English devil. He has had a lot to put up with in his long history—the leering intimacies of hysterical witches, the cold hatred of inquisitors, the feverish fantasies of romantic poets, and the supercilious mockery of every variety of enlightened intellectual.

And now, it seems, he is in vogue again—reborn in California (that Bethlehem of nearly all novelties of our time), announced by the wise men of the communications media, on the march from West to East (in this, as in so many other things, yesterday's last cry in Berkeley is tomorrow's new wave in Stockholm). Feminist communes celebrate witches' sabbaths in his name. Books about him crowd the paperback sections of college bookstores. People stood in line to see a motion picture in which a little girl, under his influence, masturbates with a crucifix. In one of the best neighborhoods in New York City, with one of the highest incidences per square yard of readers of the *New York Review of Books*, there is a store where one can buy all the necessary equipment to celebrate black masses (the store, by the way, accepts Mastercharge). For the moment, at least, the devil business seems to have a bull market.

What should one make of all this? To be sure, one ought to be careful whenever the media take up a phenomenon. Frequently they produce that which they claim to discover. Even more frequently they

This chapter originally appeared in *Worldview* (December, 1974). Copyright ᶜ 1974 by The Council on Religion and International Affairs. Reprinted by permission.

suddenly notice something which has been there all along. Since they continually copy from each other, there often occurs the illusion of an avalanche. But although the media are powerful, they are not all-powerful. In this instance the media have exaggerated the phenomenon as well as distorted it, but they have not invented it. In other words, there is something to think about in the renewed timeliness of the devil.

Could it be the measure of evil in the contemporary world? Could it be horror at the realities of modern mass murder, mass hunger, or the multifaceted threat to the survival of man on this planet? Could it be new questions about the meaning of evil, a new quest for a viable theodicy? I don't think so. There are few indications that many of our contemporaries agonize very much about these matters, even less that, in desperation, they resort once more to the old hypothesis of the devil. Or, on the contrary, could it be a completely superficial and transient fad, just one more gambit to combat the chronic boredom of affluent society? Very likely this is part of it. I don't believe that it is the whole story.

A better insight may be gained into the phenomenon by looking at its psychological character. It appears that the preoccupation with the devil, along with the whole current occult wave, provides definitely libidinal gains. There is pleasure here of a very particular kind—to wit, the pleasure of eating forbidden fruit. Put differently, the libidinal gains derive from prohibited or repressed objects. Modern man doing magic resembles a Puritan in a whorehouse. Just because the activity is forbidden it is marvelously exciting. If this psychological diagnosis is correct, then contemporary occultism (of which the devil business is but a small part) is the pornography of the modern mind. As soon as one says this, another question arises: Who or what has repressed these objects? Who or what is playing the role of Freudian censor here? Without censorship there is no pornography, just as every movement of sexual liberation is bad news for the whorehouse business.

One thing should be clear: The role of censor is certainly *not* played today by the churches. These are themselves, if not exactly repressed, in a rather difficult situation. Religious faith itself is almost pornographic in wide circles today (anyone who wants to test this proposition is invited to make religious affirmations at an upper-middle-class cocktail party). The churches are increasingly reluctant to make statements of faith unprotected by redeeming sociopolitical significance. In an earlier period of Western history things were very different; thus in the Middle Ages the devil-possessed witches bared their behinds, literally and figuratively, before the altars of Christianity. Except in some hinterland locales, such a demonstration would not be very interesting today. On the contrary, I would contend, the role of censor is played today by the highly modernized and thoroughly secularized cultural apparatus. The pornographic provocation is not directed against Christianity but against its ideological successor, namely, against the world view of modern secularity. In order to blaspheme against the Good Lord, one must first believe in Him, otherwise there is no fun in it. Anyone who still thinks that the churches in Western societies are instruments of repression is living in a nineteenth-century universe of discourse—a world, say, of Thomas Huxley or Ralph Ingersoll. (The intriguing fact that a sizable portion of our intelligentsia operates with such a quaintly antiquarian frame of reference cannot, alas, concern us further here.)

Let me, then, state a simple hypothesis: *The current occult wave (including its devil component) is to be understood as resulting from the repression of transcendence in modern consciousness.* This repression is socially and culturally institutionalized—in the schools, the communications media, even in the language of everyday life (in which, for example, curses have become domesticated as merely emotional expletives). In other words, it is institutionalized secularity that is playing the role of censor. If this is so, we can learn a useful lesson from Freud: Repressed contents have a way of coming back, often in bizarre forms.

Transcendence is the experience that human life touches on boundaries. On this side of the boundaries is the world of everyday events, practical activity, and reason, a world in which one is at home in a self-evident way. On the other side of the boundaries is the world of the uncanny, of the "totally other," in which the assumptions of ordinary life no longer hold. There is ample evidence to the effect that human beings have known of this duality of experience from the earliest times. Human religions are the many-sided and gigantic effort to come to terms with the experience of transcendence. Insofar as modern consciousness has been shaped by secularization (there is much debate about the extent of this), it constitutes a radical *novum* in history. The great effort to confront transcendence is abandoned. As far as possible, everyday life is purged of the symbols of transcendent reality. Even more radically, this great purge is intellectually legitimated by denying the status of reality to all transcendent referents. Transcendence is denied, explained in different terms, finally stigmatized as illusion or wishful thinking. Secularization is a vast simplification. In the secularized world view there is only *one* reality, pervasively rational and (at least in principle) ordinary. There are no more boundaries and the mystery of what lies beyond has been abolished. Gilbert Chesterton described this world view as the way a slightly sleepy businessman feels right after lunch. The final irony of our situation is that even the churches have tried increasingly to keep their messages within the limits of this not exactly exciting perspective.

I believe that such a world view without transcendence must eventually collapse, because it denies ineradicable aspects of human experience. But it is not my intention to argue this here. My hypothesis is social-psychological, not philosophical or theological. It is on the level of social psychology that one may say the following: The world that is being constructed by the secularists is very flat. It is a world without windows on the surrounding wonders of life. It is marked (I will allow myself a new term here) by *repressive triviality*. But the boundaries that have been denied are still there, in the minds of people if not in the cosmos. Therefore this world view, like any other, has its *reality policemen*. They are the teachers, psychiatrists, journalists, and other inquisitors of the modern culture apparatus. Their job is to make sure that no contraband items are smuggled across the frontiers. It is a difficult job, for the flat world is also rather boring. It is not surprising, then, that there continue to be people who rebel against this officially decreed boredom, and that there continues to be a demand for contraband transcendence.

Repressive triviality is not functioning very well. The reality police are not too effective; they are even curruptible. It is possible to cheat the censors. As a result, transcendence keeps coming back. Often it must take refuge underground, but it keeps popping up. Sometimes only its behind is visible. It is in this context that even the old devil gets his due again. I think it would be a great mistake to understand his reappearances as a manifestation of moral evil. The embodiments of moral evil in our time look quite different; they wear the most up-to-date uniforms, speak the language of the media, and employ all the marvels of modern technology. No, it makes little sense to see this Diabolus Redivivus as a figure of moral depravity. Rather, he may be perceived as one of the Good Lord's harlequins, a not altogether unwelcome character, a reminder of transcendence.

18

New York City 1976:
A Signal of Transcendence

Different cities acquire great symbolic significance at different moments in human history. Paris was significant in this way in the eighteenth and nineteenth centuries, as was London (though perhaps to a lesser degree), and Rome, over and beyond anything that was actually going on there, has retained its powerful symbolic character over many centuries. New York City undoubtedly has a comparable symbolic significance today. It is perceived as a symbol of modernity, of Western civilization, and (despite the often-repeated statement that "New York is not America") of the civilization of the United States. The curious thing is that it is widely perceived as a negative symbol, that is, as a metaphor of everything that has gone wrong with our society.

Much of the rest of the country sees New York City as one gigantic agglomeration of social ills: crime, poverty, racial hatred, mismanaged and corrupt government—not to mention dirt, pollution, and traffic congestion of virtually metaphysical dimensions. The same perceptions have been widely diffused abroad, and foreign tourists come to the city with the piquant ambivalence of apprehension and fascination that used to go with dangerous expeditions into the jungles of central Africa. (Such an attitude can be quite profitable to the tourist industry. I know of a German tourist, a middle-aged woman, who went for solitary walks in Central Park every evening, in thrilled anticipation of being sexually assaulted. She was, alas, disappointed. The worst—or best—result of her effort was that an inept mugger tried unsuccessfully to snatch her purse.) Interestingly, New York has negative symbolic value right across the political spectrum: As seen from the right, New

This chapter originally appeared as "In Praise of New York" in *Commentary* (February, 1977).

York is the habitat of an anti-American intellectual and media establishment, bent on converting the entire nation into the decadent welfare state that the city, supposedly, has already become. Seen from the left, New York is, above all, Wall Street—the heart of the beast, headquarters of capitalist imperialism, cosmic cancer *par excellence*; Madison Avenue has a slightly lesser place in this particular demonological vision.

And yet, despite all this, New York City continues to be a magnet and even an object of love, sometimes fierce love. People, especially the young continue to come in large numbers, irresistibly drawn to the city by expectations of success and excitement. And New Yorkers themselves, although they too frequently share the negative views of their own city (indeed, they relish topping each other's horror stories—"You think *you* had a parking problem today, well, let me tell you what happened to *me* this morning"), nevertheless continue to be inexplicably, perhaps dementedly, attached to the cesspool of perdition in which they reside. Such ambivalence suggests that the reality of New York is more complicated than its symbolic imagery. And so, of course, it is. From a sociological viewpoint, I could now proceed to delve into the welter of empirical facts that underlie the various perceptions of this city. My purpose here, though, is not sociological but theological.

Specifically, I propose to talk about New York City as a signal of transcendence—*not* New York in some romanticized past, *nor* New York in some utopian future, but New York *today*, a time of disillusion and of many fears, but also a time of promise and of hope. To speak of a signal of transcendence is neither to deny nor to idealize the often harsh empirical facts that make up our lives in the world. It is rather to try for a glimpse of the grace that is to be found "in, with, and under" the empirical reality of our lives. In other words, to speak of a signal of transcendence is to make an assertion about the presence of redemptive power in this world. Let me begin by telling you the most New York joke that I know. It comes, of course, from the pen of Woody Allen, and it concerns the hereafter. There are really only two questions about the hereafter, Woody Allen suggests: *How long does it stay open? And can you get there by cab from midtown Manhattan?* In a quite *non*jocular way, the rest of this chapter may be taken as a *midrash* on this text.

New York is no longer the world's largest city, but it is still the world's most potent symbol of urbanism and urbanity (two related but distinct matters). It seems to me that an exploration into its possibilities as a signal of transcendence must begin with this root fact: Here is not only a vast and vastly important city, but *the* city *par excellence*, the prototypical cosmopolis of our age. In think this is why visitors and new arrivals feel at home there so quickly. Every urban experience that they have had before has been, in a way, an anticipation of New York, and the encounter with the real thing thus has a strong note of familiarity, of déjà vu (apart from the fact that the major landmarks of New York are known everywhere and serve as instant orientations for the newcomer). Wherever skyscrapers reach up toward the clouds, wherever masses of cars stream back and forth over steel-girded bridges, wherever heterogeneous crowds pour through subways, underground concourses, or cavernous lobbies encased in glass, there is a bit of New York. Conversely, the New Yorker visiting other cities finds everywhere the sights and sounds, even the smells, that remind him of home. The mystique of New York City is, above all, the mystique of modern urban life, concentrated more massively than anywhere else.

It is not accidental, I think, that the biblical imagery of redemptive fulfillment is so persistently urban. Jerusalem became the focus of religious devotion from an early period of the spiritual history of ancient Israel, and it has remained the holy city in both Jewish and Christian religious imagination ever since. And this same Jerusalem, of course, came to be transformed into an image of eschatological expectation—the Jerusalem that is to come, the heavenly city, "its radiance like a most rare jewel, like a jasper, clear as crystal." Biblical scholars disagree on the precise origins and status of the Zion tradition in the Old Testament, on the religious significance of Jerusalem at, say, the time of David and Solomon, and on the significance of the various images in the Apocalypse. Yet there is, I believe, far-reaching consensus on one simple point: The city as a sociopolitical formation marks a transition in human history from bonds based exclusively on kinship to more comprehensive human relationships. Perhaps this was not the case everywhere, but it was clearly so in the ancient Mediterranean world. Here cities—as markets, centers of political or military administration, and amphictyonic sanctuaries—served to weaken and eventually to liquidate the archaic bonds of blood, of clan and tribe. Max Weber has argued that, in this, cities are incipiently "rationalizing," that is, they constitute a social and political order based on reason, as against an older order based on magical taboos. This development reached a dramatic climax in the emergence of the Greek *polis*, but it is not fanciful to suggest that the biblical imagery of the city served as a religious legitimation of the same underlying liberation from the magic of the blood. Whatever else the city is, it is a place where *different* people come together and find a new unity with each other—and, in the context of the ancient world, that is a revolutionary event. But let me not get entangled here in historical controversies. Instead, let me make this proposition: *The city is a signal of transcendence inasmuch as it embodies universalism and freedom.*

If universalism is a root urban characteristic, then surely New York is the most universalistic of cities. And, of course, it is this quality of universalism that most impresses the newcomer and that is so often bragged about by the native. In this small space are pressed together all the races and all the nations of the world. A short subway ride separates worlds of mind-boggling human diversity—black Harlem borders on the Upper West Side, the *barrio* on the territory of East Side swingers, the Village on Little Italy, Chinatown on the financial district. And that is only in Manhattan, beyond which lie the mysterious expanses of the boroughs—places like Greenpoint, Bay Ridge, or Boro Park, each one a world of meaning and belonging almost unpenetrated by outsiders. In this city you can enter a phone booth shaped like a pagoda and make a reservation in a Czechoslovak restaurant (or, more precisely, in one of *several* Czechoslovak restaurants). You can spend weeks doing nothing else, if you have the leisure, than savoring the world's greatest concentration of museums, art galleries, musical and theatrical performances, and other cultural happenings of every conceivable kind, from the sublime to the unspeakable. When I first lived in New York as a student, I had a job as a receptionist in a now-defunct dispensary on the Lower East Side. I still recall with pleasure my lunch hours: I would buy a bialy with lox in the old Essex Street Market, munch it while strolling through the teeming street life at the foot of the Williamsburg Bridge, and then have a quiet coffee with baklava in one of several Turkish cafes on Allen Street, surrounded by old men smoking waterpipes and playing checkers (apparently their only occupation). What I recall most of all is the exhilarating sense that here I was, in New York City, where all these things were going on and where, in principle, everything was possible.

Are these sentimental trivialities, fit only as copy for tourist promotion? I think not. For the mundane facts contain a mighty promise—the promise that God loves the human race in *all* its incredible variety, that His redemptive grace embraces *all* of humanity without any exception, and that His Kingdom will mean not the end but the glorious transfiguration of every truly human expression. The heavenly city, too, will contain every human type and condition, and in this it will necessarily resemble New York; needless to add, it will *not* resemble New York in that it will be without the degradations and deprivations that afflict human life in this aeon. Also, God's promise is one of perfect freedom. There is no such freedom short of the Kingdom of God; in this aeon, every liberty is bought at a price (often an ugly one), every liberation is incomplete, and some liberations are illusory. It is important to remember this. Nevertheless, wherever human beings are liberated from oppression or narrowness to wider horizons of life, thought, and imagination, there is a foreshadowing of the final liberation that is to come. Thus, I believe, New York City is a signal of transcendence also in the exhilaration of its freedom—and let me assure you that, in saying this, I do not forget for a moment the sordidness that may also be found here.

To some extent, the characteristics of universalism and freedom are endemic to urban life nearly everywhere, in varying degrees. The distinctiveness of New York comes from the enormous magnitude of these features. The same may be said of another characteristic which, I propose, may be taken as a signal of transcendence: *The city is a place of hope.*

If there is any New York legend that is generally known, it is that of the immigrant, and the legend, of course, has its most famous physical representation in the Statue of Liberty. This legend is, above all, a story of hope. I arrived in America a short time after World War II, very poor and very young, after a long ocean voyage that sticks in my memory as an endless bout with seasickness. The ship sailed into New York Bay in the early morning, in a dense fog, so that very little could be seen at first. Then, dramatically, the fog was pierced, and we saw first the Statue, which seemed perilously close to the ship, and then the skyline of lower Manhattan. All the passengers were assembled on the deck, and there was a hushed silence. But, curiously, what impressed me most at the time was not these majestic sights; I had, after all, expected to see them. There was something else. As the ship sailed up the Hudson toward its pier, I was fascinated by the traffic on what I later learned was the West Side Highway. All these cars seemed enormous to me. But, more than their size, it was their colors that impressed me. This was before New York taxis all came to be painted yellow; then, they came in all the colors of the rainbow, though yellow was pre-

dominant. I didn't know that these garish cars were taxis. The exuber-
ance of color, I thought, was characteristic of ordinary American auto-
mobiles. This, then, was my first unexpected sight in New York, and it
pleased me greatly. I don't think I put it quite this way to myself, but
implicit in my visual pleasure was the notion that someday I, too,
might be driving past the skyscrapers in a bright yellow car of surrealistic proportions, engaged (no doubt) in some business of great
importance and enjoying the company of the most beautiful woman
imaginable.

As immigrant stories go, mine has been lucky although I've never
driven a yellow cab. Indeed, I could say that New York has kept all its
promises to me. I know full well that this has not been so for all new-
comers to this city. If New York has been a place of hope, it has also
been a place of disappointed hope, of shattered expectations, of bitter-
ness and despair. It has been fashionable of late to stress this negative
aspect of the American dream—mistakenly so, I believe, because
America has fulfilled far more expectations than it has frustrated. I
would go even farther than that: The currently fashionable intellectuals, who decry the hopefulness of America, are far more in a state of
"false consciousness" than the millions of immigrants who came and
who continue to come to America full of hope. Nevertheless, just as it
would be false to speak of the universalism and the freedom of this city
without also speaking of the sordid underside of these facts, so would it
be dishonest to pretend that the hopeful message emblazoned on the
Statue of Liberty is an accurate description of empirical reality. Of
course it is not. And yet the proclamation of hope to all those who came
here across the ocean is a signal of transcendent portent. For all of us,
men and women of this aeon, are on a long journey, across vast and
dangerous seas, toward a city of hope.

There is more: *This is a place of useless labor.* Just compare New
York with an honest-to-goodness industrial city like Detroit or Pitts-
burgh, or even Chicago. In these cities most people are engaged in labor that has at least an indirect relation to economic utility. Certainly
there are such people in New York. The peculiarity of New York,
however, is the large portion of its labor force employed in activities
which only the most ingenious economic theory can interpret as a contribution to the gross national product. Leave aside the enormous
number of people working in municipal government and other public
services (and leave aside the timely question of how long the city will be
able to afford this); you are still left with legions of people making their

livelihood, or at least trying to do so, through activities which, economically speaking, are bizarre. Look at them: Promoters of Renaissance music, producers of nonverbal theater, translators of Swahili literature, purveyors of esoteric erotica, agents of nonexistent governments, revolutionaries in exile, Egyptologists, numismatic experts, scream therapists, guidance counselors for geriatric recreation, Indonesian chefs, belly dancers and teachers of belly dancing (and, for all I know, belly dancing therapists)—not to mention individuals who are on university payrolls to provide instruction in phenomenological sociology (I have frequently thought that a society that can afford *me* must somehow be heading for an economic crisis). Let me make a practical suggestion in this matter: Go for lunch someday to one of my favorite restaurants in New York, the Russian Tea Room on West 57th Street, in the heart of the music and ballet district. Study the customers. A few will be easy to place; these, most likely, are tourists from the Bronx. An attempt to guess the occupations of the rest should be enough to induce a nervous breakdown in any labor economist, especially if he also tries to figure out how such occupations can generate enough income to pay the price of a beef Stroganoff preceded by blinis with caviar.

A Chicagoan will know what to say to all of this: These people can't be serious. Precisely! The opposite of being serious is being playful; the invincible playfulness of New York City is, I believe, in itself a signal of transcendence. *Homo ludens* is closer to redemption than *homo faber*; the clown is more of a sacramental figure than the engineer. In the heavenly Jerusalem there will be no need for psychotherapy and geriatrics, but I confidently expect that there will be an unbelievable variety of restaurants—metaphysically transfigured restaurants, to be sure, but restaurants nonetheless—and, if so, there is certain to be the Platonic prototype of the Indonesian *rijstafel*, its pure ideal, its *Urform*, its ultimate culmination. May I also confess to the (perhaps crypto-Muslim) expectation that there will be *something* like belly dancers? Anyway, I think it is good theology to expect the Kingdom of God to be a very playful affair—and in *that*, at the very least, it will resemble New York more than Chicago!

New Yorkers, like the inhabitants of other large cities, are supposed to be sophisticated. The word, of course, is related to sophistry—the ability to be clever with words, to be quick, to be surprised at nothing. This notion of sophistication is closely related to that of urbanity, and it is as much a source of pride for the urbanite as it is a provocation to others. Somebody once defined a true metropolis as a place where an individual can march down the street wearing a purple robe and a hat with bells on it, beating a drum and leading an elephant by the leash, and only get casual glances from passers-by. If so, then surely New York is the truest metropolis there is. To some extent, of course, this is but another expression of the aforementioned universalism. But there is more: *The city is a place of magic.* And in that, too, I would contend, it offers us a signal of transcendence.

I don't mean occultism, though there is enough of that around as well. I mean magic in a more ample sense, namely, the quality of the surreal, the intuition that reality is manipulable, unpredictable, subject to the strangest metamorphoses at any moment. If you will, I mean what Rudolf Otto called the *mysterium fascinans*. The British author Jonathan Raban, in his curious book *Soft City*, argues that modern urban life is characterized by magic, and *not* (as it is more customarily thought to be) by rationality. I think that there is much to be said for this view; Raban also maintains that New York has this magic in a particularly potent form. The magic of the city can be summed up in a sentence that sums up a recurring experience: *Anything can happen here — and it could happen right now.*

Magic always has its dark side, and it is hardly necessary to spell out the sinister possibilities of the insight that anything can happen. But it would be a mistake to limit the experience to its negative aspect. The city is a place of strangers and of strangeness, and this very fact implies a fascination of a special kind. Ordinary-looking houses contain unimaginable mysteries within. Casual encounters are transformed into revelations of shocking impact. Passions explode in the most unexpected occasions. All of this helps to account for the excitement of the city, but it also makes for a general vision of the world: Reality is not what it seems; there are realities behind the reality of everyday life; the routine fabric of our ordinary lives is not self-contained, it has holes in it, and there is no telling what wondrous things may at any moment rush in through these holes. This vision of the world is perhaps not itself religious, but it is in close proximity to the root insights of the religious attitude. The magic of the city should not, then, be identified with religious experience, but it may be said to be an antechamber of the latter. Thus, when people say that New York City is a surrealistic place, they are saying more than they intend. They are making an ontological statement about the reality of human life: Behind the empirical city lurks *another city*, a city of dreams and wonders. They are also making a soteriological statement, for redemption always comes into the world as a big surprise—I would even say, as a cosmic joke. Anything at all can come through the holes in the fabric of ordinary reality—a man leading an elephant by the leash, or a man riding on a donkey to inaugurate the mystery of our salvation.

Some of the above may sound as if I have become a latter-day convert to some version of secular theology (maybe a sort of North American centrist adaptation of the theology of liberation?). Let me say as strongly as I can that this is not at all the case. Indeed, the theological considerations in this chapter are directly opposite to the procedure that has been characteristic of the various expressions of secular theology. That procedure, in the final analysis, is always the same: The symbols of transcendence in the Christian tradition are reinterpreted to become symbols of the human condition, the divine becomes a metaphor of the human, the metaempirical of ordinary empirical reality. I'm suggesting here the precisely opposite procedure: The human condition itself is to be seen as the penumbra of the transcendent, the human points to the divine, the empirical is a metaphor of the metaempirical. Whatever have been the shifting contents of secular theology—philosophical, psychological, most recently political—they have served as the substratum to which the traditional symbols are reduced. I strongly reject this reductionist procedure. I suggest the precise opposite of reduction, namely, a hesitantly inductive procedure which begins with the empirical realities of human life, but which intends from the start to transcend these realities.

Nor am I proposing that these or any other signals of transcendence be taken as the substance of our faith. Rather, they are particular experiences which, for some of us, may serve as auxiliaries of faith. Contrary to what some may think, I'm not suggesting that my particular vision of New York City be incorporated in the *kerygma* of the church. And I'm definitely willing to remain in full Christian communion with all those who fail to understand the deeper significance of this city. If there is a polemical edge to what I have written here, it is against those who would provide a theological rationale for the antiurbanism that is rampant today in the radical wing of the ecology movement—but this was certainly not foremost in my mind.

There is a route I drive regularly, between Rutgers University in New Jersey, where I teach, and Brooklyn, where I live. It crosses from Staten Island over the Verrazano-Narrows Bridge. It has often occurred to me, especially in the evening when the light is soft and the contours of visual reality seem to lack firmness, that the entrance to heaven may well look something like this wonderful bridge, with its majestic arcs and its breathtaking vistas on both sides. I wish for all of us that we will be part of this traffic in the evening of our lives, that we will be forgiven the toll at the gate, and that we will know that, in the city on the other side of bridge, what awaits us is home. I, for one, will not be overly surprised if the gatekeeper addresses me in a Brooklyn accent.

Notes

Chapter 1

1. The present chapter has come out of a larger project on which the authors have been engaged in collaboration with three colleagues in sociology and philosophy. The project is to produce a systematic treatise that will integrate a number of now separate theoretical strands in the sociology of knowledge. (This project led to the book by Peter Berger and Thomas Luckmann, *The Social Construction of Reality* [Garden City, N.Y.: Doubleday, 1966].)

2. *Cf.* especially Max Weber, *Wirtschaft und Gesellschaft* (Tuebingen: Mohr, 1956); Idem, *Gesammelte Aufsaetze zur Wissenschaftslebre* (Tuebingen: Mohr, 1951); George H. Mead, *Mind, Self and Society* (Chicago: University of Chricago Press, 1934); Alfred Schutz, *Der sinnhafte Aufbau der sozialen Welt* (Vienna: Springer, 1960); Idem, *Collected Papers*, I (The Hague: Nijhoff, 1962); Maurice Merleau-Ponty, *Phénoménologie de la perception* (Paris: Gallimard, 1945); Idem, *La structure du comportement* (Paris: Presses Universitaires de France, 1953).

3. *Cf.* Schutz, *Aufbau*, pp. 202–220; Idem, *Collected Papers*, I, pp. 3–27, 283–286.

4. *Cf.* Schutz, *Collected Papers*, I, pp. 207–228.

5. *Cf.* especially Jean Piaget, *The Construction of Reality in the Child* (New York: Basic Books, 1954).

6. *Cf.* Mead, *Mind, Self and Society*, pp. 135–226.

7. *Cf.* Schutz, *Aufbau*, pp. 181–195.

8. *Cf.* Arnold Gehlen, *Die Seele im technischen Zeitalter* (Hamburg: Rowohlt, 1957), pp. 57–69; Idem, *Anthropologische Forschung* (Hamburg: Rowohlt, 1961), pp. 69–77, 127–140; Helmut Schelsky, *Soziologie der Sexualitaet* (Hamburg: Rowohlt, 1955), pp. 102–133. Also, *cf.* Thomas Luckmann, "On Religion in Modern Society," *Journal for the Scientific Study of Religion*, Spring 1963, pp. 147-162.

9. In these considerations we have been influenced by certain presuppositions of Marxian anthropology, as well as by the anthropological work of Max Scheler, Helmuth Plessner, and Arnold Gehlen. We are indebted to Thomas Luckmann for the clarification of the social-phychological significance of the private sphere.

10. *Cf.* Talcott Parsons and Robert Bales, eds., *Family, Socialization and Interaction Process* (New York: Free Press, 1955), pp. 3–34, 353–396.

11. *Cf.* Philippe Ariès, *Centuries of Childhood* (New York: Knopf, 1962), pp. 339–410.

12. *Cf.* Kurt Wolff, ed., *The Sociology of Georg Simmel* (New York: Free Press, 1950), pp. 118–144.

13. *Cf.* Schutz, *Aufbau*, pp. 29–36, 149–153.

14. *Cf.* ibid, pp. 186–192, 202–210.

15. David Riesman's well-known concept of "other-direction" would also be applicable here.

16. *Cf.* Maurice Halbwachs, *Les cadres sociaux de la mémoire* (Paris: Presses Universitaires de France, 1952), esp. pp. 146–177; Also, *cf.* Peter Berger, *Invitation to Sociology—A Humanistic Perspective* (Garden City, N.Y.: Doubleday-Anchor, 1963), pp. 54–65.

17. *Cf.* Schutz, *Collected Papers*, I, pp. 72–73, 79–82.

18. The phenomena discussed here could also be formulated effectively in terms of the Marxian categories of reification and false consciousness. Jean-Paul Sartre's recent work, especially *Critique de la raison dialectique*, seeks to integrate these categories within a phenomenological

analysis of human conduct. Also, *cf.* Henri Lefebvre, *Critique de la vie quotidienne* (Paris: l'Arche, 1958–1961).

19. *Cf.* Renate Mayntz, *Die moderne Familie* (Stuttgart: Enke, 1955); Helmut Schelsky, *Wandlungen der deutschen Familie in der Gegenwart* (Stuttgart: Enke, 1955); Maximilien Sorre, ed., *Sociologie comparée de la famille contemporaine* (Paris: Centre National de la Recherche Scientifique, 1955); Ruth Anshen, ed., *The Family—Its Function and Destiny* (New York: Harper, 1959); Norman Bell and Ezra Vogel, *A Modern Introduction to the Family* (New York: Free Press, 1960).

20. *Cf.* Talcott Parsons, *Essays in Sociological Theory* (New York: Free Press, 1949), pp. 233–250.

21. In these as well as the following references to empirical studies we naturally make no attempt at comprehensiveness. References are given as representative of a much larger body of materials. *Cf.* Paul Glick, *American Families* (New York: Wiley, 1957), p. 54. Also, *cf.* Idem, "The Family Cycle," *American Sociological Review*, April 1947, pp. 164–174. Also, *cf.* Bureau of the Census, *Statistical Abstracts of the United States*, 1956 and 1958; *Current Population Reports*, Series P-20, No. 96 (Nov. 1959).

22. *Cf.* David Riesman, *The Lonely Crowd* (New Haven: Yale University Press, 1953), pp. 29–40; Frederick Elkin, *The Child and Society* (New York: Random House, 1960), *passim*.

23. *Cf.* references given above under note 21.

24. *Cf.* W. Lloyd Warner and Paul Lunt, *The Social Life of a Modern Community* (New Haven: Yale University Press, 1941), pp. 436–440; August Hollingshead, "Cultural Factors in the Selection of Marriage Mates," *American Sociological Review*, October 1950, pp. 619–627. Also, *cf.* Ernest Burgess and Paul Wallin, "Homogamy in Social Characteristics," *American Journal of Sociology*, September 1943, pp. 109–124.

25. *Cf.* Gerhard Lenski, *The Religious Factor* (Garden City, N.Y.: Doubleday, 1961), pp. 48–50.

26. *Cf.* Leonard Cottrell, "Roles in Marital Adjustment," *Publications of the American Sociological Society* 27 (1933): 107–115; Willard Waller and Reuben Hill, *The Family—A Dynamic Interpretation* (New York: Dryden, 1951), pp. 253–271; Morris Zelditch, "Role Differentiation in the Nuclear Family," in Parsons and Bales, eds., *Family, Socialization and Interaction*, pp. 307–352. For a general discussion of role interaction in small groups, *cf.* especially George Homans, *The Human Group* (New York: Harcourt Brace, 1950).

27. *Cf.* Waller and Hill, *The Family*, pp. 253–271, for an excellent summation of such data.

28. *Cf.* Dennison Nash and Peter Berger, "The Family, the Child and the Religious Revival in Suburbia," *Journal for the Scientific Study of Religion*, Fall 1962, pp. 85–93.

29. *Cf.* Bureau of the Census, *Statistical Abstracts*.

30. *Cf.* Talcott Parsons, "Age and Sex in the Social Structure of the United States," *American Sociological Review*, December 1942, pp. 604–616; Paul Glick, "First Marriages and Remarriages," *American Sociological Review*, December 1949, pp. 726–734; William Goode, *After Divorce* (New York: Free Press, 1956), pp. 269–285.

Chapter 2

1. *Cf.* George Wilbur and Werner Muensterberger, eds., *Psychoanalysis and Culture* (New York: International Universities Press, 1951); Benjamin Nelson, ed., *Freud and the 20th Century* (New York: Meridian, 1957); John Sutherland, ed., *Psychoanalysis and Contemporary Thought* (New York: Grove, 1959); C. P. Oberndorf, *A History of Psychoanalysis in America* (New York: Harper & Row, 1964). (Since this chapter was written, there has been a proliferation of various new versions of psychologism and therapeutic cults. The analysis made here can cover these more recent phenomena without strain.)

2. *Cf.* Gordon Hamilton, *Theory and Practice of Social Case Work* (New York: Columbia University Press, 1940).

3. *Cf.* Martin Gross, *The Brain Watchers* (New York: New American Library, 1963).

4. *Cf.* Thomas Szasz, *Law, Liberty and Psychiatry* (New York: Macmillan, 1963)

5. *Cf.* Samuel Klausner, *Psychiatry and Religion* (New York: Free Press, 1964).

6. Hendrik Ruitenbeck, ed., *Psychoanalysis and Social Science* (New York: Dutton, 1962), particularly the articles by Talcott Parsons and John Seeley.

7. *Cf.,* for example, the treatment of the relationship between society and personality in Talcott Parsons, *The Social System* (New York: Free Press, 1951), with that in Maurice Stein *et al.,* eds., *Identity and Anxiety* (New York: Free Press, 1960).

8. *Cf.,* as examples of these, William Rushing, *The Psychiatric Professions* (Chapel Hill: University of North Carolina Press, 1964); John Seeley *et al., Crestwood Heights* (New York: Basic Books, 1956); J. L. Moreno, ed., *Group Psychotherapy* (New York: Beacon, 1945).

9. August Hollingshead and Frederick Redlich, *Social Class and Mental Illness* (New York: Wiley, 1958); Erving Goffman, *Asylums* (Garden City, N.Y.: Doubleday-Anchor, 1961); idem, *Stigma* (Englewood Cliffs, N.J.: Prentice-Hall, 1963)

10. Richard LaPiere, *The Freudian Ethic* (New York: Duell, Sloan & Pearce, 1959); Eric Larrabee, *The Self-Conscious Society* (Garden City, N.Y.: Doubleday, 1960); Philip Rieff, *Freud—The Mind of the Moralist* (Garden City, N.Y.: Doubleday-Anchor, 1961). For a European study of the diffusion of psychoanalysis, *cf.* Serge Moscovici, *La psychoanalyse—son image et son public* (Paris: Presses Universitaires, 1961).

11. The authors of a sociological study of religious best sellers have suggested "mentalism" for roughly the same complex of phenomena in the area of popular culture, but this is at least as ambiguous a term as "psychologism." *Cf.* Louis Schneider and Sanford Dornbush, *Popular Religion* (Chicago: University of Chicago Press, 1958).

12. *Cf.* Arnold Gehlen, *Die Seele im technischern Zeitalter* (Hamburg: Rowohlt, 1957); Thomas Luckmann, *The Invisible Religion* (New York: Macmillan, 1967).

Chapter 7

1. Richard Hammer, *The Court-Martial of Lt. Calley* (New York: Coward, McCann, and Geoghegan, 1971).

2. George Bishop, *Witness to Evil* (Los Angeles: Nash, 1971).

Chapter 8

1. The term "intellectual-industrial complex" has previously been used to describe the situation in the early 1960s, when intellectuals related much more positively both to government and to the economic elite. As will be clear from what follows, my contention is that a quite different symbiosis is emerging now; the phrase is still useful.

2. I have deliberately used the term "Sovietization" rather than "Finlandization." Finland is a democracy, as the Finns are always quick to point out. They are less quick to point out that this fortunate condition is due to the position of the country *in between* the Soviet and American orbits of power. If American power disappeared from Europe, Soviet policy there is likely to be much less gingerly. In other words, "Finlandization" will then be a luxury that the Europeans may have to forego.

Chapter 10

1. Benjamin Barber, *The Death of Communal Liberty* (Princeton, N.J.: Princeton University Press, 1974).

Chapter 13

1. Will Herberg, *Protestant—Catholic—Jew; An Essay in American Religious Sociology* (Garden City, N.Y.: Doubleday, 1955).

2. Robert Bellah, "The Civil Religion in America," in *The Religious Situation: Nineteen Six-ty-Eight*, ed. Donald Cutler (Boston: Beacon, 1968).

3. Peter Berger, *The Noise of Solemn Assemblies* (Garden City, N.Y.: Doubleday, 1961).

Chapter 14

1. This chapter was first published in 1967. The most important "translation grammar" added since then has been Marxism (in various forms). The basic analysis of this chapter continues to be applicable.

Chapter 15

1. Peter Berger, *The Noise of Solemn Assemblies* (Garden City, N.Y.: Doubleday, 1961).

Index